Deadly sounds, deadly places

PETER DUNBAR-HALL is Chair of the Music Education Unit of Sydney Conservatorium of Music, University of Sydney. His major interests include Aboriginal music, Australian cultural history and Balinese gamelan repertoires. He is the author of *Strella Wilson: The Career of an Australian Singer* (Redback Press, 1997).

CHRIS GIBSON is a Senior Lecturer in the Geography Program at the University of New South Wales. His research interests include geographies of the cultural industries, popular music and place identities, and Aboriginal economic development. His other books include *Sound Tracks: Popular Music and Identity* (Routledge, 2003) and *Music and Tourism* (Channel View, 2004).

Deadly sounds,

Peter Dunbar-Hall and Chris Gibson

deadly places

Contemporary
Aboriginal music
in Australia

UNSW
PRESS

A UNSW PRESS BOOK

Published by
University of New South Wales Press Ltd
University of New South Wales
Sydney NSW 2052
AUSTRALIA
www.unswpress.com.au

All author royalties from sales of this book
contribute to a scholarship fund established
to support Aboriginal students at the University of New South Wales.

Every effort has been made by the authors to
contact the copyright holders of material
reproduced in this book and the publishers
welcome any further information.

National Library of Australia
Cataloguing-in-Publication entry:

Dunbar-Hall, P. (Peter).
Deadly sounds, deadly places: contemporary
Aboriginal music in Australia.

Includes index.
ISBN 0 86840 622 8.

1. Aboriginal Australians – Music.
I. Gibson, Chris, 1973– .
II. Title.

781.629915

Design Di Quick
Printer BPA Print Group

Cover Image courtesy Bangarra Dance Theatre
Photograph greg barrett.com
Dancer Patrick Thaiday

DEADLY: ABORIGINAL ENGLISH,
ADJECTIVE: FANTASTIC, GREAT, TERRIFIC

This book contains references to and/or images of deceased Aboriginal and Torres Strait Islander people. Discretion and the seeking of advice from relevant members of Indigenous communities are recommended if this causes offence.

Contents

Acknowledgments

Work on this book would not have been possible without the assistance of: Katherine Blackwell; Vanessa Bosnjak; Kev Carmody; Greg Castillon (Casso and Reggae Dave); Tony Collins (Triple J, Darwin); John Connell; Mick Connolly (Troppo Sound, Broome); Georgia Cordukes (Vibe Australia); Deborah Davidson; Warren Fahey (Larrikin Records); Floros Floros (So Music, Newtown); Kevin Fong (Goolarri Media Association, Broome); Kerry Gardiner (Kulumindini Band); George and Neil (Warumpi Band); Margaret Gummow; Carla Hurford; Buna Lawrie and the members of Coloured Stone; Carolyn Lowry; Ed Matzenik (Enrec Studios); Richard Micallef (Central Australian Aboriginal Media Association); Alice Moyle; Peter Apaak Jupurrula Miller (Blekbala Mujik); Tony Mitchell (University of Technology Sydney); Karl Neuenfeldt (University of Central Queensland); Samantha-Jane Norris; Ronnie Peters (Goolarri Radio, Broome); Doug Petherick (Centre for Aboriginal Studies in Music, Adelaide); Bob Randall; Chris Ross (Central Australian Aboriginal Media Association); Chester Schultz; Eric Scott (Hadley Records, Tamworth); Belinda Skinner; all at Skinny Fish Records; Martin Smith (Aboriginal Islander College, Perth); Sher Williams (Western Australian Academy for the Performing Arts, Perth); Gaye Wotherspoon (Chinatown Music, Broome); Ali Wright.

Some sections of *Deadly Sounds, Deadly Places* are based on our work in other sources. Chapters 1 and 2 draw on an article on geographies of Aboriginal popular music in *Environment and Planning D: Society and Space*, no. 16, 1998, pp. 163–84; analysis of the music/place nexus in songs by Warumpi Band in chapter 5 is a recasting of an article in *Perfect Beat*, vol. 3, no. 3, 1997, pp. 55–74; sections of chapter 6 are based on an article on the sociolinguistic aspects of contemporary Aboriginal songs in *Popular Music and Society*, vol. 27, no. 1, 2004, pp. 41–48; parts of chapter 9 appeared first in *Ethnomusicology*, vol. 44, no. 1, 2000, pp. 39–64; chapter 10, on the Kimberley region, expands on an article in *The Australian Journal of Indigenous Education*, vol. 29, no. 1, 2001, pp. 1–11.

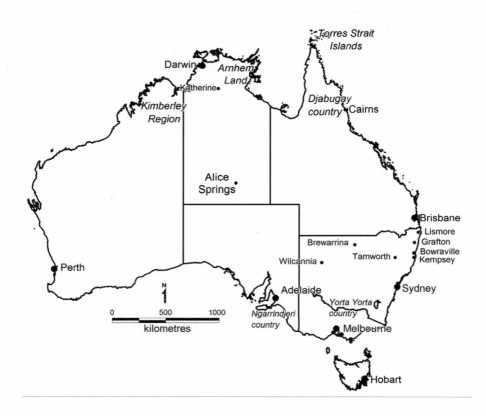

Torres Strait
Islands

Darwin

Arnhem
Land

Katherine

Kimberley
Region

Djabugay
country   Cairns

Alice
Springs

Brisbane

Brewarrina   Lismore
              Grafton
              Bowraville
Wilcannia   Tamworth   Kempsey

Perth

N

Adelaide   Sydney

0   500   1000   Yorta Yorta
                    country
kilometres

Ngarrindjeri
country   Melbourne

Hobart

Abbreviations

ABC	Australian Broadcasting Corporation
ABS	Australian Bureau of Statistics
AIATSIS	Australian Institute for Aboriginal and Torres Strait Islander Studies
ATSIAB	Aboriginal and Torres Strait Islander Arts Board (Australia Council)
ATSIC	Aboriginal and Torres Strait Islander Commission
BAMA	Broome Aboriginal Media Association
BRACS	Broadcasting for Regional Aboriginal Communities Scheme
CAAMA	Central Australian Aboriginal Media Association
CASM	Centre for Aboriginal Studies in Music
CDEP	Community Development Employment Program
KLC	Kimberley Land Council
NAISDA	National Aboriginal and Islander Skills Development Association
NIAAA	National Indigenous Arts Advocacy Association
NIMAA	National Indigenous Media Association of Australia

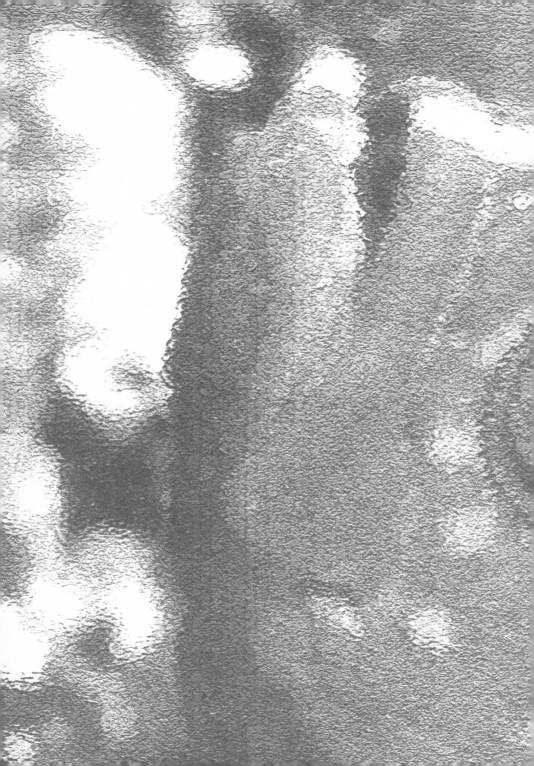

Introduction

This book was written with a number of aims. As a study of music created by contemporary Aboriginal musicians, it responds to a need in
Australian cultural history to document an often neglected aspect of
Australian music. Although some discussion of contemporary forms of
music by Aboriginal performers appears in edited collections of work on
either Aboriginal music or popular music in general (Pearce, 1979;
Garofalo, 1992; Hayward, 1992; Breen, 1994; T Mitchell, 1996), currently there are only two texts specifically on this topic. At the time of
the 1988 commemorations of white invasion of Australia, Breen edited
a book on popular music by Aborigines (Breen, 1989). Just over a
decade later, Walker (2000) released his biographical work on Aboriginal country musicians. Between these two publications, Neuenfeldt
(1997) edited *The Didjeridu: From Arnhem Land to Internet*, dedicated to one instrument. These texts have been supplemented sporadi-
cally by publication in academic journals of research into various aspects
of contemporary music by Aboriginal artists. Full-scale publication on
this topic remains rare; an absence of comprehensive analysis of the sites
and texts of contemporary Aboriginal music was an impetus for the production of this book.

In addition to documenting musical developments among Aboriginal
musicians, this book acts as a lens through which aspects of Aboriginal

cultural politics can be viewed. These include uses of music to fulfil political objectives, to record traditions and to educate within Aboriginal communities and the wider public. In addition, music as representation or expression of Aboriginality is discussed. In this book we seek to explore music not only in terms of musical texts, but also in terms of its social, economic and political contexts. Understanding the links between musical expressions and the wider sociopolitical situations within which they are made and consumed is one way of mapping contemporary Aboriginal experiences, in this case articulated by musicians and consumed by different audiences. The music we discuss is one device that Indigenous Australians utilise to enact self-determination and cultural identity and to negotiate the impacts of colonisation. By acknowledging Aboriginal ways of seeing the country and telling history, we seek to introduce a post-colonial perspective to our work.

What is 'contemporary Aboriginal music'?

The topic of this book is 'contemporary' music, although our use of this term is practical rather than universal or comprehensive. We would argue that attempts to define Aboriginal expressions through Western concepts such as 'traditional' and 'contemporary' are futile, and possibly damaging. Although we use the term 'contemporary', we are keen to avoid the implication that a dichotomy can be drawn between music deriving from the pre-colonial past and that of the present. Our position, resonant with that of many Aboriginal musicians, is that Aboriginal music is a thread of expression that has always, and is continually changing. In the live music context, for example at festivals, divisions between 'traditional' and 'contemporary' music are not necessarily apparent or important, and music from the past and the present often co-exist, occurring simultaneously within the same line-up, or within individual songs. Divisions between the 'traditional' and the 'contemporary' are blurred, as discussed throughout this book. More specifically, in the music of some Aboriginal rock groups, references to earlier forms of music make a historical thread explicit as a factor of their work. Despite choices of musical style and technological mediation, which for some listeners might constitute criteria for differentiating between 'traditional' and 'contemporary' music, there are consistencies in the themes and aesthetic stances of Aboriginal music across this binary. Throughout this book we demonstrate how stylistic and technological innovations are inherent in the dynamic nature of this music.

What constitutes 'traditional' music is much contested. As we discuss in chapter 1, Aboriginal people have consumed and performed folk music, gospel and choral music for at least a century, and country music for over fifty years. At what point these musical heritages take on meaning as 'traditional' is unclear, as they may already be considered so within Aboriginal communities. That there is no accurate definition of 'traditional' music illustrates that the concept is constructed, rather than innate in music. The concept becomes more opaque when music and dance are considered parts of the same expression, such as when Aboriginal performers working in the tourism industry mobilise contemporary themes within what otherwise appears to be 'traditional' music and dance. Such performances are marketed as 'traditional', even if songs and dances have been truncated or 'simplified', or have been newly created for touristic purposes. Elsewhere, urban Aboriginal performers, such as Sydney-based Bangarra Dance Theatre, have reclaimed 'traditional' music and dance as a means of overcoming the legacy of colonialism and dispossession. That such attempts are contemporaneous should not reduce the extent to which they are taken seriously, nor should it mean that such practices are not 'traditional'.

While 'the traditional' is fluid and constructed, some cultural expressions have persisted despite, or in reaction to, cultural change. Music can and does enable the maintenance of Indigenous knowledges. Thus in parts of Australia ongoing traditional cultural practice using music and dance can be found. These are not explored in depth here, except when we discuss their impact on the agendas of the tourism industry (chapters 6 and 7), or when they are incorporated into the sounds of contemporary music groups (chapters 5, 8 and 9). Contemporary songs by Aboriginal musicians are discussed here as musical responses to relevant and current events, just as song and dance have been used in Aboriginal societies over long periods of time. As with Aboriginal references to land, through which a continuum of ownership is expressed, music is used to sing the past into the present and the future. That some musical expressions from the past resurface in contemporary forms is partly an embodiment of this, and in this way music acts as a vehicle for statement of Aboriginal beliefs and ideologies.

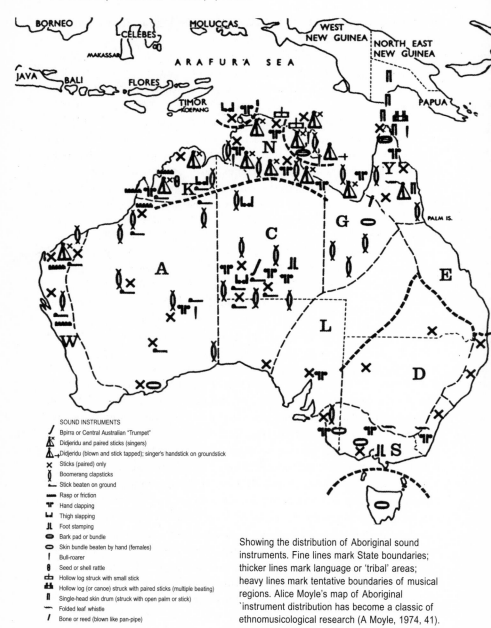

SOUND INSTRUMENTS

/ Bpirra or Central Australian "Trumpet"

⚔ Didjeridu and paired sticks (singers)

▲ Didjeridu (blown and stick tapped); singer's handstick on groundstick

✕ Sticks (paired) only

Ø Boomerang clapsticks

⌣ Stick beaten on ground

▬ Rasp or friction

⊤ Hand clapping

⊔ Thigh slapping

⨅ Foot stamping

⬤ Bark pad or bundle

⬭ Skin bundle beaten by hand (females)

| Bull-roarer

8 Seed or shell rattle

⌶ Hollow log struck with small stick

⟱ Hollow log (or canoe) struck with paired sticks (multiple beating)

∏ Single-head skin drum (struck with open palm or stick)

⌐ Folded leaf whistle

/ Bone or reed (blown like pan-pipe)

Showing the distribution of Aboriginal sound instruments. Fine lines mark State boundaries; thicker lines mark language or 'tribal' areas; heavy lines mark tentative boundaries of musical regions. Alice Moyle's map of Aboriginal `instrument distribution has become a classic of ethnomusicological research (A Moyle, 1974, 41).

Geographies of contemporary Aboriginal music

Reference to land, and to music as the means of expressing relationships between people and places, raises another aim of this book – to interpret Aboriginal music from a cultural geographical perspective. This not only illuminates representations of Aboriginality as concerned with land, but also situates music in the places where it is created, performed and received. The use of music in Aboriginal societies to articulate relationships to country underpins much published research on the music and dance that continue today from pre-colonial times. Additionally, that regional differences could be observed in music and dance has often been discussed. For example, Ellis (1985, 48) noted that:

> In pre-European Australia, Aboriginal music varied markedly throughout the continent. As with Aboriginal languages, large areas had common structural attributes with differences of dialect. For example, from what we know, the songs of the Pintupi and those of the Pitjantjatjara, Antakarinja, Wongkanguru, Arabana and Kokata-speaking peoples of northern South Australia are all accompanied only by some form of percussion beating. They are structurally similar in almost all respects ... However, this one overall song style appears to be different from ... Arnhem Land music ... in which didjeridu is used. The songs of southeastern South Australia are quite different again.

The work in the 1960s and 1970s of ethnomusicologist Alice Moyle was imbued with geographical implications. Her studies were published as regional reports on the Kimberley, north Queensland, the Northern Territory and Yarrabah (Qld); in them she discussed what she classified as regionally distinct musical practices (A Moyle, nd, 1972, 1974, 1977). This is nowhere more evident than in her description of song styles by reference to regions in Arnhem Land, and her map of the distribution of Aboriginal sound instruments (A Moyle, 1974). Alongside Alice Moyle, others whose work implies geographical dimensions of Aboriginal music include Strehlow (1971), Stubington (1978, 1979, 1994), Dixon (1984), Wild (1984), Ellis (1985), R Moyle (1986, 1997), Ellis & Barwick (1989), Keogh (1989), Payne (1989), Gummow (1994, 1995, 2002) and Marett (1994). Music as a site of expression of Aboriginal attachments to country also informs the work of researchers from various other

disciplines. This includes Williams' (1986) work on Yolngu land ownership, Rose's (1992) writing on the Yarralin mob, Davis & Prescott's
(1992) references to song as attestation of Luritja land ownership, and
Bell's (1998) investigation of song and land ownership claims by the
Ngarrindjeri people of Hindmarsh Island (SA).

Another type of geographic approach is one in which the musical
practice/s of a defined area are studied. In most cases the area nominated
for study is equated with the territory defined by the use of a language.
This is in many cases synonymous with the extent of land ownership. In
these cases land ownership, language and music are linked as a complex
through which individual and group identity are constructed, expressed
and maintained.

In this manner, research into music of the Aranda and Luritja
(Strehlow, 1971), Yolngu (Stubington, 1978), Pintupi (R Moyle, 1979)
Pitjantjatjara (Ellis, 1985), Alyawarra (R Moyle, 1986), Bundjalung and
Gidabal (Gummow, 1992), and Kukatja (R Moyle, 1997), of *nurlu* songs
from the west Kimberley (Keogh, 1989), and *mularra* clan songs from
west Arnhem Land (Anderson, 1992) are concerned with Aboriginal
musical repertoires by geographic criteria. Within these regions writers
may also identify geographically defined stylistic differences. For
example, Stubington (1979) distinguishes traditional music in east and
west Arnhem Land through the presence of two distinct didjeridu
playing styles. In addition to these large-scale works, others focus on
smaller culturally, geographically or socially delimited areas (Marett
1994; Stubington 1982, 1994; Gummow 1995).

While the body of research on the continuing tradition of pre-contact
Aboriginal music has an innate sense of material geography, studies of
contemporary music have tended to concentrate on the political and
sociological dimensions of the topic (for example, Breen, 1989, 1994).
Place-based interpretations, such as that of Ryan (1994) of Koori music
in Melbourne and Corn (2002) of songs by Top End rock group, Letterstick, have only begun to investigate possible cultural geographical readings of contemporary Aboriginal music.

There is more to a cultural geography of Aboriginal music than documenting music's origins or regional variations in style, instrumentation or
genre. Much previous work on 'traditional' music adopted an approach
where cultural variations were mapped, as with distributions of other

artefacts, objects or phenomena, and generalisations were made between regional variations and the physical and social environments apparent in different places. Beyond these types of descriptions and generalisations, there are also *symbolic geographies* (Cosgrove & Jackson, 1987; Jackson, 1989; Winchester et al., 2003) of Aboriginal music, where maps of meaning – of identity, myth, emotion and imagery – hold sway over everyday understandings of place and cultural difference. These symbolic geographies are not 'objectively' mappable in the ways that populations, languages or physical objects might be. Rather, they are composite impressions of the cultural attachments people hold to place, amalgams of tradition and cultural change, identity and conflict. Symbolic geographies are varied and dynamic. They are also sources of conflict, in the sense that different groups may hold opposing points of view about places and their meanings and the social issues through which those places are shaped. This can be seen in native title conflicts in Australia and in differing perceptions of land. Symbolic geographies also seek to examine links between representations of places and representations of peoples – these created and contested through filters of race, national identity, gender and class. In this book, we explore Aboriginal music by describing what musical activities take place and how these vary across the country, and by discussing the symbolic geographies of contemporary Aboriginal music, which connect musical texts to the narratives of places and social groups who make and interpret them.

Situating musical knowledges

Writing about Aboriginal music is not unproblematic. That two non-Indigenous researchers would use a book, a way of recording and disseminating Western thinking, to explain aspects of Aboriginal cultures with their reliance on oral transmission, is in essence contradictory. This needs to be continually set against the wishes of the musicians involved to have their music made known and the benefits of providing access to a body of music which otherwise remains unacknowledged. This book is intended to provide an introduction to many Aboriginal artists, songs and recordings of which much of the general public will not be aware. We urge readers to see this book as a companion to recordings of Aboriginal music that are commercially available. This book is not the definitive interpretation of these recordings – we do not wish to claim the

authorial voice *for* Aboriginal musicians. Instead we ask readers to consider this book one among many possible interpretations of this music
and its social contexts. Our interpretation, like any, is inevitably shaped
by our own backgrounds, experiences and motivations – for one, a music
educator, for the other, an academic geographer. Our knowledge of Aboriginal music and musicians comes from many years of listening, interpreting and writing in both academic and non-academic settings, as well
as from time spent in Aboriginal communities (from Barunga to Broome)
and, above all, talking to the musicians concerned. Where possible, we
seek to discuss music and its social contexts by referring to extracts from
interviews with Aboriginal musicians – to tell the story in the words of
the producers of the music themselves.

Writing about Aboriginal people, places or themes is inherently political, in a country still dealing with its colonial past and coming to terms
with its present. Thus it is important in this introduction to acknowledge our situation in relation to the production of this book, and moreover the political motivations underpinning our approach. We
acknowledge that as non-Indigenous researchers, with security of income
and housing, we remain in positions of privilege in comparison to many
of the subjects of this book. Beyond this acknowledgment, we also see
this book as one means of widening the audience and impact of Aboriginal music, and of improving general understanding of Aboriginal culture. In undertaking to write this book, we are compelled to refute the
'naïve belief', as Langton (1993a, 27) has put it 'that Aboriginal people
will make "better" representations of [Aboriginal people], simply because
being Aboriginal gives "greater" understanding'. Although Indigenous
control over research processes is crucial, we would not have embarked
on writing this book without the support of Indigenous musicians
(see Wild, 1994; Smith, 1999). Our desire, as non-Indigenous Autralians,
is to overtly engage with contemporary culture and political struggles
that involve Aboriginal people and issues, but not, in the process, sub-
sume cultural differences within universalising frame-works of 'negative' and 'positive' interpretations of musical texts andrepertoires.

Boundaries between us as researchers, and the musicians, social practices and musical texts that are the subjects of this book are never
absolute. We have been both 'outsiders' when interviewing musicians
or interpreting texts, and at times 'insiders', particularly when sharing

stories and insights with Aboriginal artists about the Australian music industry more generally. While we are not active participants in Aboriginal music scenes, our research has benefited from lines of affiliation with musicians generated by our own insights as musicians. We cannot speak for Aboriginal musicians. Yet our own experiences and agendas frequently coincide with those of Aboriginal cultural producers.

This book is also our chance to encourage audiences to take music more seriously – to see it as more than merely trivial or frivolous distraction. Music may be seen as a 'provisional and ephemeral presence' (Lawe Davies, 1993a, 256), but in the case of Aboriginal popular music it also provides its participants with 'empowerment practices'. This occurs in many ways: in performances where stereotypical black/white, performer/audience dichotomies are inverted or by presenting images of Aboriginal people that counter discourses of them as welfare dependent or disconnected from commercial activity (Lawe Davies, 1993a, 256–57). Forms of musical production – by both Indigenous and non-Indigenous performers – might add to stereotypes, emphasising the 'exotic', while at different times music enables groups to re-appropriate essentialisms for political purposes. In the case of Indigenous groups, this can include the use of traditions linked to custom and ceremony in land claims or their settlements.

It is problematic to interpret Aboriginal cultural production, or that of any minority group, in terms of a binary of 'negative' versus 'positive' expressions. These often operate within a framework for cultural criticism imposed from outside – one that defines what is 'good' and 'bad' cultural production – and, unintentionally 'may corroborate racism' (Langton, 1993b, 41), by assuming, for instance, that 'positive' representations of Aborigines are those which are 'safe' or which more wholly incorporate Aboriginal identities within Western consumer culture and the protestant work ethic. These types of assumptions are based on 'an ancient and universal feature of racism: the assumption of the undifferentiated *Other*' (Langton, 1993b, 27, emphasis in original), which requires Aboriginal people or other minorities to produce culture within symbolic frames controlled by metropolitan cultural industries to satisfy the demands of Western audiences. Moreover, much cultural criticism assumes that all such texts must operate as representative of a homogenised Aboriginality (see chapter 2).

In addition, as we argue in various places throughout this book, contemporary music is important because it challenges the assumptions of non-Aboriginal institutions, such as the court system and mechanisms of government and land rights legislation. An example of this is the way in which anthropological 'integrity' is required in order for an Indigenous community to be successful in a land rights or native title claim. In cases such as these, 'traditional' Aboriginal culture is seen as 'authentic', while 'contemporary' Aboriginal culture is often portrayed in terms of loss, erasure and 'inauthenticity'. Such binaries are wholly regressive. Constructing Aboriginal societies as 'culturally stable since the beginning of humanity' is problematic, implying

> an ahistorical existence, an inability to change and an incapacity to survive modernity; this essentialism also entails stipulations about what is and what is not appropriately and truly Aboriginal, which marginalizes not only urban Aboriginal cultures, but any forms not closely associated with traditional bush gathering (Thomas, 1994, 176).

This book seeks to problematise this distinction, and to make a claim for the continued importance of Aboriginal cultures and sovereignties in Australia as expressed in and through the production and consumption of music. As will hopefully become obvious throughout this book, music is not merely a passing form of expression, but is connected to real people, places and issues. As Melbourne-based singer-songwriter and filmmaker Richard Frankland has said, 'Music is the true tool of understanding ... Our songs tell stories of real things, real people and real situations. Hopefully they can change attitudes' (in *Koori Mail*, 8 Oct 1997, 21).

Audiences and aesthetics

The difficulties of writing about Aboriginal music are compounded by matters of aestheticisation of contemporary music. Contemporary Aboriginal music is often perceived in terms of its Aboriginality, but is also often compared with and valued against non-Aboriginal tastes and expectations. Some Aboriginal performers such as Yothu Yindi and Troy Cassar-Daley comfortably occupy spaces in the world of mainstream Australian popular music. At other times, mainstream reviewers impose their own beliefs and perspectives upon Aboriginal musical expression, in this way reinforcing official knowledge about how contemporary music should sound and act. Aboriginal music is constrained within what van Toorn (1990) has called a 'patron discourse' – a set of normative expectations and ways of listening in non-Aboriginal society, within which minority voices must struggle for audience. As Wark (2000, 43) has argued:

> The Aboriginal artists that have become legitimate and respected all in some way mimic white middle class tastes: Aboriginal dance theatre, Western Desert dot paintings, Aboriginal literature. But what is excluded from this belated celebration of Aboriginal creativity? Anything, I suspect, that can't be accommodated to white middle-class sensibilities. The acceptable kind of Aboriginal art, to white audiences, has some trace of authentic tribal culture but mixes it with the respectable forms of middle-class taste.

What results is an uneven power relationship between Aboriginal musicians and various gatekeepers, for example, reviewers and radio disc jockeys, that enables or prevents songs being heard by the general public. When new releases from Aboriginal musicians are received by radio stations or music writers, they sometimes do not 'sound right' to Western ears, or they unsettle non-Aboriginal assumptions, biases and opinions. Thus new releases struggle to gain airplay and favourable reviews. As Murri singer-songwriter Kev Carmody has argued in relation to national youth radio station Triple J, 'while it was the youth who have been able to come through and fulfil positions as DJs and programmers, you can bet they didn't grow up in the western suburbs of Sydney or [in] Redfern – so they've still got their own set of values and choices of styles of music' (interview, 1996). When Aboriginal music does reach the public's attention, it is often only that music which fits within an existing patron discourse that succeeds commercially. We seek to look beyond the uneven power relationships existing between Aboriginal musicians and the music industry by proposing another position – that contemporary Aboriginal music, while it exists in the world of commercial production and distribution, occupies other kinds of social spaces and symbolic geographies, and that in these other spaces music has quite different identities, purposes and meanings. The success of music in these contexts is not a matter of record sales or audience sizes, nor indeed of our aesthetic judgements of whether a song is 'good' or 'bad.' Rather, it is connected to the cultural values, imperatives and political stances of performers and audiences who make meanings of these songs.

Music and country

Relating music to Aboriginal beliefs about land is an important element of this book, but it also presents another difficulty in terms of the politics of representation. Land has become a highly politicised and controversial aspect of Aboriginal/non-Aboriginal interaction in Australia. At the most basic level, Aboriginal law regarding land is inimical in many ways to government-sanctioned ways of defining land ownership, access and use (Gibson, 1999). Land exists as a tradable commodity in Australian federal law. At the same time, it exists in Aboriginal law as 'country' – a concept with a different set of connotations. The fact that in many cases Aboriginal methods for defining the ambit of specific territories relies on interpretation of topographical subtleties often unrecognisable to non-Aboriginal people, compounds this legal disjuncture. That Aboriginal sovereignty embodies religious belief, that it can be fluid and contested, and that it does not seek to reinforce rigid and absolute boundaries as in the Western, capitalist property market, only serve to make the task of appropriately representing Aboriginal beliefs in land more difficult and problematic. This in turn makes explanation of music, which we interpret as an Aboriginal way of addressing country, a complex and shifting undertaking.

While we acknowledge that representations of Aboriginal ownership of land are problematic in these ways, and that non-Aboriginal explanations are open to misinterpretation on many levels, what interests us are the ways in which contemporary music by Aboriginal people enters this discursive field and interacts with these issues. At times, this requires us to explain histories of confrontation over land, and in these situations a case can be made for reading contemporary Aboriginal music partly as response to documented events. This can be seen throughout this book when we relate songs to various historical occurrences. At other times, Aboriginal songs about country remain opaque. Trying to fathom how these songs are used to make statements about country relies on oral histories, interviews and other sources of evidence. Deconstruction of historiography is also essential, as Aboriginal song continues to function as a primary means of recording the past; whose past that is must continually be questioned.

There is a danger in all of this that by not entering into deeper levels of explanation of Aboriginal beliefs about country, we offer a simplistic reading of the music/place relationship. It must be remembered, however, that our focus is on how music is central in outlining Aboriginal sovereignty over country. We position music as one voice in Aboriginal discourse on land, and discuss only those aspects of Aboriginal land ownership that are necessary to explicate the music we have chosen to explore. Comprehensive coverage of the gamut of Aboriginal land-based belief systems, applications of these and their implications remain the territory of those researchers who specialise in those fields.

Terminology

The title of this book utilises the term 'Aboriginal'. This presents some problems. To group all mainland Indigenous Australians under the heading 'Aboriginal' implies an artificial uniformity – even though this is the method through which both state and federal governments approach these peoples. Indigenous Australians can be referred to as members of nations within the Australian polity – Aranda, Jawoyn, Luritja, Pitjantjatjara, Yolngu, etc. At the same time, other terms for naming groups of Aborigines have evolved, for example, Koori, Murri and Noongar. Where possible, we have identified musicians as members of these language-speaking nations or current groupings, and when relevant these specific Aboriginalities are discussed. Sometimes, however, the term 'Aboriginal' is appropriate to our work – particularly when issues which affect mainland Indigenous Australians as a whole are discussed, or when there is the need to refer to disparate groups of people at the one time. We use the term 'Indigenous' to refer collectively to Aborigines and Torres Strait Islanders. The term 'indigenous' is used to refer to native peoples internationally. It should be noted that music by Torres Strait Islanders is not a focus of this book – although at times it is impossible not to include it in our discussions. This is especially so when there are crossovers between Aboriginal music and Torres Strait Island music, or when musicians, such as Torres Strait Islander Christine Anu, are involved in aspects of both. Readers interested in contemporary Torres Strait Island music are directed to the work of Beckett (1981), Connell

(1999) and Neuenfeldt (2001a, 2001b, 2002).

In light of the above discussion of meanings of 'contemporary' and 'traditional' music, we have used the former to describe musical practices that involve aspects of commercial production, performance and distribution, and which are influenced to some degree by Western sounds and instrumentations. We have generally avoided the term 'popular music' and derivatives such as 'Aboriginal popular music' or 'popular Aboriginal music', because of possible confusion and long-winded debates about style and definition, for example, whether 'country music' or 'jazz' are distinct from 'popular' music.

Occasionally we discuss musical practices that can be classified as 'traditional', although in our use of examples these largely involve instances where such sounds accompany, or are contained within, 'contemporary' expressions and commercial activities. Terms such as 'country', 'rock', 'folk' and 'hip-hop' are derived from Western popular music criticism and analysis, and are generally applied in this book in the ways understood in that context, although such distinctions are characteristic of a global music industry that has been criticised by Aboriginal musicians for overly categorising musical releases. As Murri singer-songwriter Kev Carmody has argued:

> I think it would be terrible to be handcuffed to one style or make of music, there's just so many different ways we can utilise musical expression. At the moment I'm right into the quartertone stuff like North African, Indian and Asian music ... I'm so jack of this whole idea that the music industry reckons it's got to be country music or rap music so we can jam it in some category and market it. It's like bloody cattle in a yard (McCabe, 1995, 51).

The co-existence of stylistic markers both within artists' repertoires, and within songs themselves, attests to these definitional problems. Meanwhile a range of categories used by Aboriginal musicians to describe their own work exists, from the 'desert surf rock' of Santa Theresa Mob and Coloured Stone to J-Boy's 'indijiblu', a mix of soul, R&B, funk and dance (*Koori Mail*, 5 Sep 2001, 23). Often the terms 'Koori music' and 'Koori rock' are used as stylistic descriptors by Aboriginal musicians and as a means of distinguishing their music from other genres. Wild Water, from Maningrida and Darwin, call their music 'saltwater style', because,

> it is the saltwater which links them and which has brought them all together ... Labels and categories are not easy for the Wild Water mob. They are not strictly 'Aboriginal' though their songs deal with indigenous issues; they do not fit into the mainstream industry trends ... So instead of using established terms of stylistic reference, which would clumsily attempt to describe their music as multicultural/indigenous/reggae/funk/rock fusion, Wild Water are staking a claim on their own name for their creation: 'Saltwater style' (Pearse, 1997, 29).

A note is also necessary at this point on the spelling of Aboriginal words. As Australian Aboriginal languages are not originally written languages, consistency does not always occur when they are transcribed into written form. For example, the language of the area near Cairns, on the Queensland coast, is usually given as 'Djabugay' – however the spelling 'Tjapukai' is also used. Similarly 'Aranda' appears in various sources as 'Aranta' 'Arrente', 'Arrernte' and 'Arunta'. We have aimed for consistency, but where necessary have indicated alternate spellings of Aboriginal words in brackets.

A third matter of terminology concerns the naming of aspects of Aboriginal cultures. Two issues require clarification in this: the Dreaming, and terms used to refer to land. The term 'the Dreaming' (also 'the Dreamtime') is used by many Australians to name the period in Aboriginal history when the world and living things were brought into being. Rules governing how country was to be looked after and by whom were also formulated at this time. These were given to people by the spirit beings responsible for creation activities. Each Aboriginal language has its own terms for this time, its personnel and their activities (for example, *altjiranga ngambakala* in Aranda, *burr* in Jawoyn, *tjukurrtjanu* in Pintupi; see Hume, 2002). The problem with the terms 'Dreaming' and 'Dreamtime' is that they can imply a fictitious nature for a static period – that the events described as Dreaming activities are no more than stories from a distant epoch. Yet in Aboriginal belief systems, the Dreaming continues in the present; the results of Dreaming activities are observable as features of the physical world; the songs and dances which recount these events continually exercise the power to recall and re-enact events of the past, and to give them relevance in the present. Because Dreaming events refer to the forming of features of the physical landscape, and because the songs and dances which retell these events also embody them, song and dance are a means of recording Aboriginal rights and responsibilities as expressed in land – hence their significance, and often legal discount-ability as oral evidence, in court cases over land rights.

Our topic cannot be covered without recourse to a range of terms to discuss land and land ownership. While terms such as 'property', 'own-ership', 'country' and 'sovereignty' may appear as words in standard English, they also infer ranges of meanings in Aboriginal English. 'Own' (and 'ownership') is used to mean 'to have a spiritual and material responsibility for a place; to acknowledge an identity with one's country and accept one's obligations [for it]' (Arthur, 1996, 125). 'Country' defines 'the tract of land where an Aboriginal person or community belongs, to which they have a responsibility, and from which they can draw spiritual strength' (Arthur, 1996, 11). Specifically to refer to country that is apportioned to a clan (a subgroup of a language speaking group), we use the term 'estate', as is the custom in some anthropolog-ical writings (for example, Williams, 1986; Sutton, 1995; Corn, 2002). 'Sovereignty' has become a more common term in Aboriginal use since the land rights movement of the 1970s, where it refers to the range of collective naming and owning practices that govern territory. As dis-cussed elsewhere (Gibson, 1999; Gibson & Dunbar-Hall, 2000) its use is often more fluid and negotiated – to be constantly reproduced through cultural expression – compared with more static Western meanings of sovereignty in international law. 'Site' also presents prob-lems. It has become a regularly used term for referencing a location of significance to an individual or to a group in Aboriginal Australia, often in the composite term 'sacred site'. At the same time, 'site' has assumed an identity as a term in post-structuralist thinking: texts are often defined as sites of meaning. Hopefully our contextualisation of this term makes its intended usage clear. Other terms – 'boundary', 'frontier', 'land', 'region', 'territory', 'territoriality' – are used more or less with their standard English semantic ranges.

Finally, another aim of this book, which also brings with it difficulties, is the attempt to describe a diverse body of songs, many dozens of performers, different languages and musical styles, and the complexities of issues specific to Aboriginal communities and language speaking groups. Attempting to capture this diversity is compounded by the tensions between Aboriginal musical aesthetics, the agendas of recording companies, the intentions of the musicians involved, and the non-Indigenous desire to document Aboriginal contemporary cultures. As the inclusion of Aboriginal music at the Sydney 2000 Olympics indicates, it can reach into the day-to-day lives of large populations, implicating wide audiences in the reception of contemporary Aboriginal music and the issues it raises. These issues are never unilateral. While some songs refer to topics that affect all Aborigines, such as land rights, many refer to localised interests. These themes are variously interpreted by different audiences, and are influenced by the 'gatekeepers' that enable musical expressions to reach audiences. To overcome problems such as these, rather than attempt to cover music by all contemporary Aboriginal musicians, we have identified songs and repertoires that represent key themes of our topic and act as examples of music's centrality as the medium for statement of opinion. Where possible, the opinions of musicians are quoted, and their local concerns explained. This connects musicians to the areas, languages and communities they represent, and emphasises attachments between music and country. While many themes are raised in this book, we cannot do justice to all of them, nor would we want to claim to be authoritative about a form of cultural production that is always subject to a range of interpretations.

Structure of the book

With this in mind, our first two chapters discuss a range of themes that resonate throughout the remainder of the book. Chapter 1 locates contemporary Aboriginal music in historical contexts and discusses the role of the popular music industry in relation to Aboriginal musicians in different eras. This provides perspectives through which the more specific cultural expressions that occupy later chapters can be read. Chapter 2 supplements the opening chapter, and is also general in scope, providing an explicitly cultural geographical perspective of Aboriginal music across Australia. This involves discussion of the links between music and place, both materially and symbolically, and also of the created and 'intersubjective' nature of Aboriginalities expressed in and through contemporary music. Subsequent chapters either provide detail on regions within which music is made, or present interpretations of the texts of particular musicians. In effect these chapters are a set of case studies. We have avoided the temptation to limit discussion of female Aboriginal performers to a separate chapter, in the same way that we have avoided separate chapters on 'urban' and 'remote' musical styles. Instead, women's music is discussed throughout the book where relevant to discussion, and explanations of 'urban', 'rural' and 'remote' music are dispersed throughout various chapters.

Chapters 3 and 4 examine particular musical styles used by Aboriginal musicians: country music (chapter 3) and hip-hop and R&B (chapter 4). We position these two chapters contiguously for the ways in which they contrast a historical aspect of Aboriginal musical expression (the continued use of country music over a number of decades) with newer musical trends (hip-hop and R&B). In chapter 5 we give a number of readings of a song about a place, 'Warumpinya', by Warumpi Band. We interpret this song as a means of expressing Luritja identity and mapping Luritja country. At the same time, to demonstrate that 'Warumpinya' can be located in other contexts, the song is presented as an example of the development of world music in the 1980s. The work of Djabugay musicians since the time of the 1988 bicentennial is the focus of chapter 6. In this chapter, ways in which Djabugay cultural revival surface in contemporary music, education, language reclamation and cultural tourism are critiqued. Cultural tourism also features in chapter 7, in which we discuss the work of the Central Australian Aboriginal Media Association (CAAMA) and aspects of Aboriginal tourism in Alice Springs. Chapter 8 describes music activity in the Top End. A specific study of one song by a Top End group, 'Nitmiluk' by Blekbala Mujik, is the focus of chapter 9. As with 'Warumpinya' in chapter 5, our reading of this song places it in a number of musical, social and political contexts. The Kimberley region is the topic of chapter 10 – a chapter in which contemporary music activity is linked to a nascent regional Aboriginal politics. Our final chapter, chapter 11, addresses land rights as both an ongoing issue of Indigenous politics and a topic of contemporary song.

So that readers can supplement our work by listening to the artists and songs we mention, we have recommended a number of recordings at the beginning of each chapter. Full details of these, and those of all recordings we discuss throughout the book, are provided in a discography following chapter 11.

In this book we hope that readers (particularly those who are not Aboriginal) are challenged in terms of their perceptions of place, as well as in their understandings of Aboriginal music. The title of the book uses the term 'deadly', meaning terrific or fantastic in Aboriginal English, to refer to Aboriginal music and the places from which that music comes. All too frequently, Aboriginal communities get 'a bad rap' in the main-stream media, whether towns such as Brewarrina and Bowraville in New South Wales, or ex-mission settlements such as Maningrida and Yuen-dumu in the Northern Territory. Often these places and their communi-ties are depicted as dysfunctional or dangerous. Such representations of culture and place are rarely challenged by non-Indigenous commentators. Yet in the music of bands and in the words of singers from these places, it is clear that despite social problems and the lack of basic services, such communities are often places of pride, family life and cultural survival. Aboriginal depictions of place in music are very different from the stereo-typical images that dominate non-Indigenous media reporting – it is these perspectives that are at the centre of this book. Thus, adopting the Aboriginal English use of the term 'deadly', we seek consciously to rede-fine music *and* places, inverting non-Indigenous media definitions to emphasise new and unsettling ways of thinking about place, culture and music.

Peter Dunbar-Hall
Chris Gibson

Suggested listening

The Best of Koori Classics

Kev Carmody ▲ *Images and Illusions*

Joe Geia ▲ *Yil Lull*

Jimmy Little ▲ *Messenger*

Jimmy Little ▲ *Yorta Yorta Man*

No Fixed Address ▲ *From My Eyes*

Herb Patten ▲ *Born an Aussie Son*

Warumpi Band ▲ *Big Name, No Blankets*

Warumpi Band ▲ *Too Much Humbug*

Warumpi Band ▲ *Warumpi Band Go Bush!*

Dougie Young ▲ *The Songs of Dougie Young*

CHAPTER 1

Origins, institutions, industries

Contemporary Aboriginal music is a defining feature of Australian cultural expression. It is found in airport souvenir shops, heard on mainstream and community radio stations, and is a part of major events and festivals. Contemporary Aboriginal music adorns movie soundtracks, is on offer to tourists in theme parks and hotels, and is also a crucial means of expression in Aboriginal community life. This chapter discusses the historical development of contemporary Aboriginal music in the nineteenth and twentieth centuries. We begin by tracing what is known about the origins of Aboriginal/non-Aboriginal musical interactions, and then contextualise the emergence of contemporary Aboriginal music in relation to institutional arrangements and policy developments in Australian federal politics. The final section of this chapter discusses the Australian music industry and its relationship with Aboriginal musicians, a relationship fraught with tensions. These insights then help to inform more detailed discussions of artists, songs and regions in subsequent chapters.

Origins

The recognition currently afforded many Aboriginal performers is comparatively recent. A similar situation exists in the other arts such as writing, painting, theatre and dance; all of these have benefited from expanded awareness and acknowledgment of Aboriginal cultures in Australia since the late 1980s.

This relatively recent recognition of national Aboriginal creative expression belies a longer history of engagement between Aboriginal people and various non-Indigenous musical influences, though nothing is known of the exact origins of Aboriginal 'contemporary' fusions. Aboriginal people who lived in or at the fringes of new colonial cities and towns most certainly came into contact, either directly or indirectly, with imported music throughout the nineteenth century. Little is known about how these sounds were received, or if any Aboriginal performers took the styles and idioms of these imports into their own musical practices. Music became a dominant form of international cultural exchange during the late nineteenth and early twentieth centuries, largely due to the availability of mass-produced, printed sheet music, and particularly with the advent of the phonogram and recorded music (Clarke, 1995). Musical styles such as minstrelsy, vaudeville and bush balladry grew out of their North American and European roots and were distributed and replicated in a variety of other places, particularly after the widespread dissemination of radios in the early twentieth century. Aboriginal communities in Australia most likely absorbed these styles during this period (see Gummow, 1987; Sullivan, 1988). Traces of this can be seen in the presence of bush ballads, gospel-influenced hymns and 'household' songs in Aboriginal communities (Breen, 1989). Despite the emergence of early forms of Indigenous popular music within their own network of communities, prevailing attitudes would have limited the boundaries within which wider audiences could receive early Aboriginal musical expression, and few Aboriginal artists were recognised in the major cities and towns.

Any current understanding of a history of contemporary Aboriginal music must therefore be explained in relation to a history of changing relationships between Aboriginal musicians and non-Aboriginal institutions and audiences, including those recording Aboriginal music since the introduction of sound recording technologies in the late nineteenth century. In this history, relationships between Indigenous performers and uses of sound recording have fluctuated from the purely anthropological to that of explicit commercial support.

The invention of mechanical means of recording sound in the late nineteenth century reinforced the collecting of Indigenous musics as an

academic activity, one which previously had relied on handwritten tran-
scriptions of Aboriginal songs (see Kassler & Stubington, 1984). A significant event in the use of the newly marketed technology from an
Australian perspective was an expedition from Cambridge University to
the islands of the Torres Strait, led by Alfred Cort Haddon, in 1898 (A
Moyle, 1985). On this expedition, ninety-seven wax cylinders of Islander
singing and an amount of silent film footage of dancing were made, initi-
ating the sound recording of Australian Indigenous musics. In 1899 and
1901, Fanny Cochrane Smith, a Tasmanian Aborigine, recorded a
number of wax cylinders (A Moyle, 1960), and between 1894 and 1927,
Sir Baldwin Spencer and Frank Gillen, on various expeditions from Adelaide into South Australia and the Northern Territory, recorded approximately one hundred wax cylinders of central Australian traditional
music (A Moyle, 1959; Mulvaney et al., 1997). Following Spencer and
Gillen's work, Theodor Strehlow collected hundreds of songs on tape
and film between the early 1930s and the early 1950s in central Australia, enabling the writing of his seminal *Songs of Central Australia*,
which, however, was not published until 1971 (see Hill, 2002).

Recordings of Aboriginal performances made by 'explorers', and recordings and film footage resulting from anthropological and musicological
undertakings in the mid twentieth century and after the second world war,
such as those of Strehlow, AP Elkin and subsequently Alice Moyle, primarily recorded traditional music, although Moyle's recordings include introduced and hybrid guitar accompanied songs which she noted 'seem
destined to play a larger part in the song repertoires of Northern Territory
Aborigines' (A Moyle, 1974, 35). These and subsequent recordings of traditional material have been important for their potential to document music
that may no longer be performed or remembered. In some areas of Australia, recordings such as these have been used to assist Aborigines to revive
traditions, and therefore have had a beneficial effect (Gummow, 1995). At
the same time, recordings made by early researchers have often been criticised for the ways they did not acknowledge the names of performers, the
owners and cultural significance of the music, or the offence which listening
to songs might cause. More recently, early field recordings have been reis-
sued by unscrupulous producers without the permission of the descendants
of the original performers, the approval of the group/s who own the music
and the topics sung about, or the setting up of methods for returning

royalty payments to performers and their families. In some cases didjeridu and vocal tracks have been sampled by DJs and record producers for use as backing tracks or for electronic manipulation in other recordings. As with the appropriation of Aboriginal art and design, these activities have led to legal action by and on behalf of Aborigines whose ownership rights have been violated (Janke, 1999; Jopson, 1999).

Music hall, vaudeville and gum leaves

In the 1890s, a new genre of music connected to an emerging colonial nationalism – the bush ballad – developed in Australia. Bush ballads were 'brought from the homelands of the stockmen, drovers and shearers' (Petherick, in Breen, 1989, 20–1) and included traditional songs, reels and jigs and a new style of melody and musical form: narrative verse with chorus and four or eight bar phrases in harmony, melody and rhythm. Influenced by wider Australian developments, an Aboriginal bush folk tradition emerged, linked to 'claypan dancing', busking and community gatherings. In this tradition, string bands used instruments such as banjos, fiddles, tin whistles, accordions, spoons and harmonica, with regional variations: Tasmanian Aborigines even developed a unique hybrid form of country/bluegrass music on the Cape Baron Islands, with songs based on sea shanties.

In places such as Gumbainggir country on the New South Wales North Coast and in Yorta Yorta country near the NSW/Victorian border, gumleaf playing became popular (Ryan, 1999). The then well-known Wallaga Lake Gumleaf Orchestra, which formed a union with a touring vaudeville troupe in the town of Cummera in the 1920s, eventually performed in Melbourne and Sydney, made a film appearance in *The Squatter's Daughter* and marched at the opening of the Sydney Harbour Bridge in 1932 (Walker, 2000). The family of Jimmy Little (b. 1937), to date the most successful Aboriginal country musician, once toured with the Wallaga Lake Orchestra. As Little recalls:

> Music was an automatic family thing. Mum and Dad were vaudevillians. They used to arrange entertainment at the various Aboriginal mission settlements, and my father would also organise teams of our people to give concerts throughout the district to raise funds for the mission. My uncles were vaudevillians, and that's how I got started (in Walker, 2000, 26).

Music hall was the dominant entertainment form of the time, prior to radio, thus minstrel shows and spirituals were among the musics performed on regional tours in Australia, first by visiting American and English troupes, and later by Australian companies. There were parallels between the cultural politics of these styles in Australia and in the United States, where, influenced by 'plantation melodies', African-American artists performed in contexts that allowed for black expression, but expected those artists to appear in stereotypically racist caricature. In Australia, Aboriginal performers took up minstrel acts, sometimes as extensions of re-creating 'traditional' dances and songs on stage. As Jimmy Little remembers:

> My father was a dancer, in terms of traditional dance, and he was a comedian, a natural comedian and storyteller. As a boy in the audience, I'm watching Dad on stage with a lantern and a little fan, and some crepe paper and this was fire, on stage with all the lights out and they're dancing around the fire ... I would see him add charcoal colouring ... like that Al Jolson thing? Blackface, what did they call them? Minstrels. So Dad saw the movie minstrels, and related, I can do that, I'll do that. Mum would come out in a lovely evening gown, and she'd yodel in a clear voice, sing Swiss yodelling songs (in Walker, 2000, 28).

Common to music hall and vaudeville were 'household' songs, performed by touring artists in order to promote sales of the sheet music version of the same song. These were

> typically narrative songs with chorus, similar in form to the bush ballads but with more sentiment ... they were Empire songs, drinking songs, humorous ballads like 'Daddy Wouldn't Buy Me a Bow-wow', ballads of sentiment like 'Home, Sweet Home'... They celebrate the lost love, the lost homeland, mother (who is usually old or dead) and the loss of the good old times (Schultz, in Breen 1989, 23).

While these were the emerging 'universal' themes of a twentieth century international popular music repertoire, they were rooted in a 'sense of exile and hopeless nostalgia' that 'dominated the imagination of the nineteenth century west'. Minstrel songs too, 'expressed the same loss of homesickness ...These songs were adopted by Aboriginal communities, speaking to their hearts from the hearts of another displaced people' (Shultz, in Breen 1989, 24). Aboriginal minstrels changed lyrics to refer to local places, rivers and people, making this imported music relevant to local audiences and their experiences, yet still somewhat contradictorily reinforcing colonial rela-tions. Many music hall songs, though they resonated with experiences of dispossession, were also filled with references to 'coons', 'jacky-jackys', 'gins', and 'piccaninnys', mimicking and degrading Aboriginal culture; to some extent 'the oppressed come to believe the degrading stereotypes of themselves and agree that all beauty, virtue and value go with being white' (Schultz, in Breen, 1989, 27). These songs, however, were always capable of being injected with a dry, understated humour by performers who nego-tiated their intended meanings.

Evangelical sounds and the influence of missions

The establishment of Christian missions across Australia during the nine-teenth and early twentieth centuries brought new musical influences to Aboriginal communities. These influences were linked to the denomina-tions concerned – Lutheran, Anglican, Presbyterian and Roman Catholic. Evangelical colonialism differed in its ideologies and impacts from other forms of invasion and conquest, although it also served to legitimise British expansion. Secular forms of colonial ideology portrayed Aboriginal peoples as racially inferior and incapable of governing or owning land. Evangelical ideologies, which underpinned the establishment of missions, portrayed Indigenous people in contradictory ways: they were both equal humans under God, and humans plagued by an absence of enlightenment – posi-tioned as 'pagans' distanced from a civilised centre: 'While missionaries no doubt regarded Australian Aborigines ... as baser or more degraded than the heathens of Asiatic civilisations, the premise of their efforts was an ethic of human equality in Christendom' (Thomas, 1994, 141). Missionaries sought to 'elevate' Aboriginal society and instil Christian values and behavioural norms, commonly treating an Aboriginal constituency as their 'children', thus patro-nisingly portraying Indigenous cultures as uneducated or undisciplined. Formal training in religious doctrine, English language, sports and cultural performance were all practices through which such conversions occurred:

> the mission was not simply a religious instrument but rather a total social fact ... it sought to impose a new temporal regime of work, leisure, celebration and worship; through education it offered a new

Jimmy Little's early career was founded on songs such as 'Royal Telephone'. Evangelical pop songs like this were not uncommon in the 1950s and 1960s.

global and local history ... it produced not just a population of Christians, but a people that engaged in periodic plantation work, who were notionally subject to rigorous behavioural codes and who had notionally brought their social and domestic habits into conformity with Christian norms ... The white missionaries were the parent to native boys and girls, who were instructed and brought up, not in specifically religious or technical training, but in the whole field of practical, recreational and spiritual living (Thomas, 1994, 140).

Music was a part of missionary life, as training and entertainment. Standard English hymn repertoires were introduced, although 'far more widespread and long lasting than these in its impact on Aboriginal people was the repertoire introduced by the conservative evangelicals, whose presence dominated the mission scene in many parts of Australia' (Shultz, in Breen, 1989, 15). Harmonic part singing, choral arrangements and urban gospel music became common in missions, particularly throughout central Australia. Aboriginal opera singer Harold Blair, from a mission background, became well known, eventually performing around the world, including in shows with American Paul Robeson. In some Queensland missions, including Yarrabah, Mapoon, Weipa, Cherbourg and Palm Island, brass bands were formed as early as the mid 1800s (*Koori Mail*, 2 Oct 2002, 33), although gumleaf bands were more prevalent because of the comparative affordability and portability of instruments. These musical forms, like minstrelsy, were not simply a crudely imposed idiom submissively absorbed by local Aboriginal populations: 'Aboriginal people were comparatively receptive to sacred music because of its function as a form of ritual communication with the powers of creation' (Ellis, in Streit-Warburton, 1995, 309). English hymns were translated into Aboriginal languages, and their words and meanings adapted to local circumstances:

> people related to the hymns at times when something had happened; the passing of a loved one, or a joyous occasion, singing in a soulful way. It was the manner in which we sang that made them really meaningful to the people involved. Even today the hymns are sung in the same fashion, according to whatever's being celebrated at the time. We've accepted them as part of our cultural heritage ... (Rankine, in Breen, 1989, 17).

In Ngarrindjeri country in South Australia, 'The mission school choir would serenade visitors and the passengers on paddle steamers that regularly pulled into the Raukkan jetty' (Bell, 1998, 182). Although the church played an important part in providing 'a forum in which people could sing', it nonetheless transformed local power relations: 'the democratic nature of this forum – one did not need to be an elder to sing – must have undermined the authority of the older generation ... one did not need to dedicate a lifetime to learning the songs and their significance. Once could attend the service and sing' (Bell, 1998, 182).

Gospel influences would shape the current careers of artists such as Jimmy Little and Buna Lawrie, lead singer-songwriter with Coloured Stone:

> I can remember when I was three years old at Koonibba [South Australia], my father used to sing the old gospel songs, like *Just a Closer Walk With Thee*. I knew those songs when I was three years old. Then growing up in the community, listening to the community people playing the old acoustic guitars and picking songs off the old battery wireless. We pretty much had a musical community (Lawrie, in Rintoul, 2002, 16).

Evangelical choirs still sing in ex-mission settlements today, sometimes incorporating elements of traditional dance and song into performances; while gumleaf playing is still apparent in parts of Victoria and New South Wales (see Ryan, 1999).

A new mobility

Songs were often mobile, travelling throughout communities as a result of missionary activities and migration. Whether European in origin, or as hybrids of Aboriginal and Western styles, songs could easily become part of the 'traditional' repertoires of quite different communities. Tiddas, a contemporary vocal group from Melbourne, were pleasantly surprised when a song recorded on their 1996 self-titled album, 'No Goon No Pah', was recognised when they performed live in Australia's far north:

> 'No Goon No Pah' was a song that Lou's aunties had taught her when she was quite young. It was a song that had actually travelled, because whenever we sing that song in Northern parts of

Australia, the Aboriginal mob up there always say 'Hey, we know this song! We sing it a little bit differently, but we know that song too' ... It lets people know that the song is not gonna stand still, that it's travelled for a few hundred years, and it's changed each time. (in *Form Guide*, 1996, 26).

Radio and cinema would both have a profound influence on Australian music and on Aboriginal performers in the 1930s and 1940s. Radio brought imported styles such as hillbilly, gospel and folk to both urban and remote audiences, while wind-up gramophones became popular in Aboriginal communities. Hillbilly music eventually mutated into country and western when it was visualised as a music of frontier in early 'singing cowboy' and western films. These songs and films, as well the performances of Australians such as Tex Morton and Slim Dusty, would have a significant influence on Aboriginal musical practices. Early Aboriginal country musicians, such as Billy Bargo (originally from Queensland, later settling in Melbourne), made their names on the rodeo circuit in Australia, and were often comedians, whipcrackers and boxers as well as musicians. Aboriginal country lyrics also started to incorporate new and sometimes unusual figures into their songs – Afghan camel traders, who first arrived in the desert interior of Australia in the 1840s, started to appear in songs: 'because Afghan cameleers congregated and built their houses at various railheads they became involved in local life in many outback communities such as Alice Springs' (*Koori Mail*, 4 Sep 2002, 31). Aboriginal artists sang about camels and cameleers, as well as the intermarriage of Aboriginal and Afghan people.

By the 1950s country music would become the most popular contemporary style in Aboriginal communities, and the most performed by Aboriginal musicians. The careers of two Aboriginal country musicians, Dougie Young and Jimmy Little, demonstrate different experiences of contemporary Aboriginal music and the involvement of the recording industry with it.

Singer-songwriter Dougie Young (1935? – 1991), born in Mitchell, southwestern Queensland, was only eventually recorded in Wilcannia (NSW) in the 1960s by Jeremy Beckett, Athol McCoy and Glen Vallance. Some of these tracks were released as an album by Wattle Records

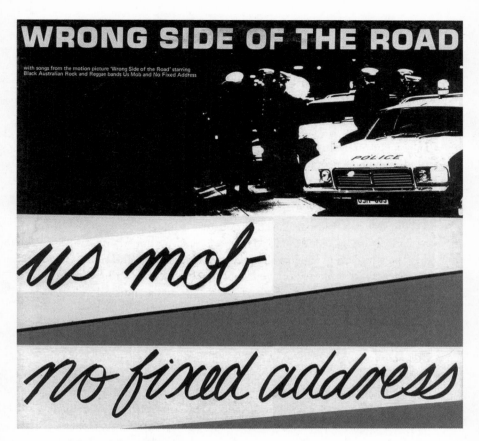

Soundtrack recording of the feature film
Wrong Side of the Road. The film followed
Aboriginal rock and reggae bands Us Mob
and No Fixed Address on a tour throughout
regional centres. The film depicted the hos-
tility and racism experienced by Aboriginal
bands in the 1970s.

in 1964, and this became one of the few available recordings by an Aboriginal singer-songwriter at that time. A complete recording of songs by
Young, released jointly by the Australian Institute of Aboriginal and
Torres Strait Islander Studies and the Australian National Library,
appeared only in 1993 (Beckett, 1993).

Young's songs are important in the *oeuvre* of contemporary Aboriginal music. In the style of guitar accompanied ballads, they present views of the lives of country town Aborigines. In a manner that presages many of the issues raised in the songs of later Aboriginal musicians, Young's songs refer freely to the effects of alcohol and to spending time in prison. They mention Young's Aboriginal background and the treatment from non-Indigenous people this caused, for example, in 'Halfcaste' Young sings autobiographically about the position of the children of mixed parentage:

> But to be an halfcaste you're an outcast
> Why it brings you shame and disgrace
> The white man laughs out upon you
> And you're never welcome in your own black race ...

While Young's songs were known to a limited audience and were concerned with Aboriginal identity and living conditions, the recordings of Jimmy Little represented a different experience of the music industry. His recording career began in 1956 and included the famous 1963 hit, 'Royal Telephone'. Although recognised and promoted as a famous Aboriginal performer, it was not until his albums of the 1990s, for example *Yorta Yorta Man* (1995) and *Messenger* (1999), that Little's output became explicitly Aboriginal in the sense of overt thematic exploration of Aboriginal issues and perspectives. Previously, Little was better known as a country performer singing about generic rural and Christian themes, although these songs may still have been 'made Aboriginal' in the ways that Aboriginal audiences understood and attached meaning to them (see chapter 2). It is Jimmy Little above all others who represents Aboriginal recording activity from the late 1950s until the more widespread commercial support for Aboriginal popular music recordings in the late 1980s, releasing over seventy separate albums, in the form of 78s, 7" singles and CDs, since 1956. There were, however, other Aboriginal musicians making recordings at the same time – among them George Asang, Heather Pitt, Lionel Rose and Georgia Lee in the 1960s; and Ernie Bridge, Col Hardy, David Page, Vic Simms, and Harry and Wilga Williams in the 1970s (Dunbar-Hall, 1995; Walker, 2000; see chapter 3).

Reggae and rock in the 1970s and 1980s

The anthemic 'We Have Survived' by No Fixed Address, is now widely sourced as one of the first recorded Aboriginal songs to break away from the country/gospel canon. If it was not the first, it was certainly the most overt *politicisation* of Aboriginal music at that time, recorded for the soundtrack of the 1981 film *Wrong Side of the Road*, a film that follows two Aboriginal rock/reggae bands on a tour of remote areas and country towns, and exposes the racism and discrimination they face. As Lawe Davies (1993a, 252) argued, No Fixed Address 'enunciated a new urban politics, a new swagger, in the style and patois of an internation-alist black roots movement', linked to the rising land rights movement in Australia. While studying at Adelaide's Centre for Aboriginal Studies in Music (CASM), members of No Fixed Address were heavily influ-enced by Bob Marley's 1979 tour of Australia. Their songs connected narratives of pan-Aboriginal survival with reggae's global diasporic tones, to call for greater black political action and communication with other oppressed peoples around the globe: 'By embracing reggae as an expression of solidarity with black people everywhere, [No Fixed Address] presented its Aboriginal audience with the possibility of a way out from under this oppression. They were in effect turning the logic of Australian individualist nationalism against itself' (Castles, 1992, 30). Bart Willoughby's lyrics encompassed many of the political themes that would later emerge throughout contemporary Aboriginal music: cul-tural survival, resistance to colonisation, cultural loss and Indigenous rights to negotiate distinct status within the Australian nation:

> You can't change the rhythm of my soul,
> You can't tell me what to do,
> You can't break my bones by putting me down
> Or by taking the things that belong to me ...

In 1984, Warumpi Band, from Luritja country, released the 45rpm 'Jailanguru Pakarnu'/ 'Kintorelakutu'. This recording, supported with airplay from Sydney ABC radio station Double J (later national youth broadcaster, Triple J), contributed to a new beginning of the nationwide appearance of recordings by Aboriginal rock groups and their recogni-tion by the wider listening public (see chapter 5). Warumpi Band were in many respects groundbreakers – gaining legitimacy for recording rock songs in Aboriginal languages, and carving out new touring networks throughout Aboriginal communities in the Northern Territory and Kimberley, bringing music recorded by an Aboriginal group to remote settlements. In a 1996 interview, lead singer George Rrurrambu and guitarist Neil Murray described the nascent Aboriginal rock scene in some of those communities:

CG: So what were those early gigs like?

NM: Lots of fun!

GR: Yeah, we just jump onto the car, piss off, with no blankets, no spare clothes, it was good!

NM: A lot of excitement. 'Cause about the only bands that communities had seen were the country showbands that came through, they hadn't had many visiting bands who were Aboriginal bands too, who come in and play music for them, especially original music. Everywhere we went we probably inspired their local bands to do the same thing – a whole lot of bands sprang up around the centre at about that time – Ilkari Maru and Titjikala Band, Coloured Stone were hanging around there, there was a whole heap at that time.

GD: We'd just say, 'let's go ... go there, play there'.

NM: Yeah, we might just ring up on the radio telephone beforehand, 'oh, we're coming in a couple of days' time'. We'd turn up, we'd have a few photocopied posters we'd made at the school [in Papunya] – little sheets, give them to a kid on a pushbike who'd take 'em and scatter them round the community, round the town.

In the same decade, Coloured Stone, who started performing in rural South Australia in 1978, and Scrap Metal, from Broome, received major label support, and Yothu Yindi's first album, *Homeland Movement* (1989) was released, introducing to the Australian public a band that would become one of the most successful in Australian musical history.

At around the same time that Warumpi Band released 'Jailanguru Pakarnu'/'Kintorelakutu', two albums by central Australian singer-songwriter, Bob Randall, appeared – *Ballads by Bob Randall* and *Bob Randall*. Both of these were recordings by the Central Australian Aboriginal Media Association (CAAMA), based in Alice Springs. Randall's songs were close to folk or country ballad style, accompanied by acoustic guitar. Although some cassettes had been produced by Imparja Records (an early incarnation of CAAMA) prior to this, these two albums represented the full-scale entry of CAAMA into the recording and sale of contemporary Aboriginal music, and date the establishment of this media company as the major agency in this field. While the style of folk/country acoustic ballads continues in the work of CAAMA artists such as Bill Wellington, Warren Williams and Frank Yamma, the beginning of CAAMA's recording activity occurred at a time of change in much Aboriginal music. This change was from a repertoire of acoustic accompanied ballads to a sound which relied on a rock group line-up of electrified guitars and drumkit – whether the music produced was country, reggae or rock music. The appearance of numerous contemporary Aboriginal music groups in the mid 1980s, in part a sign of increasing exposure to Western/American music and other forms of entertainment in Aboriginal communities, defined a significant period in the history of Aboriginal music, and initiated musical practices through which large numbers of listeners would gain access to aspects of Aboriginal cultures.

While songs by Bob Randall and his contemporary, Herbie Laughton, also an early CAAMA recording artist, represented an older, ballad oriented repertoire, they used topics and musical practices which would recur in the songs of the rock groups and country bands who followed them into CAAMA's and other recording studios. Topics such as the removal of Aboriginal children from their families in Randall's 'Brown Skin Baby', and the loss of traditional ways of life heard in Laughton's 'Arunta Man's Dream' were echoed in numerous songs by later Aboriginal groups. Also featured on albums by Randall and Laughton were songs that expressed attachment to places, songs such as 'My Island Home' by Randall (not to be confused with the song of the same name by Warumpi Band) and 'McDonnell Ranges' and 'My Finke River Home' by Laughton. The practice of writing contemporary songs in Aboriginal languages, or of combining sections of different languages in songs, also appeared on these recordings from the early 1980s.

Contemporary music in the era of self-determination

A number of reasons help explain the increased availability and accept-ance of Aboriginal arts among the broader Australian public during and since the 1980s. First, in this period there was greater exposure of Abo-riginal arts created for the purposes of protest, of declaring Aboriginal ownership of Australia, and of explaining Aboriginal histories and cul-tures to non-Aboriginal people. This can be partly related to Aboriginal reactions to the 1988 commemorations of the bicentenary of white inva-sion of Australia, galvanising protest movements that had grown over the previous decades. Subsequent events that helped to continue this agenda included the 1992 Mabo decision, the 1993 *Native Title Act* and the 1996 Wik judgement, all relating to Aboriginal ownership of land.

While Aboriginal views on land rights and land-related issues have always been at the centre of Aboriginal/non-Aboriginal interaction in Australia, attention given to land rights intensified in the 1990s with Mabo, and again after the 1996 return to power of a conservative Lib-eral government, under John Howard, after many years of Labor rule. The Labor Party in Australia had been more sympathetic to Aboriginal issues than their Liberal counterparts, and under them the first national mechanism recognising land rights had been passed − in response to the 1992 Mabo decision of the High Court. This ruling was a refutation of the Eurocentric doctrine of *terra nullius* ('empty land', or 'land owned by no-one'). The subsequent *Native Title Act* (1993) officially legislated Indigenous native title and instigated 'the potential to add considerably to the Australian Indigenous land base, by recognition of customary ownership' (Rowse, 2002, 102). Attempts by the Howard government to retrospectively alter or overthrow these decisions, and to challenge the subsequent 1996 Wik decision, another court ruling guaranteeing forms of access to leasehold land for Indigenous Australians, resulted in increased uses of music and the other arts as ways of communicating Aboriginal opinions to the Australian public (discussed in greater depth in chapter 11).

Mabo, the *Native Title Act* and Wik were only three of numerous court decisions and government policy enactments affecting Indigenous Australia in terms of country. They can be positioned as achievements in a long running history of contestation on this issue. Placed in the context of ongoing tensions between Aboriginal and non-Aboriginal Australia, they sit alongside the establishment since the 1970s of infra-structures to support handling of Indigenous affairs at the national level. This infrastructure, referred to by Rowse (2002, 1) as 'the Indige-nous sector', had its impetus in policy directions set 'some time ... between Prime Minister McMahon's Cairns Statement of April 1971 and the earliest decisions of the Whitlam government in December 1972 and January 1973'. Rowse saw the growth of the Indigenous sector as representative of government policies replacing agendas of Indigenous assimilation (in force approximately from 1930 to 1970) with those of self-determination. The development of this sector, and resultant exposure of Indigenous issues which this has fostered, have functioned as a significant influence on increased acknowledgment of Aboriginal peoples, expectations and cultures.

In the area of government policy direction as it affects Indigenous Australians, Stevenson (2000) identified a number of ways in which Aboriginal and Torres Strait Islander peoples and their cultural expres-sions have been constructed and manipulated by Indigenous and non-Indigenous interests. Among these are ways that Indigenous arts feed into 'cultural tourism ... and the representation of national identity' (Stevenson, 2000, 150). She positioned acknowledgment of Indigenous arts practitioners as contributing to the reconciliation process in Aus-tralia, and demonstrated how since the early 1990s, Indigenous arts, among them music, have become an object of federal and state govern-ment policy. Indigenous perspectives, implied objectives of inclusiveness, and potential advantage to governments through being seen to support Indigenous people, have informed the agenda for arts management in Australia.

Another factor that aided in the acknowledgment within Australia of Indigenous cultures and their representations in creative arts has been the growth of similar movements in other countries where indigenous peoples have affirmed survival and co-existence (Patterson, 1996; Keillor, 1996; Neuenfeldt, 1996). This worldwide trend, often defined as post-colonialism, refutes ways that colonised countries such as Australia have been perceived as the domain of their colonisers at the expense of their Indigenous inhabitants. Recognition and support of Indigenous arts that result from post-colonial positions has meant substantial availability of and access to Aboriginal music for listeners who would not normally encounter it. This can be seen in greater amounts of airplay for some Aboriginal bands, national and international tours by Aboriginal rock groups, the use of Aboriginal musicians in the soundtracks of films, and increased media attention to Aboriginal music events and personalities. Coverage and support, while still a long way from that for non-Aboriginal musicians, represents a significant improvement over the situation before the 1990s. Many Aboriginal musicians during this period have sought to create and sustain links with indigenous musicians in other countries. Tiddas, while on a North American tour in 1996, took time to meet and discuss music with musicians at the Canadian Music West Festival in Vancouver, eventually writing the song 'Musqueam', inspired by the people they exchanged stories and experiences with. Other musicians pursued similar inspirations and collaborations: Archie Roach and Kev Carmody have performed with George Telek, from Papua New Guinea; Jason Lee Scott undertook a cultural exchange program with Native American communities; indigenous broadcasters from Australia, New Zealand and North America have held joint symposia to exchange ideas and experiences; several Aboriginal festivals in Australia have invited Native American performers and groups from First Nations Canada to participate in cultural celebrations.

The 1980s and 1990s were also characterised by greater diversification of styles of music distributed by recording companies. Aboriginal music both constituted a new 'niche' in an ever-fragmenting popular music market, and was popular within new and revitalised genres. The influence of the popular music style labelled 'world music', for instance, enhanced the availability of contemporary Aboriginal music to the general public. Leaving aside for the moment criticisms of it as irrelevant to the intentions of the musicians involved (something we return to in later chapters), in world music, aspects of indigenous musics were blended with the sounds of mainstream popular music. Often this occurred through the integration of musical instruments of traditional provenance into rock group line-ups, or adaptations of existing repertoires into newer, popular music sounds. The world music trend developed in the 1980s, with music groups from Africa, South America, Asia, Europe, the Middle East and Oceania producing music which multinational record companies marketed under the world music rubric (Connell & Gibson, 2003). While the record industry and many purchasers of recorded music might have seen the rise of 'world' music in terms of a new commercial trend, to many of the musicians involved the music was not a new worldwide phenomenon or discrete style. Rather, it was contemporary expression of their cultures, modern compositions that utilise electrified sounds as additions to existing instrumental and vocal resources. Whatever the intent of musicians and recording companies, the world music trend of the 1980s and 1990s was one way through which attention was paid to the music of Indigenous musicians on an international level.

Releases of contemporary Aboriginal music were popular under other stylistic headings during this period. Most notably, the initial success of Yothu Yindi was partly linked to a global wave of popularity for electronic dance music in the early 1990s, especially following the international success of a remix of their 'Treaty' by dance music producers, Filthy Lucre. Meanwhile the careers of singer-songwriters such as Kev Carmody, Kerrianne Cox, Ruby Hunter, Archie Roach and the all-female groups Tiddas and Stiff Gins, can be read as benefiting from an international resurgence of acoustic folk music in the 1990s. Indigenous country music performers also benefited from an upsurge in the worldwide popularity of and interest in country music in the 1990s. Through this trend Aboriginal country musicians such as Troy Cassar-Daley found new audiences in Australia and overseas, while older stalwarts such as Jimmy Little had revivals in their careers (chapter 3).

A further influence on the acceptance of contemporary forms of music by Aboriginal performers was increased academic recognition of Aboriginal everyday/popular cultures alongside a history of research into what is generally referred to as 'traditional' song and dance (Newsome, 1998). The appearance of published research in this field since the late 1980s represents a reversal of earlier notions of 'acceptable' research agendas. This could be interpreted in various ways. It possibly represents a genuine movement in academia to support investigation of current Aboriginal cultural expression; it might represent the musical version of the 'new

phenomenon of "Aboriginal history" [which emerged] in the late 1970s'
(Jopson, 2003, 9); it also aligns with worldwide trends in research through
which popular music became a *bona fide* object of investigation; it could be
perceived as one application of minority studies, as political correctness, or
as an analysable component of the Australian Indigenous sector.

Access to electronic media technologies in Aboriginal communities
since the 1970s also provided means through which contemporary
musical expression was supported and fostered. Discussing the introduction of these technologies into central Australian Aboriginal communities, Eric Michaels (1986, 103) noted that the wide availability of
inexpensive cassette recorders in the 1970s led to their use among

The National Aboriginal and Islander Skills
Development Association trains dancers in
Sydney but also travels extensively to Indige-
nous communities to study music and dance.
(Courtesy NAISDA)

THE UNIVERSITY OF ADELAIDE'S CENTRE FOR ABORIGINAL STUDIES IN MUSIC

presents

CASM SHOWCASE 98

SATURDAY 28 NOVEMBER, 8pm

AN EXCITING NIGHT OF MUSIC & DANCE
FEATURING STUDENTS FROM CASM

LION THEATRE & CAFE BAR
CNR MORPHETT STREET
& NORTH TERRACE
CITY

MEALS AVAILABLE 7pm - 9pm
BAR FACILITIES AVAILABLE

$5 WAGED
$3 UNWAGED

Artwork by Inawinytji Williamson, Kunytjitja Brown and CASM students & staff

The Centre for Aboriginal Studies in Music
(University of Adelaide) has become one of
the most prominent training grounds for
Indigenous musicians.

Aborigines 'for a variety of purposes ... country and western pre-recorded
tapes became popular [and] local music was also recorded, both traditional
and modern'. In a subsequent discussion, he showed how the adoption of
television production and broadcasting by Warlpiri Aborigines at Yuendumu in 1985, incidentally among the first public television services in
Australia, demonstrated 'considerable creative interest among Aborigines
in the new entertainment technology' (Michaels, 1989, 11). Considered
in combination with the instigation of broadcasting from Alice Springs
through CAAMA in 1980, similar local television production and broadcasting in other central Australian communities, and the introduction
of ABC TV to remote Australia via satellite in 1984/1985, a picture

emerges of simultaneous media developments and utilisations in Aboriginal communities. Recording and broadcasting of contemporary forms of music were only one use to which these technologies were put.

In addition to these reasons for increased acknowledgment of forms of contemporary Aboriginal music is one which is perhaps the most important: the use of contemporary musical expression among Aborigines as interventionist texts, making music as deliberate re-representations of themselves, Aboriginal cultures and places, and a desire to broadcast these ideas nationally and internationally. Such a use of music may be seen as responding to myths about Aboriginal people and culture, the result of a need to counteract degrading images and treatment of Aboriginal people. Taken another way, this music is sometimes more overtly *protest* music. At the same time it becomes a proactive use of music as a means of affirming identity, and of reviving and reinterpreting cultural practices, some of which had been limited to older generations. In Aboriginal English this concept is summed up in the term 'survival', and music has played a large part in this agenda, both as expression of culture, and expression about culture (chapter 2).

A national geography

As a culmination of these factors, there is now a national geography of Aboriginal contemporary musical expression – a map of Aboriginal music production and performance that, while it may often intersect with that of non-Indigenous Australian music, is appreciably different from it.

The capital cities of the eastern side of Australia – Adelaide, Brisbane, Canberra, Hobart, Melbourne, Sydney – constitute a network through which much of the commercial and 'high art' music industry is supported. This includes state orchestras, international music recording and production facilities, opera and ballet companies, festivals, and the touring circuits undertaken by artists. An eastern seaboard musical geography of largely non-Indigenous music, with a history dating from the early nineteenth century, dominates Australian commercial musical life. Another important musical cartography is that shaped by country music, with its main institutions in the northeastern part of New South Wales and southeastern part of Queensland. This represents the traditional 'heartland' of Australian country music. Here a regular cycle of country music events, rodeos, musters, festivals and competitions keeps the country music industry vital. This map intersects with a cartography of Aboriginal country music, especially during the annual Tamworth Country Music Festival, at which both Aboriginal and non-Aboriginal musicians perform, even if on different levels and to different forms of acknowledgment (see chapter 3).

Distinct from these networks, there are vibrant Aboriginal music scenes with their own networks of production and dissemination. One of these is derived from centres for teaching. Important locations at which Indigenous musicians study are in Adelaide (Centre for Aboriginal Studies in Music/Wilto Yerlo, University of Adelaide); Brisbane (Aboriginal Centre for the Performing Arts); Sydney (Eora TAFE College); and Perth (Western Australian Academy of the Performing Arts; Aboriginal Islander Music College, usually known as Abmusic). Dance companies based around the training of Indigenous students, such as the Aboriginal Dance Theatre, Bangarra Dance Theatre and the National Aboriginal and Islander Skills Development Association (NAISDA), all three in Sydney, and centres at which Indigenous students undertake training in theatre arts (for example in Brisbane and Perth) also belong to this network. Often training at one of these institutions leads directly to recorded output and public performances. The Centre for Aboriginal Studies in Music (CASM), at the University of Adelaide, has been perhaps the most productive in this respect, former students including Jimmy Chi, Arnold 'Puddin' ' Smith, Bart Willoughby, and members of the groups Aroona, Artoowarapana Band, Coloured Stone, Kuckles, No Fixed Address and Us Mob.

Another network links locations of Aboriginal recording facilities and institutions, often also the sites of Indigenous cultural tourism – Alice Springs, Broome, Darwin, Fremantle, Tamworth. In some cases, these places are also the locations of Aboriginal broadcasting facilities and/or media associations. There are more than a hundred Aboriginal media associations administered through the federal government's Broadcasting for Remote Aboriginal Communities Scheme (BRACS), and overseen by the National Indigenous Media Association of Australia (NIMAA) (National Indigenous Media Association of Australia, nd; Meadows, 2002). They fulfil a number of agendas. They are primary sites for the dissemination of contemporary Aboriginal music. Through Indigenous control of broadcasting, they are a direct arena of empowerment, enabling Aboriginal interventions in publicly available media and representations of Aboriginality. Their role in the 'preservation, development and promotion of [Indigenous] arts, cultures and languages' (Aboriginal and Torres Strait Islander Commission, 1997a, 90) refers not only to the provision of information and communication services to Indigenous Australians, but also to an objective of 'foster[ing] understanding between Aboriginal and Torres Strait Islander people and other Australians through communication of Aboriginal and Torres Strait Islander issues ... to all sections of society' (Aboriginal and Torres Strait Islander Commission, 1997a, 90–91). Moreover, reflecting utilisations of contemporary music by Aboriginal people, as part of the overall manipulation of the media by Indigenous communities, they provide an 'opportunity for counter-hegemonic processes to operate, challenging dominant ideas and assumptions about the world' (Meadows, 2002, 257).

Another geography of contemporary Aboriginal music is that consisting of festivals at which Indigenous musicians perform. Some of these, such as Barunga Festival (NT), Barambah Beltout (Qld), Stompen Ground (WA) and Survival (NSW) are almost exclusively Indigenous. Others are festivals at which strong support for Indigenous performers is found. Indigenous and non-Indigenous festival networks coincide in events such as Croc Fest (various locations), Port Fairy Folk Festival (Vic), Tamworth Country Music Festival (NSW), Womad (SA) and Woodford Festival (Qld), although these festivals are distinct and express different audiences, priorities, agendas, commercial interests, politics and cultural expectations (see chapter 2 for further discussion of festivals).

Recording companies and the music industry

The role of the music industry in the promotion of contemporary Aboriginal music cannot be underestimated (Mitchell, 1992; Neuenfeldt, 1993a; Kukoyi, 1999). Through it, musicians receive public exposure, and access to the infrastructures and profits of recording, advertising and touring, and to radio, television and internet appearances. In these ways Aboriginal thoughts and opinions are mediated into the wider public domain. In addition, Aboriginal cultures are generally oral traditions not preserved in writing, but maintained and passed on in spoken and sung forms. Recording – a contemporary form of preserving and spreading ideas and traditions through sound – is a method of cultural dissemination of great appeal to Aboriginal musicians and listeners. However, it must be remembered that the recording industry is based on commercial enterprise, that it does not merely distribute recordings in a 'hands-off' fashion. The recording industry is made up of a range of 'gate-keepers' such as managers, promoters, sound engineers, reviewers and disc jockeys, who all to various degrees influence the production of music, sometimes dictating stylistic and ideological positions that may be at odds with the intentions of Aboriginal musicians. There are also differences in the way music is marketed, distributed and consumed in cities and in remote areas. For example, the prevalence of cassette recordings of albums (rather than CDs) in record outlets in remote parts of Australia is evidence that recordings by Aboriginal popular musicians are primarily intended for local communities rather than for worldwide distribution. Limited commercial accessibility to albums in remote communities, where they can only be purchased in community stores, is further evidence that recordings are aimed at local listeners. Buying patterns among Aboriginal youths reported by shop owners confirm the regional appeals of certain recordings, with purchases often reflecting family links to performers, or to knowing that a performer or group is from the purchaser's community or mob. The use of Aboriginal languages with limited numbers of speakers for the lyrics of popular songs, a recognised strategy for preserving languages, is another indication of intended audiences of many recordings, and that the possibility of widespread commercial release might not be the primary reason an Aboriginal music group enters the recording studio.

Sometimes changes to Aboriginal music brought about through the wishes of the recording industry are not completely approved of by Aboriginal musicians and listeners. At the same time the involvement of the recording industry in Aboriginal music brings with it interactions with commercial cultures, and degrees of participation in and membership of contemporary Australian society. It is a means of interacting with and utilising current forms of communication; its adoption by Aboriginal musicians is an indication of the dynamism of Aboriginal cultures. In these ways contemporary Aboriginal music exists in numerous fields of intent and interpretation and cannot be divorced from the financial agendas of some of the companies through which it is marketed. At the same time, without these record companies, musics that are at risk of lack of attention might not reach wide audiences. In these ways the relationship between contemporary Aboriginal music and the recording industry that supports it is one of tensions and contradictions.

The recording industry falls into three broad sections in relation to contemporary Aboriginal music. There are national and international record companies that market the music of numerous Australian artists, Aboriginal and non-Aboriginal, such as Festival/Mushroom Records, now a part of Rupert Murdoch's News Corporation (who release recordings of Torres Strait Islander Christine Anu, and Aboriginal musicians Warumpi Band, Ruby Hunter, Archie Roach and Yothu Yindi); Sony Music (Troy Cassar-Daley; Shakaya); RCA Victor (Coloured Stone) and Larrikin (Mark Atkins, Indijjinus, Bobby McLeod). On the other hand there are companies such as CAAMA and Goolarri Media that market music only by Aboriginal musicians and may be the sole commercial support network for many Aboriginal performers. Between these two poles of Indigenous recording are companies such as Moondog Records (Fremantle, WA) and Skinny Fish Records (Darwin, NT) who cater for both Indigenous and non-Indigenous artists. These types of companies have different cultural, economic and political agendas.

Until the mid 1990s, recording and dissemination of contemporary Aboriginal music was not generally in the domain of mainstream recording companies. Rather it was undertaken by specialist labels. While Festival Records recorded Jimmy Little and Warumpi Band, much work was done by companies such as Enrec Studios, Hadley Records and Opal Records – all originally based in Tamworth (NSW), the recognised centre of the Australian country music industry. Between them, these three studios produced and released the recordings of a significant number of Aboriginal musicians. Their recordings from the 1980s provide important documentation of the period immediately before the entry onto the music scene of groups such as Yothu Yindi through whose careers the profile of Indigenous music rapidly expanded. They also indicate the continuing importance of country music as a stylistic mainstay of Aboriginal performers.

Enrec Studios released recordings of country singer Roger Knox and his group, Euraba. This studio also produced a series of albums strongly oriented towards country music under the collective title *Koori Classics*.

Some albums in this series presented an artist (for example, Ian Atkinson), others were compilations of Aboriginal performers, including Sarina Andrew, Kathy Kelly, Roger Knox, Sharon Mann, Mac Silva and Vic Simms. Enrec Studios also released recordings by didjeridu players David Hudson and Mark Atkins. Hadley Records has recorded a number of Aboriginal performers, among them Dave Thulina and the Moon-dusks, and Harry and Wilga Williams and their group, The Country Outcasts. The success of Hadley recordings of Harry Williams led to this studio being sought out by other Aboriginal artists and groups, among them Gus Williams and Country Ebony, from Ntaria (Hermannsburg) west of Alice Springs (Scott, Eric, interview, 1999). Opal Records spe-cialise in recordings of country and western musicians. Consequently their contribution to Aboriginal popular music has focused on record-ings of well-known Aboriginal artists such as Col Hardy, a mainstay of Aboriginal country music performances and festivals. More recently Lar-rikin Records has shown its support of Indigenous musicians through a number of recordings, including a double CD compendium of historic Aboriginal country music performances released in conjunction with the publication of Walker's (2000) book, *Buried Country: The Story of Abo-riginal Country Music.*

Through these various means numerous Aboriginal artists from all regions have been recorded and distributed throughout Australia and overseas. The number of Aboriginal artists signed to 'major' record com-panies peaked following the success of Yothu Yindi in the early 1990s, declining somewhat since then, although the amount of Aboriginal pro-duction has not ceased, with many more regional broadcasting agencies now involved in recording local bands. This has been made easier by the advent of more accessible and affordable recording technologies. Nonetheless, there are persistent structural and cultural problems with the recording industry that hinder the successes of contemporary Abo-riginal musicians, ranging from explicit racism to factors associated with geographical distance.

Contemporary Aboriginal musicians share with others in the music industry conditions of work that are, generally speaking, intermittent and under-remunerated. Well-paid musicians do exist in the music industry, and a limited group of Aboriginal musicians (such as Yothu Yindi and Troy Cassar-Daley) have signed national and international recording contracts. These examples act as exceptional proofs of success, interpreted by many Aboriginal musicians at the grass roots level as examples of possible ways to develop careers in music, particularly for those who might seek similar fortunes. Yet, for most, the lure of such possibilities is linked to their willingness to remain unpaid for current activities, traded against promised future gains. For Troy Cassar-Daley, this was demonstrably the case: 'I had about four or five years of really living on the breadline. At different times I had to do funny sorts of jobs to keep myself existing' (in *Deadly Vibe*, 2003, 6–7). Very few musicians (whether Aboriginal or non-Aboriginal) make a reliable income from their efforts (see Gibson 2003). For Kev Carmody, 'It's only the big festivals where I pick up money. When I was on the road recently the roadies picked up $450–$500. Rory McLeod and I picked up $150' (quoted in George, 1992, 36). Despite being a recording artist for over twenty years, Buna Lawrie, from Coloured Stone, has received little reward for his efforts:

> Two years ago, Lawrie was awarded the Don Banks Music Fund Award for his contribution to Australian Music, but asked what he has made from music, he replies acidly 'Just enough for food and petrol'. Through the years he has sold about 250,000 albums, but says if he had been 'treated equally' it would have been closer to 5 million. 'I am bitter', he says. 'You do all the hard work and then you get turned away. They don't want to play your music. You get an anger in you. I've got to be strong enough to keep going' (Rintoul, 2002, 16).

Similarly, Rose Pearse, songwriter, filmmaker and manager of Darwin-based group Wild Water, has argued that

> in Darwin and in Australia, there is little real support for developing indigenous musical talent. Few venues want to employ black bands unless they come from overseas. Many Australian festivals seem to have adopted the 'got one Aboriginal act, we've covered that side of things' attitude to programming. [Australian] record companies are slow off the mark – they only ever follow the global trends, they never lead them (Pearse, 1997, 29).

Aboriginal women involved in the music industry face a particularly difficult set of circumstances. Gender relations in the mainstream music industry are already highly uneven. Women have far fewer opportunities for full-time work, and gendered notions of musicianship, credibility and musical skill work against women.

Beyond structural barriers with the music industry, the nature of Aboriginal musical expressions is often seen as a problem within the music industry. Kev Carmody has argued that the Australian music industry has an 'inbuilt censorship mechanism'. Mainstream radio, for instance,

> has an obsession with 'radio friendly' music; promotional singles just get thrown in the bin. They won't even touch anything that's not 'safe' to play. They don't like anything or anybody that's singing from outside the system and communicating messages that criticise that system (interview, 1996).

This inbuilt censorship is present at the level of choices made about the make-up of albums, track listings, and methods of marketing releases to audiences. For Kev Carmody,

> with the last album [*Images and Illusions*], I had a whole list of songs which were finished, and they decided the best thing to do to market the songs would be to release an EP. So I said 'OK, which songs would you want on it?'. All these execs sat round the boardroom table and went 'this one, this one, this one' – it was all the safe, depoliticised, radio-friendly stuff' (interview, 1996).

In some cases, the efforts of Aboriginal musicians are hampered by out-and-out racism. According to Blackfire's Grant Hansen:

> Racism is rife in the music industry. Most hotels don't want Aboriginal clients or audiences because Aboriginal music is still thought of as being purely a political tool. And, by and large, record companies don't think there's a market. Most indigenous performers are self-managed artists who find trouble negotiating gigs and staging their work (quoted in Evorall, 1999, 22).

Richard Micallef, then head of CAAMA Music in Alice Springs, said in 1996 that

> Racism is something very difficult to prove. It is easy to hide the racism issue behind the marketing issue. 'They don't fit our format', is being used very regularly when it comes to Aboriginal bands. There is a reasonable suspicion that people look at the colour of the band before booking them. As a result, there are a lot of disgruntled bands. One of our bands had a residency in Melbourne. It was a great night but at the end someone knocked someone else onto the ground, a punch. Later it was found that the person that was knocked out was harassing black girls all night. But the point is, this one blow led to 8 police cars turning up and the cancellation of the band. Now if you were a white band, and there was a fight in the pub, you wouldn't cancel the band. You'd just find the bloke who was fighting and kick him out. People think that the problem is related to the fact that there was a black band. If there is a large black following, people are worried. When you're touring there are restricted opportunities because as soon as a black band gets popular and they get a black audience, people don't want to book them (quoted in Gledhill 1996:12).

Racism also works in other ways, including expectations imposed on Aboriginal artists to emphasise 'traditional' elements of culture over those that outsiders might perceive as 'too Western' or 'inauthentic'. At the 1993 Womad ('world of music') festival in Adelaide, for instance, 'two weeks before the festival, an Adelaide Womad organiser announced that she had decided to drop Rough Image (a band from Point McLeay near the Murray Mouth) from the line-up. The stated reason for excluding them was that "their music doesn't sound Aboriginal, it sounds western" ' (Hollinsworth, 1996, 64). Uneven relations of power continue to work within the music industry in defining Aboriginality, and expectations are brought to bear about which elements of 'authentic' Aboriginal culture should be promoted or silenced.

In this chapter we have attempted to chart interactions between Aboriginal musicians and the various outside influences and industries through which songs and performances are mediated – the arrangements of power, both historically and in the current era, which shape the terrain upon which musicians undertake their art. Aboriginal artists are, in general, acutely aware of their particular positionality in relation to these axes of power, as well as the racism and stereotypes that must be battled throughout their everyday lives. Their efforts to overcome these disadvantages and contribute to a continually unfurling geography of Aboriginal cultural expression are explored in the following chapter, which engages in more depth with the Aboriginalities, and spatialities, created and contested through music.

Suggested listening

Bangarra Dance Theatre/David Page ▲ *Fish – The Music*

Bangarra Dance Theatre/David Page ▲ *Ochres – The Music*

Kerrianne Cox ▲ *Just Wanna Move*

Fitzroy Xpress ▲ *Little Bit Country Little Bit Rock 'n' Roll*

Ruby Hunter ▲ *Thoughts Within*

Mixed Relations ▲ *Love*

North Tanami Band ▲ *Warlpiri Warlpiri People*

Archie Roach ▲ *Charcoal Lane*

Tiddas ▲ *Sing about Life*

Stiff Gins ▲ *Origins*

CHAPTER 2

Music, place and identity

The variety of styles and concerns articulated in contemporary Aboriginal music, and associated social practices, thwart attempts to pigeonhole Aboriginal music by style, purpose or theme. Rather than displaying 'cardboard' versions of Aboriginality that are static or stereotyped, Aboriginal musicians sing about a diverse range of issues – as performers and as individuals in heterogeneous circumstances. Generalising about the thematic intentions of Aboriginal musicians is problematic, as outlined in the introduction of this book. Notwithstanding this concern, contemporary Aboriginal music is geographical in many ways, both as a cultural practice linked to particular places, regions and community activities, and as musical and lyrical text, expressed through language, musical referents, lyrics about land rights struggles, self-determination, cultural survival and national identity. In order to explore these geographies of contemporary Aboriginal music, we argue that music needs to be understood as a text and as a social/economic practice mediating Aboriginal identities, the various representations of Aboriginality communicated through music.

Discussions of Aboriginality generally deal with debates about 'race', 'identity' and 'inheritance'. Since European colonial invasion, both Aboriginal and non-Aboriginal people have perceived identity in various ways. For some, biological concepts such as 'blood' inheritance apply — thus the use of terms in the past such as 'half-caste' and 'octa-roon' to measure racial heritage. Increasingly, other interpretations have been emphasised:

> 'Aboriginality' is not just a label to do with skin colour or the par-ticular ideas a person carries around in his/her head which might be labelled Aboriginal such as an Aboriginal language or kinship system. 'Aboriginality' is a social thing ... It is created from our his-tories. It arises from the intersubjectivity of black and white in dialogue (Langton, 1993a, 31).

Indeed, 'Aboriginality' as a notion only came into being with colonisa-tion — it distinguished those peoples that Europeans thought of as 'natives' or 'originals' from themselves. In pre-colonial times, Aboriginal people were part of linguistic tribal groups, clan systems or families — there was no overarching collective identity for these groups before Europeans started to generalise about them. Rather than an innate and fixed identity automatically inherited at birth, Aboriginality is a perva-sive *idea*, or a set of ideas, created and sustained in the public realm by various actors, both Indigenous and non-Indigenous. Hence 'the most dense relationship is not between actual people, but between white Australians and the symbols created by their predecessors. Australians do not know and relate to Aboriginal people. They relate to stories told by former colonists' (Langton, 1993a, 33). Rather than an innate or biological concept, Aboriginality, therefore, is 'a field of intersubjec-tivity in that it is remade over and over again in a process of dialogue, of imagination, of representation and interpretation' (Langton, 1993a, 33–4).

This more social/cultural perspective on Aboriginality is important for many cultural, legal and political reasons. Biological metaphors inevitably shroud discriminatory ideas of 'purity' of inheritance, and emphasise 'race' over 'ethnicity', setting the stage for other essentialised, exoticised or simply degrading images of Aboriginal people (for instance, arguments of genetic predisposition to drunkenness). On the other hand, social conceptions of Aboriginality provide theoretical tools to uncover discriminatory representations of Aboriginal people and to empower Aboriginal people to negotiate and resist these images in a variety of ways. As Langton (1993b), Michaels (1986; 1989) and others have argued, media such as film, literature and music are important arenas through which to understand how Aboriginality is intersubjectively constructed by both Aboriginal and non-Aboriginal people. While racist stereotypes often dominate representations of Aboriginality in mainstream media, Aboriginal people represent themselves in different ways, sometimes as efforts to counteract repressive representations, at other times to celebrate Indigenous life and culture. Aboriginality is thus a site of resistance as well as oppression:

> As an invention, both of tradition and ethnicity, contemporary Aboriginality is syncretic and operates across time, space, and situation, endeavouring to meld a sense of group and self for Aboriginal consociations and individuals in the face of persistent degradation by powerful vested interests in the dominant culture (Neuenfeldt, 1995, 25).

It is thus important to understand Aboriginality as socially constructed. Moving on from this recognition, Aboriginality is also mediated by geography. All cultural identities are spatial, in that they are always connected to perceptions of place and scale, from the human body to region, nation and beyond. Because identities of all types are constructed, performed and contested in physical and symbolic spaces, the context matters (see Jackson, 1989; Pile & Thrift, 1995; D Mitchell, 2000). We begin our discussion of geographies of Aboriginality in music by examining those Aboriginalities linked to country and complex sets of social structures and laws; these are depictions of Aboriginal identity inherited and adapted from pre-colonial times, but communicated through the means of contemporary Aboriginal music. We then discuss other less literal ways in which Aboriginality can be understood as spatially constructed. This includes music in 'urban' contexts and music in community life, as well as ways in which Aboriginalities interact with other identities, most notably those associated with gender.

Music and the Aboriginal significance of place

In his introduction to a collection of essays on land rights by Indigenous writers, Yolngu elder, Galarwuy Yunupingu, wrote that 'our land is our life — this belief is central to Aboriginal people's existence'

(G Yunupingu, 1997, xv). This idea forms a continual basis through which writers have tried to understand Aboriginal music and dance.

A central concern of Aboriginal culture is expression of attachment to, responsibility for and the significance of place. Place, in the form of a region, the ambit of the use of a language, a named site, or generically as the concept 'land' or 'country', is an ongoing topic of Aboriginal cultural expression, whether in the visual arts, story, song or dance. Examination of the meanings of music through its ability to refer to a place, and through that to express the importance of place, is a standard means of discussing Aboriginal musical aesthetics in literature on Aboriginal cultures across various academic disciplines.

Place is central to Aboriginal identity on many levels. A person's conception site, the region from which a person or a group of people come, the physical sites formed by historical personages during the creation period, all contribute to constructions of individual and group identity. Singing about these places affirms their existence and the connections between them and their owners. As Dixon wrote in the Introduction to *The Honey-Ant Men's Love Song and Other Aboriginal Song Poems*, 'Song was, and still is, a central component of Aboriginal culture, often marking the connection between a people and their country' (Dixon & Duwell, 1990, xiv). This was echoed in comments by other writers, such as Richard Moyle (1986, 4) when he pointed out in his work on the Agharringa of central Australia that

> the linking of songs to the land is a feature of central Australian society generally. ... the Agharringa men consider the bond between certain of their own ceremonies and Agharringa Country to be such that ownership of the former is a *sine qua non* for ownership of the latter.

This premise is borne out in Australian courts when songs are sung as evidence to establish Aboriginal land claims, and in anthropological writings in which songs are used as research material to investigate the significance of land in Aboriginal cultures (for example, Morphy, 1984; Davis & Prescott, 1992). The significance of land in this respect is explained, for example, by Toyne and Vachon (1984, 5–6) in their work on Pitjantjatjara land claims:

For Pitjantjatjara men and women, their land is the central and inseparable part of their being ... When [they] talk about them-selves relating to the land, they express these relationships in a single concept known as ngura. Ngura can be a single camp or a community, the places where people make a living and renew their existence in dance and song ... [ngura] is a focus of day-to-day living and philosophical ideas and speculation. And it is a key to understanding the people, their culture and their rights to land.

This naming of places is found not only in traditional songs, but also in contemporary Aboriginal songs, where singing about sites and the events of the past associated with them are a means of affirming group and individual identity and of stating relationships to places (Corn & Gumbula, 2002). In this way, Aboriginal sites become songs.

This summary explanation of some aspects of Aboriginal links to country is only an introductory indication of a complex and fluctuating situation. As Sutton (1995) shows, general statements such as this require qualification if the range of Aboriginal relationships to country are to be properly acknowledged. For example, that areas of country can be named and defined from the language spoken in them is not always the case. Further, systems of land ownership and responsibility differ across regions of Aboriginal Australia, and levels of descent through either a person's father or mother affect subsequent levels of attachment to country − these are not uniform. In some cases, Aboriginal people from different but physically close areas indicate allegiance to 'shared land, shared identities' (Sutton, 1995, 53) − this challenges a perception of Aboriginal ownership of country as unilateral and unchanging. Attachment to country is thus a general theme which is articulated in unique and specific ways around Australia, particularly given that colonisation was not a singular process enacted identically across the continent (Thomas, 1994).

The roles that music plays in the expression of the various links between a person or a group of people and place is complex. In Aborig-inal cosmologies the creation of the physical world and the rules by which it could function and be managed were simultaneous, the work of Dreaming beings who figure in the texts of songs, the topics of dances and the imagery of design and painting. The places created through this activity are owned by the Aboriginal people to whom they were given, who inhabit them and who affirm their identity through that posses- sion. In most cases, concomitant with that ownership of land is the pos- session and use of language/s within a region – a key element of continually maintained sovereignty. In these instances, ownership of country is continually attested in acts of speech when a language belongs inextricably to the place where it is spoken. Singing a song in a language establishes sovereignty on these two initial levels: songs about a place define that place as belonging to specific owners; songs sung in the language of a place delimit ownership to the speakers of that lan- guage. In this way songs act as *territorialisations* across both traditional and contemporary Aboriginal musical expression.

The manner in which these aspects of Aboriginal culture and sover- eignty are transposed into contemporary song are numerous. On a widely recognised public level, songs that call for the return of alienated lands to Aborigines through statement of land rights, or refer to specific cases of dispute over ownership or use of country, are initial examples on which a broadly geographical reading of contemporary Aboriginal music can function. On less widely recognised levels are songs that cel- ebrate Aboriginal communities' responses to the return of sites to their owners, songs that praise a site as the home of a community, and songs that express personal relationships to and responsibilities for a place. Each of these types of relationship to place can also be interpreted as a statement of individual and group identity, as proactive expression of Indigenous cultures, and as notification of political positions and agendas. Political interpretation of these songs is particularly relevant when they are heard in conjunction with the actions and policies of fed- eral and state Australian governments, as responses by Aboriginal com- munities to these, and as musical reification of political movements through which Aboriginal nationhood is sought. Contemporary music plays a large role in negotiation over and notification of these issues.

In contemporary forms of music by Aborigines, topics of land, country and sovereignty resurface continually in a number of ways. In a fashion similar to that heard in traditional music, rock songs exist about the importance of a place, a site, or town to an individual or group. When Wirrinyga Band, from Milingimbi (NT), sing about Galiwinku in their song 'My sweet Takarrina' they express their attachment to this place and its importance to them. In the same vein, North Tanami Band sing about their membership of the Warlpiri in the opening song of their 1990 album *Warlpiri Warlpiri People* through an appeal to the place where the Warlpiri live, the Tanami Desert. Reference to lineage ('our Fathers') in this song as proof of ownership of a place, is one means of expressing a group's rights to a place, and a recurring method for this in contemporary Aboriginal expression:

> Right in the centre there's a desert
> That belongs to our Fathers ...
> We are the Desert people
> We are the Warlpiri tribe.

Another link between contemporary music and geography is in the use of rock songs to express generalised Indigenous calls for the return of country. In these cases, songs align with those of indigenous musicians from other colonised countries at the same time that they accord with protest genres of folk and rock music in general. The special choice of land as their topic is both a statement of Indigenous relationship to and alienation from country, and symbolic of the treatment of Aborigines on many other fronts. What becomes clear when listening to Aboriginal songs about land from various regions is that two broad symbolic devices are used. There are songs about specific places and their significance to the members of communities from which musicians come. Another set of songs is about country in general; these songs do not name specific sites or language speaking areas. While the first set of songs may use lyrics wholly or in part in Aboriginal languages, thus connoting areas of country and affirming rights to it, the second set of songs tends to be in English. We perceive this distinction as representative of the provenance of songs as either expressing an individual language speaking community's attachment to named sites, or as representative of a national, pan-Aboriginal land rights ethic. In the case of the first set of songs, links between the traditional music of an area, such as the use of specific musical instruments (for example, pairs of boomerangs or didjeridu), are analysed here as giving such songs relevance through aural factors to the sites named in songs, as with 'Warumpinya' by Warumpi Band (chapter 5) and 'Nitmiluk' by Blekbala Mujik (chapter 9).

Naming practices among Aboriginal music groups

In the context of the lives of Aboriginal musicians and their communities, the naming of bands provides an insight into how musical activity is linked to expression of relationship to country. This is especially so in those areas of Australia away from the major cities – areas where links to country continue to form the basis of life. While some Aboriginal groups, such as Coloured Stone and Nokturnl, use names that can be interpreted as typical of rock groups worldwide, other Aboriginal groups name themselves through locally understood terms or phrases. In many cases the words chosen for music group names have specific meaning/s for Aboriginal communities or language speaking groups, and in this way a group can be identified with a community, issues which affect it, or places significant to it. This is done by using a term from a locally understood Aboriginal language for a group's name, by referring to a place, community, or significant site, or by reference to a totem such as an animal or natural occurrence. As reference to any one of these implies reference to the area in which it is known, a group's name becomes intertextual and can make a statement about a place. For example, the country-rock band, Fitzroy Xpress, indicate their location in the township of Fitzroy Crossing in the south Kimberley region of Western Australia. To Aboriginal people of this area, the name implies more than simply that of a township: it is where local Aboriginal people dispossessed from their traditional lands moved to set up shanty suburbs in the 1970s, and where today celebrations of contemporary Aboriginal cultures (through a local festival featuring Aboriginal country music bands) take place. Such names resonate with meaning and implied connections to localities and communities.

Other groups utilise the names of Aboriginal languages in their names. In this way the Tjapukai Dance Theatre label themselves as members of the Tjapukai (Djabugay) people of the northern Queensland coast. Like the Tjapukai Dance Theatre, Arrente Desert Posse and Pitjantjatjara Country Band draw attention to their links to Arrente and Pitjantjatjara speakers respectively. The Wedgetail Eagle Band, from Fregon in the Pitjantjatjara lands, name themselves after a bird common in the central Australian region, while the group Wairuk have used the Wayra language name for a Dreaming personage, the fish tail eagle, as the name of their band. Other less explicit naming practices exist. In the name of their group, Yothu Yindi reference aspects of Yolngu cosmology and social organisation. This locating of a music group is in reference to local knowledge rather than to a place.

The most common method of naming a rock group is by reference to place names. Some groups use place names that appear on official government maps. Thus the North Tanami Band, from Lajamanu, use a name found on maps as both the title of the Tanami Desert and a settlement, Tanami Downs, northwest of the Alice Springs area. The Areyonga Desert Tigers use the name of a community, Areyonga, southwest of Alice Springs. In both cases the names, although Aboriginal in origin, appear on official maps. Other bands utilise Aboriginal names for places or regions that do not appear on government sanctioned maps. These are the original names of places as they are known to their Aboriginal inhabitants and owners. This choice of an Aboriginal place name can carry with it objectives of support for the community named, and steps to counter government interference in the control of Aboriginal communities. This practice can be seen in the names of numerous groups. For example, Amunda, from Alice Springs, use a term derived from the Aranda name for a place in the Alice Springs area; Ulpanyali use the Pitjantjatjara name for what non-Aborigines call King's Canyon; Titjikala Desert Oaks Band have chosen the place name Titjikala, shown officially on maps as Maryvale; the Kulumindini Band use the name of a dreaming site of the Jingili people near the Northern Territory town of Elliot. Through this method of naming themselves, music groups express links with local communities and languages, contravene 'official' government cartographies and situate themselves geographically within networks of Aboriginal Australia. Band names can thus rewrite Australian place identities.

'Aboriginalisation' and music

Geographies of contemporary Aboriginal music are symbolic as well as literal. Territorialisations in music can be overt – as with naming practices of groups, or in songs about places – but can also be interpreted in other ways. For example, cultural theorists Deleuze & Guattari (1987) have argued that forms of territorialisation are enacted symbolically through repetition, through people or individuals occupying spaces repeatedly over a period of time, building up associations with

National Indigenous Arts Advocacy Association Inc proudly presents

SURVIVAL '96

FRIDAY, 26TH JANUARY 1996

PROTECT OUR CULTURE

celebrate with Indigenous music, art and culture

- Koori art & craft
- Food stalls
- NO GROG!!

$10 Adults & $7 Conc.

(Kids under 12 yrs free)

- 10am - 6pm

(Gates open 9am)

Tickets on sale at gate

For bookings & info,

ring NIAAA Hotline -

(02) 281 2144

Bus info: from

Central #393 &

Circular Quay #394

SURVIVAL '96 is also supported
by the Australia Council for the Arts,
ATSIC, the NSW Ministry for the
Arts & Festivals Australia.

ATSIC   Australia Council for the Arts

Festivals Australia   New South Wales Government Ministry for the Arts

Featuring...
- Leah Purcell
- Christine Anu
- Kev Carmody
- Archie Roach
- Footprince
- Coloured Stone
- Rygela
- Blekbala Mujik
- Phil Moncrieff
- Aim 4 More
- Ruby Hunter
- Adrian Ross
- Pauline McLeod
- Aboriginal & Islander Dance Theatre
- Roger Knox & Euraba
- Brenda Gifford
- Peter McKenzie
- Desert Sea
- Maree Peters
- Bangarra Dance Theatre

and many more...

Artwork by: George Milpurrurru
"The Goose Egg Hunt", 1983,
reproduced with the kind
permission of artist and the
Australian National Gallery.

WOOMERA OVAL, BUNNERONG ROAD, LA PEROUSE

The annual Survival Day concert makes statements about Aboriginal readings of history and Aboriginal control of contemporary cultural and social agendas.

place or continuously unsettling assumed meanings of places (see also Duffy, 2000). No Aboriginal musical event has more significance in this regard than the annual Survival Day concert in Sydney, held on January 26 on the site of white invasion. Survival Day celebrations of Aboriginal people deliberately invert the nationalist undertones of officially designated 'Australia Day' as a commemoration of colonial 'settlement' on 26 January 1788. Organised by the National Indigenous Arts Advocacy Organisation (NIAAA), the Survival Day concert, usually referred to as Survival, has hosted many major Aboriginal performers and groups over its eleven-year history. For NIAAA festival co-ordinator, Robin Cowburn, Survival celebrates 'something a little "deeper" than colonial nostalgia – the survival of the oldest continuing human civilisation ... The annual concert ... is similar in form to traditional Aboriginal gatherings where several tribes would meet at the same place to eat, dance, marry and/or exchange knowledge and lore' (in Condie, 2000a, 17).

Territorialisations may be physical (as with festivals) or textual – for instance in songs. Musical practices can thus constitute acts of owning in a symbolic, if not literal, sense. This is a more subtle version of place attachment – one achieved through repeated performances in particular venues and through attachments and senses of ownership established over time. Songs can be less overtly about traditional links to country, but through a body of work made over a period and in the reactions of audiences to those events and musical texts, places are remade and refashioned through music.

Legal reclamation of place through land rights mechanisms is currently almost impossible for urban Aboriginal groups, yet 'Aboriginalisations' of place emerge in symbolic ways through creative expressions, which 'open out possibilities for repossessing place that acknowledges Aboriginal prior occupation and the history of dispossession. In addition such projects express ... the contemporary reality of cultural survival through the active revival of traditions' (Jacobs, 1995, 212). Songs cannot reverse the impacts of colonisation, but are a means of negotiating colonial legacies in the contemporary context.

Some contemporary Aboriginal songs and expressions seek to unsettle Australian national identity in this way, providing challenges to the way we see 'the nation' and its meanings. The national anthem has been treated in exactly this way. 'Advance Australia Fair' is for many an outdated remnant of colonial sentiment in an increasingly multicultural society aware of its Indigenous past. Melbourne group Tiddas challenge its proclamations of 'boundless plains to share', youth, freedom and abundant natural resources, clearly indicating the persistence of unre-solved Indigenous claims to sovereignty over land in their song 'Anthem' (1996):

> ...This land may be beautiful
> But it cannot be called fair
> So don't sing me your anthem
> 'Til we've learnt how to share.

Trevor Adamson's 1994 version of 'Waltzing Matilda', sung in Pitjant-jatjara on CAAMA's *In Aboriginal* series of recordings in languages, inverts the meanings in another song that many non-Aboriginal Aus-tralians might consider Australia's 'genuine' national anthem, while Yothu Yindi's song 'Treaty' (1989) became for many Australians an alter-native anthem at a time when reconciliation became firmly established as a national obsession (see chapter 11).

Aboriginalisations of place are most apparent at the local level. Bell (1998, 189) discusses ways in which this is so in Ngarrindjeri country in South Australia. Within a community that had suffered dispossession and been heavily influenced by missionaries to the extent that much cer-emonial knowledge had been lost, music provided an important link and means of cultural persistence. Even though

> there have been generations of Ngarrindjeri raised with little knowledge or regard for the music and stories of their forebears ... [contemporary songs] are an important moment in the history of Ngarrindjeri singing and, although they are unlike the traditional songs of Milerum recorded by Tindale, they nonetheless tell of Ngarrindjeri lands ... The language is English and the musical form non-Indigenous, but the people and places are Ngarrindjeri.

New songs such as Dorothy Shaw's 'The Dreaming of a Ngarrindjeri Memini' have since become community staples, performed by Ngar-rindjeri applicants in land rights hearings, at government inquiries and in special concerts. Contemporary song constitutes one means of 'learning back' of heritages 'continuously reworked, redirected and enjoyed in new ways'; Aboriginal music serves 'as a site for creative and sustaining cultural responses to the facts of that history itself' (Donaldson, 1995, 157), and is thus a form of interpretative, mutable historiography.

Songs that rewrite place pervade urban Aboriginal music, although often calling different imagery into play than in remote settings. When Mixed Relations refer to inner-city Sydney in their 'Newtown Dreaming' they combine aspects of the Aboriginal past ('Dreaming') with the present day realities of urban life. Aspects of Sydney's transition from Aboriginal place to colonial outpost and contemporary city are mapped in this song, the city reclaimed by Aboriginal people in the song's conclusion (Gibson & Connell, 2000), which celebrates continued spiritual attachments to place in spite of dispossession.

References to place in the work of other urban performers are less obvious. Ruby Hunter alludes to a place of origin when she sings 'Kutjeri lady, so far from home' – also exemplifying an Aboriginal nostalgia for a home that is somewhere else. Archie Roach, in 'Took the Children Away', names the place he was removed from as a child ('One dark day in Framligham ...'), although in his other songs the sense of place is more cryptic. For example, in 'Morning Star', Dreaming travels of creation spirits form the basis of the song's imagery, conjuring up oblique references to the places they visited. Even though it is not directly a song about place, 'Took the Children Away' would have a resonating impact on Australian music far beyond the author's initial intentions by becoming a 'soundtrack' of urban Aboriginal experiences. The song outlines the effects of assimilation policy on Aboriginal families. In it the histories of colonialism that litter contemporary Aboriginal Affairs take on a sharp-edged frankness when expressed in such personalised contexts:

> Mother's tears were falling down
> Dad shaped up he stood his ground
> He said you touch my kids and you fight me
> And they took us away from our family.

Roach's politics of empowerment rely on the listener to respond individually to the narratives of dispossession and injustice outlined in the song.

After No Fixed Address, Bart Willoughby (pic-
tured here holding a didjeridu) formed Sydney-
based group Mixed Relations. Reggae
continued to be a major influence on
their music.

Unlike more direct geographies of Aboriginality connected to traditional
roots, this song seeks a more private, solemn identification from the audience. The structure of the song exemplifies this, with its shift from a personal narrative of injustice to celebration of survival. The song ultimately
calls for the recognition of the persistence of Aboriginality in urban circumstances.

Urban Aboriginal music is not inauthentic because it of its absence of
tribal linkages and themes. In it Aboriginalities are constructed in relation to histories and events that span both traditional and contemporary
circumstances.

Some Aboriginal musicians discuss such themes in interviews, and in
liner notes to their albums. Thus for Melbourne's Blackfire, their 1994

release, *A Time to Dream*, was introduced to the listener in the following way: 'We sing for the Aboriginals in the city. Where we hunted now there's traffic, where we gathered seed now there are supermarkets, where we loved and played now there are factories. Now we need a Time to Dream. We hope you can hear us'. Jacinta Tobin's 2001 album, *Yarra-mundi and the Four Leaf Clover*, sought to capture a history of Western Sydney's Darug (Dharug) people in music: 'This CD has no breaks in the music; it becomes a continual Darug song covering the history of Darug people ... This CD is for all to see that we as Darug people are very strong in our culture and that we are still living in our homeland and we are not going away' (in *Koori Mail*, 3 Oct 2001, 22). Location influences cre-ativity, inspires reclamation or evokes nostalgia for past homelands – for many urban Aboriginal musicians, music is one way of reclaiming history, culture and place.

Many urban Aboriginal performers are thus keen to continue to sing about Aboriginality. Jason Lee Scott, for example, even though he grew up in urban surroundings, says, 'I'll continue, because it is a part of us. We want to be able to express ourselves and promote our culture, and put it out there to keep it going, keep it alive through our music' (in Rin-toul, 2002, 17). Scott felt 'remorse for not being able to grow up in that traditional life, or look traditional today, because our world has changed ... losing that identity, but still holding on to our culture and still being able to learn the culture, being able to go back there and find that and get it all happening again'. For his father, Buna Lawrie of Coloured Stone, music has more recently been an avenue to rediscover and incorporate traditionally inspired Aboriginal content: Coloured Stone's live perform-ances now begin with 'Mouydjengara', a 'traditional whale-dreaming song' in language (Rintoul, 2002, 17). For Lawrie: 'I feel the responsi-bility of being the modern day song and dance man, following in the foot-steps of my grandfather. I feel the responsibility of singing language songs'. This approach, of deliberately fusing 'tribal' and 'urban' expres-sions, underpins the recordings of Maroochy Barambah, who uses the term 'modern-tribalism' to describe her combination of elements from Gubbi Gubbi traditional culture and current dance music trends. It was and is still central to the philosophy behind the activities of CASM, in Adelaide, where many Aboriginal bands formed and crystallised the cre-ative agendas in their work.

BANGARRA DANCE THEATRE

DANCE CLAN

Breaking the barriers between traditional and
contemporary is an ongoing agenda of
Sydney-based Bangarra Dance Theatre.

One of the most important urban institutions in Australia is Sydney-
based Bangarra Dance Theatre, established in 1989, 'when it operated
from the living room of its founders'. Bangarra has 'developed an electri-
fying and distinctive style through which to tell the contemporary stories
of urban Aboriginal and Islander people: modern day Dreaming fused
with the sacred myths and traditions of the past' (Bangarra Dance
Theatre, 2002, 3). Their 1999 production, *DanceClan 2*, for example,
included 'Minymaku Inma' (created by Frances Rings), which brought
together the dance theatre's female dancers and 'traditional' women, all

members of the Ngaanyatjarra Pitjantjatjara Yakunytjatjara Women's Council in central Australia (*Koori Mail*, 17 Nov 1999, 29), alongside performances by Archie Roach, Ruby Hunter, Stiff Gins and Jimmy Little.

Priorities linked to survival and revival underwrite Bangarra's aims. According to the then Artistic Director and Choreographer, Stephen Page:

> when I took this job I realised that it wasn't going to be about doing five, six, seven, eight Janet Jackson video kicks. I was taking on a responsibility to maintain a culture. I think of what my ancestors went through and if I'm going to take this responsibility then I'm going to do it for a long time ... I'm going to take myself through a contemporary initiation and reclaim, rebuild and rekindle an identity that's inherited (Australian Broadcasting Corporation, 2003, 2).

This involved a stated political objective to transgress boundaries between 'remote' and 'urban' Aboriginality:

> It's great that I can use this dance medium because it does give us the freedom to be quite political. I quite like the fact that we can evolve an old concept and push it through the new millennium ... I think one of the most beautiful things in the process is that we've built a relationship from real bush rule to urban. They know that I wasn't brought up with all my languages, that I was taken away from my mother and father, and they know that I'm trying to rekindle all that. So for [Bangarra dancer] Djakapurra and his Munyarryun clan to embrace the culture of knowledge with me and share that with me ... that's been a wonderful process of trust and honesty (Australian Broadcasting Corporation, 2003, 2).

This implies not only the revival of markers of Aboriginal identity in displaced contexts, such as in major cities. For Stephen Page, there is also a kind of 'reverse' process in the inter-Aboriginal exchanges that occurred in the development of Bangarra's repertoire when 'going bush' to seek permission to perform traditional pieces:

> I've always gone up to Djakapurra's homeland and sat with his mum ... and the elders love it. They love it because kids in the bush think you have to be old to maintain culture. They're into popular

culture, American culture – hip-hop and basketball and all that. And I think the elders quite love the idea that there's an urban contemporary child from the city that has talent from all over the country and they're about maintaining culture and they're evolving visual, physical storytelling through the theatrical indigenous experience. I think they find that the new form of Corroboree and it's tapping into the modern experience but it's also maintaining integrity. So there's mutual support (Australian Broadcasting Corporation, 2003, 2).

Music and dance are thus forms of exchange between Aboriginal groups across Australia. Ruby Hunter and Archie Roach have toured remote Top End and Far North Queensland communities on a number of occasions since 1997, including Nauiyu Nambiyu (Daly River), Weipa, Aurukun, Hopevale and Kowanyama. Their tours include songwriting workshops, music skills and industry development talks and slide shows designed to build musical knowledges in Aboriginal communities, in addition to providing entertainment. For some urban Aboriginal musicians, boundaries between the 'traditional' and 'contemporary' need to be seen as opaque, or simply false. For Richard Frankland,

I love songs that tell a story. That's a prime thing in our culture. My songs are just as traditional a part of our culture as the culture from pre-contact days. By that I mean that our culture is amazingly strong and resilient, and that it has the ability to adapt and evolve. My songs are part of my dreaming path and that's important (in *Koori Mail*, 4 Sept 2002, 31).

Unlike other forms of knowledge, music emphasises what is fluid and inchoate, and thus has the capacity to break down boundaries and to forge new agendas, alliances and exchanges.

Gender and identity

Personal identities are not singular or fixed. That this is so is evident in a key distinction between constructions of Aboriginality that are essentialist and those that seek to empower Aboriginal people through radical 'opening-up' of the discursive field surrounding textual representation. Discriminatory representations of Aboriginality invariably converge on perpetual stereotypes and generalisations. Aboriginal people are all too familiar with these myths − of, among others, welfare dependency, 'pre-dispositions' to alcoholism and notions of a 'dying race'. In these cases, Aboriginality overrides other aspects of personal identity and marks the individual as 'other'. It is often assumed that Aboriginality is an all-defining element of identity in all circumstances.

In contrast, much work in feminism and cultural studies emphasises how personal identities are multifaceted, in that individuals are simulta-neously constructed by others and themselves through the different frames of gender, class, age, sexuality and nationality (Butler, 1990; Pile & Thrift, 1995). Identities are not static or innately present, rather they are performed, embedded in and enacted through human bodies when aspects of identity are consciously displayed or are interpreted by others. Different elements of personal identity are mobilised and concealed in various contexts for particular reasons. A person may be simultaneously perceived and interpreted by others in terms of certain aspects of their identity, while other aspects are downplayed or ignored. Drawing on an example from music, some Australian bands emphasise their national identity when performing to Australian backpackers or tourists outside of Australia, where musicians and audiences alike collectively invest in a patriotic nostalgia and homesickness. In a different context, 'all-girl' bands are invariably written about in the music press in relation to issues of gender, while 'all-male' bands are much more likely to be reviewed in terms of style, attitude, fashion, politics or lyrics. In these cases, issues of masculinity are often ignored. National identity or gender are aspects of identity highlighted or downplayed, noticed or assumed, depending on the context and the power relations between subject and observer.

Such considerations are important when interpreting Aboriginal music. All Aboriginal musicians are simultaneously men or women, from specific class backgrounds, with origins in urban, rural or remote places (or combinations of these). Some are religious, some are old, some are young. Some share ideological concerns with non-Aboriginal people that are linked to a common status as part of a marginalised group − for instance, solidarities between gay and lesbian people of Aboriginal and non-Aboriginal background. For others, their identities as elders, or as members of the stolen generation, may be as important in terms of how they see themselves and wish others to view them and their music.

This fluidity of interpretation is evident in the repertoires, and reception of, music performed by Aboriginal women. Groups such as Tiddas ('sisters' in Aboriginal English) and Stiff Gins, and solo artists such as Shelly Atkins, Maroochy Barambah, Kerrianne Cox, Ruby Hunter, Debbie Morrow and Brenda Webb have performed in many contexts for different audiences. When performing at Aboriginal festivals or events, Aboriginality may be an obvious point of connection between performer and crowd, especially in songs that communicate aspects of Aboriginal experiences. This can be read in the song 'Malcolm Smith', performed by Tiddas on their 1993 album, *Sing about Life*, a song that evokes images of the trauma of an Aboriginal death in custody. At other events, these groups may be interpreted as part of the feminist movement. Tiddas and the Stiff Gins act as examples of this, being popular among female audiences, both Aboriginal and non-Aboriginal, in straight and lesbian settings. Melbourne's Hot Jam Cooking festival was set up as a space for Aboriginal and non-Aboriginal women performers, as Ruby Hunter explained: 'many women musicians at the time were complaining about a lack of venue support and places to play. We wanted to get together and show that women (including our Koori sisters) are creative in many areas' (in McGrath, 1996b, 29). In this respect, and in certain circumstances for some audiences, female Aboriginal musicians have been received more in sympathy with other female acts from non-Aboriginal Australia and overseas. As Streit-Warburton (1995, 307) has argued, 'music performed by Australian Aboriginal women is an effective and age honoured means of negotiating identity'. A glowing review of Debbie Morrow's 1998 solo album *Flight of the Emu* illustrates this point:

> It's all questions, probings, poking around for answers, affirming ideas like ancestry and motherhood in the context of a newly found spiritual strength ... Morrow's material is dead difficult and tragic at face value – adoption, white society's values of violence, soul sell-out, the denial of access to one's cultural birthright. Her ability to turn that into a physical force where words take on extra meaning is a talent all generic grrls need to skill up on fast (Riley, 1998, 43).

Morrow has said of her music that it

originally spawned from the anger of finding out what really happened to my people in this country ... I want to find what has been hidden from us, what has been denied us, and make connections again between women and children. Being a mother has given me the strength to be seen. Music is such a good universal tool to get messages across to people in a softer form (in *Koori Mail*, 19 Sep 2001, 32).

Here Aboriginality need not be presented in overt ways, although it was understood and appreciated by the reviewer. What mattered was how the album contributed to a developing repertoire that questioned identity and unsettled colonial silences.

Song texts sometimes make appeals to feminist politics explicit: soul/blues singer Rochelle Watson's 'Too Deadly My Sister' (1999) is 'about all the women out there who have influenced who I am today' (in Howes, 1999, 25); Lexine Solomon's album *This is Woman* (2002) was dedicated to 'the women in our lives and how they continue to love us even when we fail them ... this is my tribute to my mother and grandmother, aunties, sisters and friends in my life' (in *Koori Mail*, 26 June 2002, 43). Meanwhile, Tiddas' 'My Sister' (1993) and Ruby Hunter's 'Sister Yappa', 'Proud, Proud Woman' and 'Women's Business' on *Thoughts Within* (1994), are about solidarity between women, and allude to Aboriginal survival beyond dispossession.

For many Aboriginal women musicians, their identities as black and female are equally important. This convergence of Aboriginality and gender has been particularly apparent for many women conscious of the circumstances they face in a white, male-dominated music industry:

> [Music] provides an avenue through which musicians can explore and precipitate change. For Aboriginal women living in a society shaped by a white, male hegemony, music is like a raft that ferries them through the hazards of the mainstream. For many, it has also been a lifesaver, keeping alive important knowledge and raising spirits (Streit-Warburton, 1995, 307).

Although aware of both the Aboriginal and feminist politics their repertoire contributed to, members of Tiddas were often reluctant to see their creativity in terms of any given agenda:

We may sing a strong story about stolen children, deaths in custody or women with burdens or anything like that, but when you
put it into a musical format, it can take on any shape, and I'm glad
people will hear the music first and then listen to the words.
Instead of being taken with a song for its lyrical content. Because
it's a pretty subtle way of getting into someone's head, I reckon.
I think it's different strokes for different folks I guess. People
want to see us as being a political band and that's their opinion
that they're entitled to, but you know, we try and just be happy
musicians first (in *Form Guide*, 1996, 35).

For this reason, many Aboriginal groups resist being pigeonholed by
their Indigeneity, and often prefer that their music is not categorised as
'world music', a term plagued by problems of over-generalisation. For
Stiff Gins,

in some quarters there exists the misconception that when a given
music style does not fit the 'Western music pattern' it is labelled
'world music' ... Our music is not necessarily Indigenous or Aboriginal. It contains R&B, rock, blues and some local stuff. We are
first and foremost artists and musicians wishing to appeal to mainstream society minus isms (*City Hub*, 23 Nov 2000, 14).

Personal identities are made more complex for some women musicians
when, as with the case of Melbourne-based rapper and breakdancer
Georgina Chrisanthopoulos (aka Little G), ethnicity derives from Aboriginal and non-Aboriginal parentage. Little G has both Aboriginal and
Greek backgrounds, and looks to both, often with humour, in affirming
and making sense of her identity:

I love getting out there and freestyling. I'm inspired by my culture –
being indigenous, the political issues and just everyday issues you
go through. I'm very proud of being Aboriginal and Greek. Actually I call myself a 'wogarinie' ... I hope to inspire other indigenous
kids and show people all over the world that we're doing things –
we're not all lazy alcoholics. Let's get rid of the stereotypes and
prove people wrong. We're strong, we're still here, we can do
things (in *Koori Mail*, 11 Jul 2001, 27).

Vocalist Deborah Cheetham found her identity unsettled in other ways; as an Aboriginal woman singing opera arias by Mozart, Handel and Cilea, challenges came from those who were unsure about the authenticity of an Aboriginal woman singing music steeped in a European classical tradition:

> Yes, opera is a Western art form, but so is oil on canvas. Singing an Italian aria shouldn't be an invalidation of the fact that I'm an Aboriginal woman who's bringing her own interpretation to it ... when I took to the stage, I was standing there as Deborah Cheetham, a woman who is proudly Aboriginal. But the foremost thing in my mind was that I'm a soprano who had to do the music justice (in *Koori Mail*, 27 Jun 2001, 35).

A different kind of debate linked to Aboriginality and gender emerged in the Indigenous print media in 2001 regarding the naming of the Stiff Gins, which plays upon the notion of 'gins', historically a derogatory term for Aboriginal women. For long-time Aboriginal activist, Chicka Dixon,

> It is with a great deal of sadness that I put pen to paper to point out that I am hurt and disgusted that a performing group of Koori women call themselves 'Stiff Gins', while another group call themselves 'Black Velvet' ... for years we fought Gubbas (white people) physically for boasting (especially in racist country towns) that they were the 'king gin jockeys' of their towns and always claimed to visit the local Aboriginal camp for some 'black velvet'. I am asking these groups to stop playing Othello to white Australia and consider changing their groups' names as they are encouraging the red-necked racists to continue making derogatory remarks about our people (letter to the editor, *Koori Mail*, 17 Oct 2001, 6).

For another contributor to the debate:

> To refer to our womenfolk as 'gins' was most offensive, and to us people who lived through that era, that word is still offensive and, might I say, painful ... I ask that you younger people give some thought as to what we older ones have lived through in the days when there were no anti-discrimination laws or support groups of any kind (letter to the editor, *Koori Mail*, 14 Nov 2001, 7).

In response to these criticisms, Nardi Simpson and Kaleena Briggs, of Stiff Gins, argued that their appropriation of the term marked respect for those who had suffered its use in the past:

> The name 'Stiff Gins' came about almost three years ago when we heard someone say that their sister-in-law (a non-Aboriginal woman) did nothing without three stiff gins in the morning. At this time we were looking for a band name and when we discussed the possibility of using the phrase, we realised the responsibility we as a band were taking on. Almost all Aboriginal people are aware of the negative sexual connotations the word 'gin' has. As a band we are trying to redress this meaning. We, along with many other Aboriginal and non-Aboriginal people, no longer want the word to be associated with such hurt and negativity, and our actions are in honour of all the women, our own mothers, aunties, sisters and grandmothers included, who were abused with this word. At all our concerts and performances we explain that as young Aboriginal women, we now want the word to mean strong, proud, talented black woman, in order for all those who went before us and will come after us to enjoy and celebrate a word that originally is Dharug for 'woman'... we believe that by attempting to change the meaning of this word, we are helping to empower those we represent, and in the process are making it possible for us to control our own destiny (letter to the editor, *Koori Mail*, 31 Oct 2001, 9).

Many ensuing letters to the editor supported the Stiff Gins in their decision.

Whatever one's response is to this debate, it illustrates two points. First, that music is a means for negotiating and contesting identity, for reclamation and dissent, particularly where Aboriginality and gender are concerned. Second, that music matters, not only as a form of entertainment, but also as an important means of self and collective expression. That the naming of the Stiff Gins could elicit such debate demonstrates the extent to which Aboriginal performers represent themselves, embody stated political positions and create cultural expressions that speak for and to communities of Aboriginal people at local, regional and national scales. The debate about the Stiff Gins was important not only because of the contested nature of the word 'gin', but because it was understood that this group's music, like that of many other female Aboriginal musicians, had real currency and meaning in community life.

Conclusion – music and community

There are both immediate and symbolic geographies of Aboriginality in music. Some are connected to tribal law – ceremonial and traditional contexts reproduced in contemporary form. Some musical texts affront white colonialist ideas of nationhood, some reclaim urban spaces of dispossession and marginalisation. Others can be seen as territorialisations enacted in less overt ways, through performance itself rather than lyrical content. Beyond this, Aboriginal music is important across Australia because of the role it plays in community life. Beyond record deals and promotional tours, film clips or festival crowds, participation in music making at the family and community levels reveals most about its communicative power. For Kev Carmody:

> Music got into me. I can never remember a time in my memory where there wasn't music around. You had to entertain yourself around a campfire with music and storytelling. Some of those so-called illiterate people made up wonderful poems and rhymes and stories. There was a big technological innovation when the old fella brought out a dry cell wireless and it was portable and you had to run an aerial up a bloody tree ... the family travelled a lot, moving from camp to camp, from one mustering job to another. They would play gum leaves or bang on a bloody log or something. We had clapsticks or a mouth organ, anything you could carry in your pocket (in *Thompson*. 1997, 48–49).

For many Aboriginal musicians, their emphasis is on songwriting as storytelling or singing as a healing process. Debbie Morrow has said that: 'songs reflect many emotions – anger, hope and suppression. They are healing songs and I hope that by listening to them others will gain the will to heal. Through healing we will progress and through progression we have a future' (in McGrath, 1996a, 18).

In many respects, these social uses of music are made even clearer when it is known that many Indigenous musicians combine songwriting and performing with other activities. Music is one component of a range of expressive forms utilised to create messages, to improve community life. Joe Geia is a mural painter and an educator who visits kindergartens and primary schools to teach elements of Aboriginal culture; Leah Purcell is a musician, activist, actor and writer; Kev Carmody, alongside a successful career as a singer-songwriter, writes children's stories; Essie Coffey, Brewarrina's 'bush queen', was a singer, an actor and an activist; Melbourne gumleaf player, Herb Patten, worked as an Aboriginal cultural officer with the cities of Dandenong and Melbourne and ran Aboriginal hostels around Victoria; Richard Frankland is an award-winning filmmaker who has won three Australian Film Institute awards and was a senior advisor on the Royal Commission into Aboriginal Deaths in Custody. It is sometimes only in the context of this range of expressions of Aboriginal community combined with working and activist roles that music reveals its potential as an emotive, empowering creative form.

The role of music in community life is perhaps best illustrated by ways in which certain songs become part of an Aboriginal repertoire, performed repeatedly in different places to different audiences, but with similar reactions. These songs include Joe Geia's 'Yil Lull', Bob Randall's 'Brown Skin Baby', Archie Roach's 'Took the Children Away' and Kev Carmody/Paul Kelly's 'From Little Things Big Things Grow'. As one indication of the significance such songs develop, the last two were performed to highly emotive crowds at the conclusion of the 1998 Sorry Day commemorations, when they became one way for Indigenous Australians to work through personal and family issues associated with being taken away from their families or dispossessed, and for non-Indigenous Australians to demonstrate their support for these concerns. For Archie Roach, 'there were certain things I couldn't talk about, deal with in my life, so I started to write about it, sing about it, and it was such a release. I'm glad I discovered that – putting your feelings in songs – otherwise I'd probably be committed somewhere by now. Or dead' (in Walker, 1993, 81). While the wider sociopolitical themes of Aboriginal music resonate in the foreground in songs such as these, the empowering aspect of the songwriting process itself should not be overlooked in the process of seeking 'profound' interpretations. Despite the struggle most artists have in making a living from music, there are direct measures of empowerment accorded through the process of writing songs, working in bands, touring, performing, and receiving audience appreciation. On the release of his first album, *Charcoal Lane*, Archie Roach emphasised that 'just making *Charcoal Lane*, I said "that's it, I've made a record". It's something a lot of people never get the opportunity to do. To me it was a big thing' (*On the Street*, 24 Jan 1995, 33).

Suggested listening

Benning Brothers ▲ *Kimberley Country*

Best of Koori Classics

Ernie and Noel Bridge ▲ *200 Years Ago*

Buried Country: The Story of Aboriginal Country Music

Troy Cassar-Daley ▲ *Beyond the Dancing*

Roger Knox ▲ *Warrior in Chains*

Jimmy Little ▲ *Jimmy Little Sings the Country and Western Greats*

Wedgetail Eagle Band ▲ *Wedgetail Eagle*

Harry and Wilga Williams and the Country Outcasts ▲ *Harry and Wilga Williams and the Country Outcasts*

CHAPTER 3

Singing country

The previous two chapters have concentrated on Aboriginal music in general, discussing a range of issues affecting performance and song text. In the remainder of this book, chapters deal with case studies of particular musical styles, of music in certain places, or of specific songs. In this chapter we present the first of these case studies, focusing on what has been the most popular and persistent element of contemporary Aboriginal musical expression, country music. Interactions between Aboriginal and non-Aboriginal musicians and audiences form the framework of this chapter. We begin by examining country music in the Australian musical landscape, and by interpreting non-Aboriginal Australian country music as representative of a politics of colonialism, rurality and whiteness. This allows us to interpret Aboriginal country music in relation to the broader national country music scene and its cultural politics. Later in this chapter, we discuss country music in Tamworth, reflecting that town's position as the site of the major country music festival in Australia, a festival with both Aboriginal and non-Aboriginal profiles and the symbolic 'heart' of Australian country music.

Australian country music

In Australia, country music traditions have emerged in both non-Aboriginal and Aboriginal contexts. These contexts intersect at specific locations and through the careers of a number of artists in a variety of complex ways. Country music has become a style of music popular among white (non-Indigenous) Australians, with its own history, stars, recording infrastructures, repertoires, literature and festivals (Watson, 1975, 1983, 1987; J Smith, 1984; Dawson, 1985; Allan, 1988; Latta, 1991; G Smith, 1994; Dusty & McKean, 1996). It also became a significant component of and influence on the popular music expressions of Aboriginal Australians, accounting for approximately a third of songs on commercially released recordings of Indigenous musicians (Stokes et al., nd; Ellis et al., 1988; Knox, 1988; Breen, 1989, 1994; Dunbar-Hall, 1994; Narogin, 1990; Mudrooroo, 1997). Each of these traditions can be seen to share similar origins and means of distribution and to have emerged in distinct cultural domains that, despite the common element of a country music sound, articulate diverging musical, economic, social and political agendas. Aboriginal and non-Aboriginal musicians in Australia have utilised this genre for different ends. Thus there is a range of aesthetic positions on country music. While there are many levels of interaction between Aboriginal and non-Aboriginal actors in the Australian country music scene, for the purposes of understanding the cultural politics of country music in Australia we discuss each of these scenes in turn – beginning with non-Aboriginal uses of the style.

Non-Aboriginal country music in Australia

Narratives of 'settlement' and 'progress' have been central to Australian nationalism since the period of intense patriotism that preceded the federation of Australian states in 1901. These are reflected in Australian musical histories, including that of country music. Now often considered part of a traditionalist, politically conservative ethos, these narratives can be highlighted in the topics of songs. There is general agreement that country music was well established in Australia by the early 1930s (Watson, 1975; J Smith, 1984; Allan, 1988; Latta, 1991; G Smith, 1994) within a decade of the coalescence of this style into identifiable form in North America (Biracree, 1993; Peterson, 1997). Non-Aboriginal country songs built upon country and western traditions that originated on the 'frontier' of settler/invader North America, yet made sense of, and shaped, localised Australian experiences of place. Country music spanned the range of rural experiences and myths: displacement, loneliness and heartbreak, morality, the hardships of rural life, love of the land, and lapses into addiction. As a lyrical form it relied on storytelling as a means of expression, its lyrics populated by real or mythical characters.

Country music was also one of the ways in which Australian rural-based mythologies of national identity were constructed through archetypal figures such as drovers, swagmen, jackeroos and bushmen. Country music, originally a working-class 'cowboy' music from the American 'frontier', was blended with Celtic folk influences stemming from convict transportation and mass migration to Australia from Ireland. Celtic folk music had already worked itself into discourses of Australian nationalism by the turn of the century, after the Sydney-based *Bulletin* magazine lauded it, alongside Celtic poetry and art, as archetypal expression of a new national creative canon based around rural 'bush' life, comradery and 'mateship'. The 'bush ballad', as such songs became known, was in essence a 'template' of rural musical expression, onto which American country music was grafted in the 1930s and 1940s. Its use of guitars, fiddles and other 'rustic' instruments prefigured a rural 'authenticity' that would resurface in country music. When bush ballads became country music, the result was an Australian idiom that 'rode on the sheep's back' and posited the bush as the wellspring of all that was 'authentically' Australian. Discussing the music of Tex Morton, an early Australian hillbilly singer, Smith (1994, 300) suggests ways in which icons of the American country music tradition were appropriated and transformed to suit vernacular conditions:

> Australian place names appear, seeking the same mythological resonance that American localisation evoked: hobos became bagmen ... cowboys become boundary riders ... The western films of Gene Autry provided substantial models for dress, deportment and performer attitude and gave Australian singers a model for performance; almost all Australian performers based their persona on the singing cowboy.

In Australian country music, 'country' thus became an open-ended geographical signifier, absorbing and encapsulating 'the bush' and 'the outback', two colonial geographical metaphors that presume a white, expansionist point of reference. The following transcript, from a 1942 country music radio show, gives some insight into the ways in which music embodied these distinctly white Australian myths. In this show, Tex Morton, Australia's first widely successful country musician, talks with his 'cowboy' sidekick, Shorty, about hillbilly or country songs. They reflect on the quality of this music and locating it not only discursively as the music of the bush, but postulating on the sites of its conception:

> SHORTY: But gee, there's nothin' to beat them old bush songs that you sing. They've got the beat I like.

> TEX: Yes, they're the ones I like best too, Shorty. You know, Australia's folk songs are really typical of our great outback. Most of them aren't sung fast with slick sounding words, but slowly and rhythmically. Perhaps they were first sung to the sound of clashing shears in a shearing shed, or 'round the campfire to tell a story after a long tiring day riding after sheep or cattle ...

From another program in the same year:

> TEX: You know, folks, I like this idea of being called your friend, makes me feel that wherever you are, way out back in the bush with the boys in camp, or right in the heart of the big smoke, we're all pretty good pals, good neighbours in this grand country of ours ... (*Tex Morton: Yodelling Cowboy*)

Thus Australian country music in the 1930s and 1940s was bound up in notions of Australian national identity that were entrenched through references to precedents in North America.

Much non-Aboriginal country music in Australia has glorified a rugged Australian-ness, a continent 'settled' by hardworking rural personalities and their families. These songs equate rural lifestyles with a 'true' national character, present Australian country music as '*the* music of our country' (Country Music Association of Australia, 1997, emphasis added) and claim to tell the 'stories of our land'. Yet they are often one-sided. With the exception of occasional songs by Ted Egan, John Williamson and Slim Dusty, there are no geographies of Indigenous Australia in non-Aboriginal Australian country music. Aboriginal place names and people are largely absent, while song spaces often resonate with those places emblematic of white settlement and invasion (such as

Gundagai, Birdsville and Broken Hill). As far as incorporating Aboriginal experiences into song, many non-Aboriginal country music landscapes are rendered empty – musical versions of the concept of *terra nullius*. However, country music's narrative form, its emotional profile and connection to landscapes of rural and remote existence, also helped make it an ideal genre for addressing Aboriginal feelings for and relationships to country.

Aboriginal country music

Aboriginal country music traditions, while building on similar North American stylistic precedents, operate in social and discursive spaces distinct from those outlined above. A survey of commercial recordings by contemporary Aboriginal music performers carried out in the early 1990s revealed that of 913 songs, 310 (approximately one-third) were country songs, showed country music influence, or contained sections of country music (Dunbar-Hall, 1994). In the same survey, the sounds of Aboriginal country music were analysed as part of two broad trends – some performers utilised the sounds of traditional country music through the presence of fiddle and slide guitar, while another grouping of performers produced a sound closer to basic rock music without traditional country string instruments, generally through standard rock group line-ups. This difference in sound coincides with the geographic origins of Aboriginal country music performers in ways that invert the spatial distribution of non-Aboriginal music styles in Australia (where rock bands predominate in cities and country musicians tend to emerge from country towns and pastoral stations). Solo Aboriginal musicians, such as Roger Knox, who perform with traditional country sounds are mostly based in cities and towns of the Australian east coast (such as Tamworth, Sydney, Melbourne), while rock groups who perform country songs, such as many of the groups recorded by CAAMA, are from central and northern rural Australia and live and perform in remote Aboriginal communities. Differences in geographic origin and sound reflect the relative acknowledgment of Aboriginal country musicians by the Australian country music fraternity in general. For example, east coast performers, with their more familiar sound, are more accepted by the Tamworth Country Music Festival, while other bands who play country music alongside reggae and rock formats receive little non-Aboriginal recognition. This creates Aboriginal country music sounds and country music uses which in many cases differ markedly from those of white, mainstream country performers.

Various reasons have been offered for the popularity of country music in Aboriginal communities and its adoption by Aboriginal musicians. When asked about this, Aboriginal musicians Richard Wally, Jo Geia, and Ernie Dingo replied that the music was

> akin to the outback Koori [Aboriginal] experience. In America that repertoire includes songs about experiences like those of Kooris in the outback, i.e., songs about horses, cattle, the land, and unity, and is based on work on the land. Koori men, they said, feel closer to cowboys than they do to city people. Yet tragedy is inherent in this music, for it is rooted in hardship and racial conflict ... country-style music is nevertheless what they can best identify with, in all its levels of meaning and expressiveness (Kartomi, 1988, 21).

In addition, a number of writers have pointed out that the visits of country music performers to remote Aboriginal communities helped spread this style (Pearce, 1979; Allan, 1988; Dawson, 1985; Dusty & McKean, 1996), and that newly introduced mechanical and electric media assisted in the spread of country music to Aboriginal listeners and performers (Ellis et al., 1988). When asked about stylistic influences on Warumpi Band in the 1980s, guitarist Neil Murray mentioned how country music was heard by Aboriginal people:

> the guys [in Warumpi Band] heard straight country and western because that's what they heard out in the bush – it was largely patronised by the white pastoralist community out there – so the major form of Western music that Aboriginal people were exposed to was country and western long before they started to play rock 'n' roll (interview, 1988).

The recorded songs of Aboriginal singer-songwriter Dougie Young show that the country ballad genre was in use among Aboriginal people by at least the early 1960s, although Walker (2000) traces the roots of Aboriginal country music further back to the gospel, vaudeville and bush band traditions of the period roughly from 1890 to the late 1920s. Jeremy

Beckett, one of the collectors responsible for Young's recordings, noted that 'among black, white and brindled [sic], hillbilly songs are the real favourites in the Australian outback' (Beckett, 1958, 32), while field-work tapes from the early 1960s held in the Sound Archive of the Australian Institute of Aboriginal and Torres Strait Islander Studies (AIATSIS) contain large numbers of 'hillbilly songs' performed by Aborigines, including 'The Streets of Laredo', 'My Home's across the Blue Ridge Mountain' and 'When Jimmy Rogers Said Goodbye' (AIATSIS Tapes Nos A887–A897).

Wider academic literature, both in general on Australian popular music and specifically on Aboriginal music, acknowledges the importance of country music to Aboriginal musicians (for example, Breen, 1989; Walker, 2000). This literature remains one of the few areas of research on Australian popular music in which the work of Aboriginal musicians is credited in a major way. Watson (1983, 158–160), for example, provides a profile of the career of Aboriginal country singer Jimmy Little, yet comments rather erroneously considering the songs of Dougie Young:

> as it is, no Aborigine has yet emerged who has succeeded, or for that matter tried, to project his own racial and social background. Australian country [music] is the poorer for the deficiency.

In contrast, Allan (1988) devotes a chapter of her history of the Tamworth Country Music Festival to the contribution of Koori musicians to this event, mentioning a number of performers: Auriel Andrew, Ernie Bridge, Roger Knox and Jimmy Little. In the same way, Latta (1991) includes a chapter on Aboriginal country music in his survey, *Australian Country Music*. Here, Auriel Andrew, Kev Carmody, Col Hardy, Roger Knox, Jimmy Little and Archie Roach are mentioned, as well as the work of the Central Australian Aboriginal Media Association in promoting Aboriginal country music. Breen (1989) discusses country and western as a continuing stylistic choice of Aboriginal musicians, noting later (Breen, 1992, 156) that country and western had become 'the prominent genre used today'. To Narogin (1990, 63), this style of music was so important to Aboriginal musicians that in some contexts it 'replaced Aboriginal song structures almost completely'. Subsequently he went on to state that:

this was because the subject matter reflected the new Indigenous lifestyles: horses and cattle, drinking, gambling, the outsider as hero, a nomadic existence, country-orientation, wronged love, fighting and fucking – the whole gamut of an itinerant life romanticised in the stockman/cowboy ... (Mudrooroo, 1997, 111).

Comparing Aboriginal music in cities and country towns with that produced in central Australia, Castles (1992, 27) wrote that:

in the cities and big country towns a tradition of family-oriented C[ountry] & W[estern] outfits stretches back to Harry and Wilga Williams and the Country Outcasts, who began playing around Fitzroy in Melbourne in the 60s ... Music from the Centre has a different feel, but it is similarly dominated by C[ountry] & W[estern].

The most comprehensive analysis of Aboriginal country music to date is Walker's (2000) *Buried Country: The Story of Aboriginal Country Music*. This history of Aboriginal use of the style charts its popularity, performers and their outputs, and implications for understanding country music as synonymous with 'Aboriginal' music for many listeners. In it, Troy Cassar-Daley argued that:

It is a really universal music, country, to be able to affect a little Aboriginal kid growing up in Grafton the same way it affects, say, a kid growing up in Nashville, Tennessee. The fact that there is a story to this music and it takes a lot of pride in the lyric, I think that's the thing that really gets you in the first place. Aboriginal families love country music and I think the main reason is because of its honesty. It tells about real things. It tells about getting up in the morning and feeling down, perhaps (Walker, 2000, 286–87).

In addition to the reasons stated above, Walker (2000, 14) argues that country music requires smaller investments (both financial and musical) and less in the way of an infrastructure of production, 'country music is guitar based (thus portable) and easy to play (easy to play competently enough to get by ...)'.

Recurrent recognition in the literature that country music is a component of contemporary Aboriginal music has rarely expanded upon the range of lyrical and musical uses to which this type of music has been put, while the ways in which Aboriginal country music interacts with country music in the wider, Australian context are rarely analysed. There is a danger in generalising about Aboriginal country music of giving the impression that once adopted, country music is used for the majority of artists' songs, is employed as a whole, and is used without musical or textual discrimination. Study of the extent and uses of country music style by Aboriginal musicians, however, reveals a wide-ranging musical aesthetic, particularly in various representations of Aboriginality and the expression of opinion on issues relevant to Aboriginal listeners and pertinent to understanding current Aboriginal strategies for recognition. It implicates differences of musical sound, degrees of access to promotion by record companies with Australia-wide distribution networks or by labels exclusively concerned with recording and support of Aboriginal music, and shapes the reception of Aboriginal country musicians at the Tamworth Country Music Festival.

Aboriginal country music performers

Some Aboriginal musicians are exclusively country performers. These tend to be solo singers, often with careers dating back as far as at least the late 1950s when Jimmy Little made his first recordings (Latta, 1991). Prominent among these country singers have been Auriel Andrew, Sarina Andrew, Ernie and Noel Bridge, Troy Cassar-Daley, Kathy Kelly, Col Hardy, Roger Knox, Sharon Mann, Ceddie McGrady, Bobby McLeod and Jimmy Little. Many favour cover versions and their sound is 'traditionalist' country, produced by backing groups, often with the addition of bowed and plucked string instruments. Analysis of their recordings reveals a trend in album construction of including a mixture of two types of country songs: (1) Australian and American (non-indigenous) material, and (2) songs by Aboriginal musicians and with Aboriginal references in their lyrics. Through this Aboriginal material, country songs commonly take on roles of either reactions to white treatment of Aborigines, or positive representations of Aboriginal cultures and affirmations of Indigenous survival. Listing the contents of *Koori Classic, Volume 3: The Girls*, an album of country songs by Aboriginal women performers produced by Enrec Recording Studios, shows this method of album construction. Of the twelve listed tracks, three are Aboriginal (that is, were written by Aboriginal musicians and have Aboriginal topics): 'Arnhem Land Lullaby',

'Brown Skin Baby' and 'Streets of Tamworth'. The first of these includes some Aboriginal language lyrics. The remaining nine songs are covers of standard (non-Aboriginal) country songs.

While this pattern also appears on the albums of other Aboriginal country singers, there are differing levels of overt Aboriginality on them. Jimmy Little's recordings, for example, begin to include songs with explicit Aboriginal reference in the 1990s, despite the length of his recording career. Little, perhaps the best known Aboriginal recording artist of the period before the fame of Indigenous rock groups such as Yothu Yindi, records almost exclusively country music based around cover versions of songs. In 1995, on the album *Yorta Yorta Man*, he departed from this practice in the album's title track in an explicit reference to his Aboriginal background:

> I was born on the banks of the Murray
> Yorta Yorta is my mother's tribal name ...

A more politically motivated use of country music to express opinion on an issue of Aborginal concern occurs in the title track of the 1994 album *200 Years Ago*, by Ernie Bridge and his son, Noel. Here, of fourteen songs, only this opening track ('200 Years Ago') contains Aboriginal references, in this case to the 1992 *Mabo* decision, through which the High Court of Australia recognised that Australia was not *terra nullius* ('empty land') in 1788, and that Aborigines and Torres Strait Islanders had common law rights to the protection of native title to land. This topic appeared in numerous Aboriginal songs of the 1990s; its presence on a country album indicating an aesthetic stance of Aboriginal musicians, in which contemporary music was used for the expression of opinion and for debate over issues of relevance to Aboriginal people. In this sense, Aboriginal country music provides a lens through which cultural expressions and political shifts are articulated:

> The highest court has verified the truth of Mabo's stand
> This one man had the courage to fight his case and show
> Australia was no empty land two hundred years ago ...

In contrast to singers such as Little and Ernie and Noel Bridge, are others based in central Australia and recorded by CAAMA, including the Benning Brothers, Gus Williams and Country Ebony, Kunmanara Yamma and the Pitjantjatjara Country Band, Wedgetail Eagle Band, Wild Brumbys and Irwin Inkamala and the Country Lads. In view of CAAMA's policies of using music to address social issues (discussed in chapter 7), it is not surprising to find that country style songs by Bob Randall and Herbie Laughton, both early CAAMA recording artists with albums dating from the early 1980s, dealt almost exclusively with issues of importance to Aboriginal communities. Randall's 'Brown Skin Baby', in which an Aboriginal mother laments the forced removal of her baby by a policeman (an assimilationist practice instigated and continued by Australian governments until the late 1970s), and Laughton's 'Arunta Man's Dream', in which an Arunta elder explains the decline of his traditional culture after contact with white people, were clear examples of CAAMA's objectives articulated in song.

Songs by these musicians can also be used to demonstrate another facet of central Australian Aboriginal country music, the use of textual elements to reflect and locate Aboriginal heritages. Laughton's 'Ghan to the Alice', a ballad about a person returning to the place of his birth (the 'Ghan' is a local train service; 'the Alice' is the colloquial term for the township of Alice Springs in the Northern Territory), used a typical country song topic (Ohrlin, 1989; Rogers, 1989), one which Laughton expressed through formulaic country lyrics and rhyming patterns:

> When loneliness and sorrow and trouble come your way
> Friends you have in many to help you on your way
> When sickness overtakes you and you are all alone
> It's the only time you'll think of the old folks at home ...

While the topic and textual elements of 'Ghan to the Alice' can be read as typical of country music worldwide, they operate in ways which negotiate these standard country motifs, appropriating the myths of place and nostalgia and reinterpreting them as expressions of Aboriginality. Related to this is the idea of place, as kinship structures are generally located in networks of sacred sites, migration paths and community focal points. Through the title and text elements of 'Ghan to the Alice', such as 'the old folks at home', these features of Aboriginal identity construction can be read 'between the lines' of Laughton's song.

Covering songs, changing meanings

In many Western contemporary music cultures, cover versions are not generally associated with originality and credibility. 'Original' music is that written and performed by the same artist. It is often considered more authentic than cover versions – an entertaining but nonetheless shallow musical form, sometimes seen as an artistic sellout. These ideas of taste and credibility are closely linked to ideals of individualism, creativity and authorship that are distinctly modern and European in their orientation, as opposed to oral traditions in which ownership of musical knowledge is shared and passed down through familial and community links.

In Aboriginal Australia, cultural production is in many cases an oral tradition, with notions of authorship stemming from tribal and linguistic affiliations, community responsibilities and collective heritages. Communities own rights over song texts, like art designs; culture is maintained through revisiting cultural production and through constantly being remade in design, dance and music. In this context, cover versions, most often of country and folk songs, are interpretable in quite different ways to how they would be perceived in non-Indigenous rock music settings.

Cover versions are common in Aboriginal country music, and are incorporated into Aboriginal life in ways that reflect community ownership of cultural production. Tracing one song through various reworkings illustrates how covers perform this function. Harry Williams' 'Streets of Fitzroy' is an Aboriginal country 'classic', in which standard country motifs of a nostalgic wish to return home, the comfort of the past and a city/country dichotomy are inverted as part of an Aboriginal expression of desire for reclamation of the 'Dreaming', a symbol of pre-colonial society. This song represents the adaptation of a number of country music themes to one that remained specifically Aboriginal in intent:

> Oh I wish that I was back in the Dreamtime
> Hear the didjeridu droning through the night
> Where the corroborees are seen by the firelight
> Far away from the glow of city lights.

Inclusion of explicit depictions of Aboriginalities ('Dreamtime', 'didjeridu', 'corroborees') to express aspects of Aboriginal culture or Aboriginal

THE GHOST OF THE JOLLY OLD SWAGMAN
I DON'T CARE (Just as Long as You Love Me)
BLUE GUMS CALLING ME BACK HOME
LOVE, LOVE, LOVE
HOME SWEET HOME ON THE PRAIRIE
THE HILLS ARE TURNING BROWN

KAWLIGA
GOODNIGHT IRENE
MANY HAPPY HANGOVERS
JACKIE JACKIE
MIND YOUR OWN BUSINESS
HEARTACHES C.O.D.

and the Country Outcasts

Hadley

Recordings by Harry and Wilga Williams
and the Country Outcasts include songs by
Harry Williams and covers of country
music standards. (Courtesy: Hadley
Records and photographer Eric Scott)

policies in country songs (a subsequent repetition of the chorus includes the lines 'How I wish that I was back in the Dreamtime ... where the white man's ways won't bother me no more') are typical of the songs written and arranged by Williams, lead singer of the 1970s Melbourne-based group Harry and Wilga Williams and the Country Outcasts. The appearance of these songs on two albums conforms to the pattern noticed for singers such as Jimmy Little and Ernie and Noel Bridge: songs of identifiable Aboriginal reference occur alongside covers of country standards, in Harry Williams' case, songs by Hank Williams, including 'Kawliga' and 'Mind Your Own Business'.

Further cover versions of this song illustrate how community ownership of Aboriginal musical texts operates. 'Streets of Fitzroy' was subsequently covered by Roger Knox in 1983, and Tracey Lee Gray in 1986, this time as 'Streets of Tamworth'. Lyrics remain the same, except for place references, the site from which the lamenting singer wishes to travel back to the Dreamtime. While generic in its mobilisation of country themes, and non-specific in that it articulates pan-Aboriginal images of 'Dreamtime' and 'corroborees', the song could be reworked when covered, remade relevant for local contexts by changing the place from which the song is sung. That this is possible is also illustrated in an anecdote of one of the authors of this book. In 1997, while one author was busking in Bondi Junction, Sydney, an Aboriginal man (whose name was never offered) approached and asked to join the 'jam'. After accepting the invitation, the first song that the man encouraged us to play was a cover version of 'Streets of Fitzroy', yet this time the lyrics had again been adapted to local circumstances, as 'Streets of old Town Hall' (in reference to the popular meeting place in Sydney's central business district, where homeless Kooris are known to gather). The song is thus a fluid text attributed officially to Harry Williams, as songwriter and copyright holder, but also 'owned' more generally by various Aboriginal performers and audiences.

Prison songs

It would be deceiving to imply that only those country songs with explicitly 'Aboriginal' lyrics are genuinely 'Aboriginal', while at the same time arguing that cover versions of non-Aboriginal songs somehow have less meaning. Understanding the social contexts within which country music is

made, heard and interpreted is necessary, to go beyond the immediate textual evidence of a song, and to situate musical meaning in the communities
in which it is spread. There is more happening in the recording, distribution and consumption of Aboriginal country music than just songs with
overt Aboriginal references. Covers of non-Aboriginal songs constitute
reproductions of originals that are often simply enjoyed by Aboriginal
audiences for no specific reason other than that they are good songs but
beyond this, they are also often characterised by themes that resonate with
Aboriginal experiences. Even though in their non-Aboriginal contexts
country songs might be situated in a tradition with colonial, white, mascu-
line overtones, for Aboriginal audiences they may have different meanings.
Aboriginal interpretations of 'country', 'bush' and 'outback', for instance,
can be quite different from non-Aboriginal ones. 'Country' music, and references to 'country' in lyrics, for example, coincide with the use of that
term in Aboriginal societies to describe one's tribal/linguistic home territory, *one's country*, a real place rather than a generic rural/non-urban space.

As Troy Cassar-Daley has said, 'it doesn't necessarily have to be from
Australia. It can be an American song and you can think, Gee, I can
relate to that. That's what attracted me to the music when I was a kid, its
lyrics, its honesty' (in Walker, 2000, 287). Hence, country songs from
American artists such as Johnny Cash and Merle Haggard that bemoan
life in prisons take on meanings in Aboriginal communities when re-
covered by Aboriginal performers. These songs have revised meanings
because of the high rates of incarceration of Aboriginal people in Australian jails, relative to the non-Aboriginal population, and cultural inap-
propriateness of prisons for Aboriginal people, a situation investigated in
the late 1980s by the Royal Commission into Aboriginal Deaths in Custody (Commonwealth of Australia, 1992). Songs about hardships in
prisons, lamenting past wrongs and longing for release, take on profound
significance in this context, as with, for instance, 'I Want to be Free'
(Elvis Presley) and 'I'll Break Out Again Tonight' (Merle Haggard), both
covered by Roger Knox in 1988 on his *Warrior in Chains* album:

> These walls and bars can't hold a dreaming man
> So I'll be home to tuck the babies in
> They can chain my body but not my mind
> So I'll break out again tonight.

These songs are about a longing to be free from incarceration, but contain slippages from their original meanings when understood in Aboriginal contexts. These include, in this case, references to a 'dreaming man' (dreaming not just as a verb – that is, longing for release – but also as an adjective, as an Aboriginal man connected to the Dreaming). Given the burden faced by Aboriginal inmates with their own community responsibilities unable to be carried out when in jail, and hardship faced when, for instance, inhabiting prison spaces in which previous community members have committed suicide, one can begin to understand that this choice of cover material is not incidental. This was particularly the case for Vic Simms, who began his recording career in 1961 with his first single, 'Yo Yo Heart' at the age of fifteen. After the decline of his career and problems with alcohol, Simms ended up in Bathurst prison in 1968, perhaps the worst facility in the country and where 'prisoners were openly and systematically beaten' (Walker, 2000, 129), threatening his burgeoning recording career. However, after a demonstration tape of his songs, recorded in Bathurst prison as part of a welfare project, reached RCA Records, he eventually recorded *The Loner* in 1973 while still incarcerated. A mobile studio was given approval by the Department of Correctional Services because the recording was seen to have good PR for the prison:

> We had exactly an hour to record, because that was all the time allocated by the prison. The screws didn't like it at all. They thought it was all about pampering prisoners – and a blackfella at that! It was the end of the world for them. I had to hope and pray that I'd do okay on each of the 10 tracks because there'd be no second bidding. And I did ... I felt that if I didn't record that album, it would just prove that we were out of sight and out of mind. I wanted to show that musical talent could exist no matter where it was, out in the bush or behind walls (in *Koori Mail*, 17 Apr 2002, 60).

Later in his career, Simms would also record on an Enrec compilation entitled *Prison Songs* (1988) of cover versions of country style prison songs, including 'Branded Man', 'I Fought the Law', and 'Riot in Cellblock #9'. Many artists such as Roger Knox, Warumpi Band, Archie Roach and Kev Carmody continue to perform for prison inmates. Vic

Simms, Roger Knox and Bobby McLeod even undertook a tour in 1990 of Canadian jails, where First Nations indigenous people make up the bulk of inmates. For Vic Simms, prison performances provide important emotional support for inmates:

> You see them there, the radiance comes out of their faces. They just bop along and you can see the lifting of their hearts, you know. All the tension's gone ... maybe some of them have got chips on their shoulders, which you can't blame them for because, even though it's a lot easier today, jail is still jail. The loved ones are out here and they're in there, but we try to alleviate the sadness and the pain, through music, and they appreciate it. We try to deliver a message too, to say, We've been there, we did all that, you know, and there's a better life out there (in Walker, 2000, 136).

Kev Carmody has said of such experiences that

> performing is a two-way process of empowerment. It's not just the audience being empowered by the music but also the performer. With me, I try not to make it the kind of traditional rock 'n' roll thing – the Rolling Stones' 'Nuremberg Rally' thing where there's the performer up on stage with this huge stage and 50,000 watts of Marshall stacks, and 'you plebs' down there are going to watch from afar and there's absolutely no interaction. For example, when I go and do the prison gigs, the first thing they do is pull out the video camera, and the boys in there say 'can you play us this song', so I do it for them, and straight after the song's finished they're playing it back again, trying to figure out the chords – they'll say 'ah, that's how you do that chord'; or if they didn't get it the first time they'll get me to play it again (interview, 1996).

Music has immediate relevance in such circumstances – a link to the outside world, and a means of communicating sympathy. It also acts as an indicator to both the Aboriginal and non-Aboriginal listeners of a widely experienced aspect of Aboriginal life. Thus general phrases and themes in non-Aboriginal country music can have specific meanings and interpretations for Aboriginal audiences in certain contexts.

The Tamworth Country Music Festival

Tamworth has had an association with country music at least since the 1940s, when local radio station 2TM began to broadcast country music, including the famous *Hoedown* show, on an unusually clear signal to many parts of eastern Australia. In the 1960s, Tamworth developed a formative circuit of pub venues such as Joe Maguire's Pub, playing host to country music performances as part of a larger rural network. Thus, before the establishment of the well-known music festival in the early 1970s, Tamworth already had a country music presence. The festival itself was preceded by the Tamworth country music jamboree, which staged a number of performances and a talent quest over the January, Australia Day long weekend. Max Ellis, manager of the 2TM radio station and later Broadcast Amalgamated Limited Marketing (BAL), was responsible for transforming this mainly amateur event into a full-scale production of the magnitude of current festivals, and in 1969, was the first to describe Tamworth as the 'Country Music Capital'. This catch-phrase was not only coined to describe place and the Country Music Festival, but to encourage year-round tourist strategies of the town as a whole. The establishment of several recording studios also solidified the presence of the country music industry in Tamworth around this time. The Hadley country music studios were opened in 1970; others, including Opal, Selection and Enrec recording studios, followed soon after (Allan, 1988).

In 1973, the Tamworth Country Music Festival became an official event on the country music calendar, with 2TM announcing the winners of the inaugural Australasian Country Music Awards. In the 1970s, the festival spanned the January long weekend, and later was extended to a full nine-day program as the events and number of performances grew during the 1980s. The festival now currently runs over ten days, usually starting on the Friday or Saturday prior to the January long weekend. It attracts over 50 000 visitors to the town, and generates an estimated $40 million for the local economy. In 1997, the festival's 'silver jubilee', the festival featured over 1900 events and 650 official individual performers and bands (Gibson & Davidson, 2004). Performances take place in a range of venues, from informal busking and singing in the 'tent city' constructed by the river to accommodate extra visitors, through to the pub circuit and larger, formal venues such as the Longyard Hotel and the Tamworth Town Hall, as well as large open air, free concerts.

In many respects, the Tamworth Country Music Festival has been woven into the fabric of country music in Australia in ways that entrench the ideological background of Australian country music discussed at the beginning of this chapter. Themes of Australian nationalism, of a colonial, rural mythology of place, are amplified in relation to Tamworth given the timing of its country music festival around the Australia Day holiday, and very much celebrated as part of that day and all it represents within an overtly non-Indigenous history. The profundity of Australia Day, as a marker of invasion, colonialism and the beginning of dispossession and Indigenous resistance, is overlooked in promotions of the festival. Indeed, the major concert performance of the festival takes place not only on Australia Day but in *Bicentennial* Park, also emphasising the celebratory rather than commemorative aspects of this day. The bicentennial year 1988 (in which Tamworth's park and many others around Australia were opened) was celebrated by most of Australia's state institutions, community groups and companies as a recognition of the 'birth' of a nation while Indigenous organisations protested around Australia on 'Australia Day' (January 26), renaming the occasion 'Invasion Day' or 'Survival Day' (hence the festival of the same name, discussed in chapter 2).

Tamworth City Council has echoed the construction of Australian nationalism around tropes of (non-Indigenous) country music traditions, placing itself at the centre of these discourses. In a submission to the 1997 NSW Tourism Awards for Excellence, the Council responded to the question 'How does your event integrate with the natural and/or cultural environment?' with the following statement: 'Tamworth – it's Australia'. Further on the festival is described as 'a celebration of the Australian Identity ... manag[ing] to showcase the sum and substance of being Australian'. Throughout other promotional documents Tamworth and the Country Music Festival are variously described as: 'a celebration of the Australian entity'; 'that feeling of warmth when two strangers on a street actually bid each other nothing more than a simple 'g-day''; featuring 'happenings [that] classically illustrate the Australian character', meanwhile participants can 'fulfill the unique Aussie spirit of 'having a go', enjoy a 'juicy piece of prime beef prepared in an establishment that could have that day taken the beast from the back paddock and placed it

Much of the Aboriginal country music presence
at the Tamworth Country Music Festival occurs
in unacknowledged ways. In this photo, the
Gumbangerri Sunrise Band perform in Peel St,
the main shopping street of Tamworth (Photo:
Peter Dunbar-Hall)

onto the char grill', and experience the 'spirit of the Anzacs and images
of the Kokoda track' through assertions of 'mateship' (Tamworth City
Council files, 1997, quoted in Gibson & Davidson, 2004). Evidence
given to support this claim includes 'the spirit of competing and winning
evidenced in the awarding of the coveted Golden Guitar trophy. The
wonderful Australian character of supporting your favourite football
team is duplicated when they see their favourite star take home gold'.
The organisers claim that 'country music conjures up images of all things
rural', a sentiment that can be brought back from the festival in paintings
captured on anything from a beer bottle to a garden spade. Thus, Tamworth is depicted as the quintessential rural experience, leading organisers to the following conclusion: 'Tamworth would challenge that
nowhere else in Australia ... can the culture of our country be personified

so accurately in spirit or style ... It's where country is' (Tamworth City Council files, 1997, quoted in Gibson & Davidson, 2004). This is translated into the particular styles of music most popular and promoted at Tamworth, or chosen by promoters to feature there; what Walker (2000, 285) described as an 'almost xenophobic obsession with preserving the purity of the Australian bush ballad'.

These representations of Tamworth and associations with country music have occurred in ways that situate the town within dominant rural, non-Aboriginal discourses of Australian national identity. However, the presence of Aboriginal artists within the festival to some extent challenges this, though engagements with the 'mainstream' country music circuit remain ambiguous. Many Indigenous performers, including Auriel Andrew, Troy Cassar-Daley, Col Hardy, the Kelly Family, Gus Williams, Roger Knox and Jimmy Little have performed over the years at Tamworth, yet only relatively recently have Aboriginal shows been established at Tamworth and thus far, only two Aboriginal artists – Troy Cassar-Daley and Jimmy Little – have received widespread recognition for their work in the Golden Guitar awards. Indigenous artists have now established their own shows at the festival, organised and hosted by the local Aboriginal health service at the Mara Mara Aboriginal Centre. Indigenous presence in the formally organised side of the festival had until recently consisted of a single night, the Koori Country Spectacular, however by 2003 it had grown to include a Koori Health Concert, the 'Feeling Good' Town Hall Aboriginal showcase concert and the Aboriginal Talent Quest. These are organised and run by local health units, and by the Sydney Country Music Club Aboriginal Corporation, under the Festival's general organisational plan that sees individual proprietors and promoters staging events independently of the City Council and BAL Marketing, whose role is more of a co-ordinating and state-wide promotional committee. Within this decentralised organisational structure, Indigenous organisations have been able to carve out space for Aboriginal concerts and expressions. As Agnes Donovan, project co-ordinator of the Aboriginal showcase and talent quest at Tamworth 2003 explained, 'people want to see Aboriginal people perform, and there's a real need for us to have our own shows, because all the other big showcases don't often recognise us as Aboriginal people, and somebody's got to do it ... I felt proud to be there at the festival with all my people, and to see that we can do things just as well as anybody else, to see that the people enjoy what we do, and appreciate our music' (in *Koori Mail*, 12 Feb 2003, 30).

The extent to which Aboriginal voices are marginalised at Tamworth is less than it once was, as the success of Troy Cassar-Daley demonstrates. Nonetheless, performers at Aboriginal events generally do not play at other venues in the Festival, which remain part of a mainstream circuit controlled by individual venue owners, record companies and major sponsors. Many Aboriginal musicians have tended to participate as buskers, passers-by, and performers in generally low-key, informal environments. For example, the Kelly Family are regular visitors to Tamworth, while artists such as John Turner from Mt Isa have gained recognition for their busking efforts. He won the 1993 Golden Swaggie Award, presented by the Spirit of Tamworth collective as an alternative to the large-scale Country Music Association awards. While Tamworth is a site of convergence for Aboriginal and non-Aboriginal geographies of country music, a range of industry factors (discussed in chapter 1) limit the opportunities available for Aboriginal musicians. Moreover, symbolically, the Tamworth Country Music Festival both encapsulates conservative elements of national identity in country music, and is an event in which Aboriginal people are able to create spaces for community celebration. It thus embodies the contradictions of country music in Australia in a space for musical performance.

Conclusion

Interpreting country music in Australia is complex. It is to some extent true that country music has 'become common ground between black and white Australia', as Walker (2000, 13) argued. An Aboriginal radio station in Brisbane, 4AAA ('Brisbane's No. 1 Murri Country Radio'), has since its licence was issued ten years ago built up a significant non-Aboriginal audience because it is that city's only station to specialise in country, providing an opportunity for important cross-cultural exchanges to occur. As station manager, Tiga Bayles, noted:

> When Pauline Hanson was cracking we had a lot more calls. A lot of those rednecks love the country and western stuff, but only a few of them knew that we were just a bunch of Murris playing our

music. You've got to laugh with this country stuff ... [country music] gets us into the homes of the people who we need to reach. About 90 percent of our non-indigenous audience have never let a blackfella inside their front gate, let alone into their living rooms. The message we have to them is that we're not going to take everything off you. Check us out. If they get to know us, then there'll be better respect, and better understanding, and that's what we're all about (in Fraser, 2001, 5).

Yet there is also a sense in which there are continuing fissions, both between Aboriginal and non-Aboriginal Australian scenes, and differences in musical intent and social context of reception, even within Aboriginal society. It is too simplistic to 'write off' country music as merely a conservative music of white Australia, as is demonstrated by the appropriation of country music in creative ways by Aboriginal artists. It has long been a form of Aboriginal expression through which various concerns are voiced and cultural practices enacted. Non-Aboriginal country music (both American and Australian) is itself also diverse, as are the audiences who enjoy it. Much country music makes sense to Aboriginal audiences because of its narrative structure and themes of land, alienation and tradition, even if Aboriginal places and meanings are absent. At the same time, though, the same country music remains popular with non-Aboriginal constituencies, some of whom would consider Aboriginal rights and concerns illegitimate, and who instead would prefer to see in country music a reinforcing of conservative values and perspectives.

In this chapter we have provided an overview of the music and wider cultural debates that surround the use of country styles by musicians in Australia. Aboriginal country music is at once 'on the map' of Australian country music, and simultaneously marginalised within it — it is both 'there' and 'not there'. Nonetheless, Aboriginal contributions to Australia's country music heritage persist, well over seventy years after its widespread adoption, and in this sense country music remains a major contributing element of a history of Aboriginal musical expression.

Suggested listening

AIM 4 MORE ▲ *Aim 4 More*

All You Mob!

Shakaya ▲ *Shakaya*

CHAPTER 4

Aboriginality and transnational black culture – hip-hop and R&B

Theories of Aboriginality discussed in chapter 2 emphasise the extent to which media such as music, film, the internet and television provide avenues for Indigenous groups to maintain or revive culture by appropriating communicative technologies (Michaels, 1986; 1989). As Hinkson (2002, 216–17) has argued, however, in her revisiting of Warlpiri use of media and communications technology (in the community where Michaels' famous studies of the 1980s were conducted): 'the problem with a cultural maintenance approach to thinking about Warlpiri people's interaction with new communications technologies is that it fails to reflect the very real changes in Warlpiri sociality that are occurring as the parameters of the Warlpiri lifeworld continue to expand'. Aboriginal people such as the Warlpiri are not passive observers of the transformations enacted through such media and cultural forms. Rather,

> their ongoing engagement with new technologies suggests that at least some Warlpiri people see benefits in the new forms of articulation with the wider society that accelerated globalisation carries with it. For some there is a clearly understood political imperative to engage; for others, such engagement is comprehended as the product of a history that cannot be wound back.

The media of globalisation – internet, television, film, radio – operate as transnational spaces within which cultural exchanges and borrowings occur. These include broadcasts of Aboriginality, when representations of Aboriginal people are circulated via communications technologies. Sometimes such media allow derogatory representations of Aboriginality as 'primitivism' to be promulgated (Langton, 1993a; Kibby, 1999). At other times, Aboriginal people contribute to national and international mediascapes, for example, when Aboriginal music video clips are shown internationally. In addition, Aboriginal people, like other social groups, take elements of cultural practices and expressions that appeal to them from national and international mediascapes. One indicator of the reach and pervasiveness of some forms of globalising popular culture is the extent to which contemporary music has been transformed not only in urban, but also remote Aboriginal communities in Australia. Young Aboriginal people around the country have appropriated elements of foreign cultural expressions, and in particular those of black American culture including sport (basketball), music (hip-hop, R&B) and fashion (baseball caps, sports clothing brands).

The adoption by young Aboriginal musicians of black American musical styles, including hip-hop and R&B, is the subject of this chapter. In its currency, the use of these types of music acts as a balance to the historical perspectives of the use of country music among Aboriginal musicians discussed in the previous chapter. The significance of these black American musical practices lies not only in their popularity among younger generation performers and listeners, but also in the geography they represent. Much Aboriginal music can be interpreted through theories of cultural revival and maintenance. The examples discussed in this chapter, however, also reveal Aboriginality as constructed through dialogue with black cultural forms and political concerns that are transnational.

Black (trans)nationalism

Much has been made of transnationalism in music. Several musical styles, including rap, reggae and country, have become global styles with the advent of electronic technologies and the development of international distribution networks within major global entertainment corporations. Over time, elements of these styles have been appropriated by local musicians, constituting 'glocal' subcultures (T Mitchell, 1996) that take from and contribute to global musical languages at the same time that they produce music that resonates with local circumstances and concerns. Black musical forms that draw on African roots – including reggae, funk, rap, R&B and soul – have become popular among disenfranchised groups in Europe, throughout Asia and in Australia, where they have become especially popular among migrant groups, working class youth and Indigenous communities (Iveson, 1997; Maxwell, 1997a, 1997b). Black transnationalism moves beyond Gilroy's (1993) notion of a 'Black Atlantic' linking African diasporic communities in Europe and north America, however, to include a range of marginalised peoples throughout the world. As Stephens (1998, 163) has noted in relation to reggae:

> 'transnationalism' becomes a utopian symbolic space between the culture of the racial diaspora and the political economy of the Amer-ican nation state. For [musicians], transnationalism is not a simple transcendence of the national, but rather an expressive project that samples and mixes the identities of immigrant, citizen and refugee.

and in Australia (we would add) Aboriginal identities. This sense of sam-pling and mixing of transnational black identities is revealed both in musical practices and in social linkages enabled by global media, trans-portation and touring networks.

There has been an increasing affinity between Aboriginal Australians and black Americans since the early 1990s, although links between black America and Australia extend further back culturally, including the influence on Aboriginal performers of black jazz musicians stationed in Far North Queensland during World War II (Walker, 2000). Popular culture, including music, has been central to this new avenue of commu-nication. Many young Aboriginal people absorb images of black Amer-ican culture via television. Sports coverage and music video clips that depict empowered, black people provide role models of success. Beyond mere idolisation, many black American music stars have sought to make connections with members of Australia's Indigenous communities while touring here. Thus Michael Franti, Chuck D, the Fugees, Bob Marley, C and C Music Factory, Ice Cube, Ice-T and Ben Harper have all at var-ious times either made appearances on Aboriginal radio stations, per-formed for Aboriginal audiences, made special visits to disadvantaged communities, or alluded to commonalities between black Americans and Australians while on stage or in media interviews. Michael Franti, lyricist

and rapper with The Disposable Heroes of Hiphoprisy and then Spear-
head, has been quite vocal in this regard, arguing that: 'reconciliation
between black and white Australia is as much a global issue as a local one
... be it The Bronx or Alice Springs, the colour of a person's skin often
leads to prejudice, especially when the police are involved. Racial pro-
filing in the United States and mandatory sentencing in the Northern
Territory are part of the same global problem of racism' (in Delaney,
2001, 3). For Franti, music provides a crucial tool to negotiate margin-
ality and discrimination, 'let's use culture as a site of resistance ... with
the vulnerability of your open mouth, the energy of your sound and the
addition of your thoughts through words, you have power' (in Delaney,
2001, 3).

Hip-hop in particular has become a common feature of everyday Aboriginal life across Australia. Hip-hop combines rapping over turntable
scratching and samples of breakbeats, graffiti art, breakdancing, beat-
boxing, fashion, and more ideologically, an 'ethos' of solidarity and loyalty.
Hip-hop emerged from a fusion of elements brought to the United States
by migrants from Latin America and the Caribbean with the local
musical forms heard in deprived, inner-city neighbourhoods. From its origins in the South Bronx (New York) in the 1970s, hip-hop was quickly
taken up by residents in similar American urban neighbourhoods,
notably in south-central Los Angeles, but also other urban ghettos in
major cities (McLaren, 1995, 14). The success of this type of music relied
on the skill and dexterity of DJs, their use of original and obscure record
sources and the ability to provide breakbeats and mix several records
using twin turntables and volume faders.

With perhaps the exception of reggae and jazz, hip-hop has been probably the most widespread transnational black cultural form, distinct in its
intense territoriality and its focus on 'the ghetto' as a real and mythical
space (McLaren, 1995; T Mitchell, 1996; Rose, 1994; Dudrah, 2002; Connell & Gibson, 2003). As Rose (1994, 101) has argued, 'rap is a contemporary stage for the theater of the powerless. On this stage, rappers act out
inversions of status hierarchies, tell alternative stories of contact with
police and the education process, and draw portraits of contact with dominant groups in which the hidden transcript inverts/subverts the public,
dominant transcript.' The visual and aural elements of hip-hop cultures
have articulated a mesmerising array of urban American experiences, from

contradictory sexisms and anti-Semitic comments to stories of pleasure and violence; all of this alongside militant expressions of black nationalism.

In Australia, hip-hop never eclipsed rock music as the central style in the (Anglo-Celtic) popular music market, and it has often been ridiculed and disparaged: 'youth culture has always been fractious and tribalised, but rarely has an entire segment of it been as derided as hip-hop. NSW Premier Bob Carr complains about kids wearing baseball caps backwards, radio plays TISM's "All Homeboys are Dickheads", and the misunderstandings mean most of Sydney ignores a vibrant and growing scene' (Dunne, 1995, 13). Nonetheless, hip-hop has been a constant presence since its internationalisation in the early 1980s, popular with young people of all backgrounds, including Aboriginal youth. For MC Brothablack (aka Shannon Williams), from Sydney's South West Syndicate: 'I started out by trying to imitate Chuck D and people like that. Listening to rap music was just part of my everyday life' (in *Koori Mail*, 27 Nov 2002, 33), while for Aboriginal rapper Lez 'Bex' Beckett, from Cunnamulla: 'before Australian and Aboriginal hip-hop really took off, we [Aboriginal youth] all followed what the Americans did. It really influenced me because it was a black face on the television, and when you are a young fulla growing up in Cunnamulla in central Queensland, it is a pride thing to see another blackfella in a position of power' (in Condie, 2003, 36). Thus for Native Rhyme Syndicate, based in Brisbane and containing members from Arrente country in central Australia and Gkuthaarn clan in Gulf of Carpentaria, hip-hop is 'one of the most effective means to communicate with young people' (*Koori Mail*, 14 Jan 1998, 19).

Such sentiments were not uniquely felt by Aboriginal youth – hip-hop also quickly became popular among Australian teenagers of Lebanese, Filipino, Vietnamese and Turkish backgrounds, as well as working class white youth in poorer areas of the capital cities. For some it was a means of transcending ethnicity and forming a common youth subculture, a means of expression for young people of backgrounds otherwise marginalised in Australia's Anglocentric commercial media. At the 1995 Hip Hopera festival in Western Sydney, Naz, from South West Syndicate, emphasised hip-hop's transcultural potential: 'we've got blacks, whites, we got Middle-Eastern people, we've got all mixtures of all groups, know what I mean? There's no racism' (in Dunne, 1995, 13; see also Iveson, 1997). For Morgan Lewis, aka Morganics: 'Being a teenager is all about being oppressed. Every teenager has to be a rebel. It doesn't matter whether you're white, black, Asian or what. That's your thing; you are oppressed by school and teacher and so on. Hip-hop becomes your voice, and it's a very potent voice' (in Dunne, 1995, 13). Will Jarrett, aka MC Wire, from Bowraville (NSW) and with Gumbainggir background, emphasised the extent to which this global style had been 'made local' in Australia: 'Hip-hop subculture has been given a peculiarly Australian flavour ... infused with diverse musical and cultural influences. With its foundations in protest and adversity, it is increasingly being used by young black people from Indigenous and immigrant backgrounds in Australia to find their voice and creatively articulate their ideas' (in *Koori Mail*, 12 Jun 2002, 47). This is perhaps nowhere more potently evident than in the following rap, by MC Brothablack:

> Ha ha I'm back all with South West Syndicate so make your call
> Slappin' high fives everywhere I go with my lyrical flow that I know, so ...
> Our nation of residence is getting hesitant
> They can't do shit because they got no evidence
> 200 years of this bullshit us kooris have had enough
> So you better quit
> Got brothers like me behind bars and in the gutter
> Portraying us as stupid black fuckers
> The white man's plan is getting outta hand
> We are being hung up in your cells across the land
> Keep an eye on them drunks in the park
> Time for us to raise up outta the dark
> From Broome all the way back to Redfern
> Brothers and sistas raise up it's your turn
> (South West Syndicate, in Dunne, 1995, 13).

As with black American hip-hop, rapping enables reclamation of spaces, in the case of the Clevo St Boys' 'The Block', about the Sydney Aboriginal community's settlement of that name in inner-city Redfern:

> Stand your ground
> Black people from The Block
> We're not moving on, so rack off cops
> The Redfern Housing Company

Gonna manifest our own destiny ...
Dealers, junkies, gamblers
All bringing the cops around
Making a bad rap for our parts of town
We've had about enough
You better move along
Cos we're comin' at ya, broth ...
This is where we live, what we call home.

In recognition of the power of hip-hop as a communicative media for young people, and linked to its ethos of solidarity and community, many of Australia's well-established MCs, DJs and breakdancers have toured Australia disseminating their skills to young Aboriginal people. Bex, from Cunnamulla, is one with such aims:

> I want to teach them how to 'human beatbox', how to play guitar, how to combine riffs and beats, and how to make their way through the industry if that is their chosen path. I write about the positive changes you can make with your life, about everyday living, the struggle to survive, especially if you are a blackfella, and how you can have focus points in your life to concentrate on ... I tell them, 'keep it Australian', because while it is an American form, we can incorporate our own lives into it, we can rap our own way ... (in Condie, 2003, 36).

By far the most successful effort in this regard has been the National Indige-nous 3 on 3 Basketball and Hip-Hop Challenge, a travelling program organ-ised by *Deadly Vibe* magazine, and funded by various agencies including the NSW Aboriginal Land Council, ATSIC, Centrelink and *Koori Mail*. The 3 on 3 challenge involves a basketball, breakdancing and rapping competi-tion for Indigenous teenagers. It is hosted by leading Aboriginal MCs and DJs, and features guest sport stars in workshops and skills development ses-sions. 3 on 3 Challenges have taken place in Broome, Murray Bridge, Mil-dura, Kempsey and Minto in Sydney's outer southwest. Gavin Jones, co-organiser, emphases how sport and music contribute to a global black consciousness yet remain relevant within a refreshed Indigenous culture:

> we try to keep a balance between American hip-hop and Aborig-inal music. I think this event is bigger than American culture and

taps into a worldwide black culture that Aboriginal Australia fits into. Hip-hop is a music of the people and our young people are writing raps and rhymes about being Aboriginal, so it is an element of the black culture of this country (in Condie, 2002b, 24).

Similarly for Brothablack, one of the main role models at 3 on 3 Challenges, 'it's important to teach Indigenous young people in regional and remote communities that we have our own rapping and breaking culture. That way, we can explode the myth about it just being an American thing. We have the talent and the interest right here' (in *Koori Mail,* 27 Nov 2002, 33). Hip-hop has thus become an important part of youth welfare activities for Aboriginal communities around Australia, a means of self-expression and empowerment for disenfranchised youth in places with meagre job opportunities and, often, difficult social problems. Through these activities and the expressions that they facilitate, hip-hop moves beyond mere educational purpose to become a means for developing confidence and pride. In some cases it has enabled new symbolic geographies to emerge, as otherwise marginalised places are figured into the scripts of rap rhymes and are re-represented in sound.

This has been especially the case for two towns in rural New South Wales that were the places of origin of two of Australia's best known rap artists: MC Wire, from Bowraville, and Wilcannia Mob, a group of three young Aboriginal boys from the town of the same name in western New South Wales. A recent education and recording project that visited both towns would have an important impact as a youth welfare activity, as well as contributing to the re-visioning of the symbolic geography of these places in the imagination of the wider public.

Comin' at ya! – hip-hop projects from the bush

Whenever Bowraville is depicted in Australian media (an extremely rare occurrence for a town that generally draws no media attention beyond its own region), the images evoked are invariably negative, as the following quote from a major metropolitan newspaper attests:

> Not much happens in Bowraville on a hot afternoon. Nor any other time for that matter. A timber town on the mid-North Coast of NSW where the timber is running out, Bowraville (population: 1000; job prospects: negligible) struggles to survive. Two

BOUNCE! BEATS! BREAKS!

ARE YOU UP TO THE CHALLENGE?

The National Indigenous 3 on 3 Basketball and Hip-Hop Challenge is coming to a community near you. It's about sport, music, self-expression, health, education and most of all, FUN! The 3 on 3 Challenge is an Aboriginal and Torres Strait Islander event for our community, our family and all our friends. Everybody is welcome.

Kempsey
Melville High School
Nicholson Street

19-20 OCTOBER 2002

Register from 9am

For more information call Vibe Australia on 1800 623 430 or go to vibe.com.au

The 3 on 3 Challenges combine hip-hop music with basketball, both generally considered quintessentially American cultural forms. They have become important opportunities, though, for Aboriginal youth to meet and develop musical, as well as sporting, skills. (Courtesy: Vibe Australia)

generations back, the men all had jobs, and the farmers' daughters looked forward to a night at the pictures, a dance at the community ball, and jaunts to the beach 15kms away in Nambucca Heads. Today, the cinema stands empty and the town's many young people (one third of the population is under 18) loiter in the street, waiting. Waiting for jobs, for the pub to open, for a southerly breeze to blow through and freshen things up ... several major employers, including the meat works and two timber mills, have shut down. And the picture gets bleaker. Bowraville is also an old Aboriginal mission town and its population is starkly divided: the white folk live in town, in Federation timber homes with broad-brimmed verandas and agapanthus hedges; the 'blacks' – the Gumbaynggir people for whom the surrounding semi-tropical land has been home for tens of thousands of years and who now make up almost a quarter of the population – are mostly housed at the old mission, a littered and graffiti-strewn plot of government-issue houses with no postal service, conveniently tucked away en route to the cemetery (Wilson, 2003, 14).

MC Wire grew up in Bowraville, in circumstances of racism and marginalisation that would draw him to hip-hop:

Aboriginal people can relate to hip-hop culture because it's storytelling. I could really relate to Ice Cube. Like me, he was an angry young black man, but he was very intellectual about it and he was telling his reality which was removed from my reality, but there were parallels, you know, a black man speaking out about the white oppressor (in Wilson, 2003, 16).

He found further success in hip-hop once moving to Sydney, but has since returned to Bowraville as part of hip-hop workshops run in conjunction with local youth groups.

The workshops, organised by Morganics and Triple J's Tony Collins, were part of a wider 2002 network of tours of Aboriginal communities across Australia, including Darwin, Coffs Harbour, Grafton, Alice Springs, Maningrida and Redfern. In Bowraville, MC Wire had an important influence on youth in the town: 'When Will and Morganics came through last year it was the best thing that ever happened to this town. It changed the atmosphere here for the kids for months after. The hip-hop workshops brought them all together for the first time. A rarity for this town' (Bowraville Youth Club president Dale Hawkins, in Wilson, 2003, 15–16).

Similarly, Wilcannia has been revived through rap: Wilcannia, like nearby Brewarrina and Walgett, is an old colonial river port in the New South Wales Far West, now predominantly an Aboriginal community. The decline in river transport, which was replaced in the twentieth century by road and rail, a general loss of employment and industry in smaller rural settlements and 'white flight' from these places which are now considered violent and tough places to live, has meant that the once 'queen city of the west' (Jopson, 2002, 9) is now described in the following terms:

> Wilcannia has an image problem, to say the very least. For many travellers, Wilcannia means 'watch out'. So-called grey nomads travelling between Broken Hill, 195 kilometres to the south-west, warn each other not to stop there for fear of assault or theft. A Broken Hill service station operator tells motorists to drive straight through ... Wilcannia is now the state's Scarytown (Jopson, 2002, 9).

Socioeconomic statistics reinforce Wilcannia's image as a disadvantaged place. It has the state's highest death rate from coronary artery disease, lung cancer and diabetes; the state's highest rate of low birth weight, smoking, obesity, and death from falls, motor vehicle accidents, poisoning, homicide and suicide. With an average life expectancy of thirty-seven years for men and forty-three for women, it is the most disadvantaged area of New South Wales (Wilcannia Community Working Party, 2001). Morganic's hip-hop program visited Wilcannia in 2002, when he recorded Wilcannia Mob, made up of Keith Dutton, Buddy Blair and Colroy Johnson. Their track 'Down River' featured on a subsequent CD of hip-hop songs by Aboriginal children, *All You Mob!*, released by ABC Music in 2002. Also on this album, songs such as 'Wilcannia Comin' at Ya', 'George from Bowraville', 'Coffs Harbour Mission' and 'The Block' by groups such as Clevo St Boys, Bowraville Mob and Wongalla Boys attest to the continuing power of place to dominate hip-hop lyrics, and to explicate issues of Aboriginal identity. The Wilcannia Mob's 'Down River' reflects the simple childhood pleasures of life in an otherwise tough town:

> When it's hot we go down to the river and swim
> When we go fishing we're catching the bream
> When the river's high we jump off the bridge
> When we get home we play some didj.

Says Morganics, 'hip-hop is all about representing where you're from and your life and story. We just asked the boys what they do and they said, "when it's hot we go down to the river for a swim". And it was like, OK, there's the beginning, let's go from there' (in P Munro, 2002, 5). The song scored unlikely success and high rotation on national youth broadcaster Triple J. It attracted national media attention and secured its performers a slot at the 2002 Homebake Festival in Sydney in front of 20 000 people; their performance was afterwards lauded as the highlight of the festival in many reviews.

According to MC Wire, in contrast to much of the commercial music now dominating Top 40 singles charts, hip-hop makes sense in places like Bowraville and Wilcannia because of its original grassroots ethos:

> it originated as a form of community expression. Kids today associate [imported] hip-hop with the candy life. They haven't been made aware of what hip-hop is really about. It's about representing your story, telling the world about you, your love, your fears and the great thing about [the Morganics] project is going to communities to show them this ... not just indigenous youth, because disadvantaged youth are disadvantaged youth. You see, it's all about teaching kids confidence through self-expression and self-identification, being proud of yourself, not being ashamed, which in small town communities is a massive contributing factor to the sadness' (in Wilson 2003, 16–17).

Regardless of the political stances (or not) adopted in rap lyrics, hip-hop enables cultural expressions that can reverse patterns of domination and invert meanings of place that revolve around alienation and marginalisation.

Rhythm 'n' bounce – Aboriginal R&B

There are other elements of black American music cultures that have influenced Aboriginal artists. Though jazz, blues and funk have rarely surfaced in Aboriginal communities (with notable exceptions, such as jazz vocalists

Georgia Lee and Liz Cavanagh, and blues singer Marlene Cummins), R&B has much more recently become a highly popular style with younger Aboriginal people, with some groups achieving national recording success. This version of R&B is more a dance-oriented derivation of hip-hop, without its politicised or confronting rapping, and with added layers of harmonised vocal parts. It is tangentially linked to the rhythm and blues sound of the 1960s, associated with Detroit's Motown label, although the parallel to that era is more one of the formats of production, marketing and performance than of stylistic influence. Contemporary R&B is performed by 'boy bands' and 'girl groups' who sing and dance in choreographed style to backing sequences of drum, bass and synthesizer. Marketing of R&B is closely aligned with fashion trends and, as with Motown stars of the 1960s, groups are often 'dressed up' in matching outfits with carefully cultivated images, albeit in relation to contemporary trends, with 'street' images rather than the polished 'neat' look of earlier Motown groups.

Many Aboriginal teenagers came into contact with R&B when famous black American artists such as Bobby Brown, Boyz II Men and TLC featured on weekend video hits television shows around Australia. By the mid-1990s AIM 4 MORE ('AIM' stands for 'Aboriginal and Islander Mob') had became one of the first groups to pick up on contemporary R&B in an Aboriginal context, performing at Survival concerts and releasing singles and in 1997 a self-titled album. Since then, other R&B acts have emerged, most notably Shakaya – a duo from Cairns who sing in the mould of Destiny's Child or TLC and are marketed predominantly to teenage/young adult audiences. Shakaya (Naomi Wenitong and Simone Stacey), have had a number of successful singles releases in national charts, including 'Stop Calling Me' and 'The Way You Make Me Feel', a cover of the Michael Jackson classic. Signed to international media conglomerate Sony, Shakaya won Deadly Awards for Band of the Year, Single of the Year and Most Promising New Talent in 2002. Shakaya are important in this discussion of Aboriginality and symbolic geography, as, perhaps more so than other successful Indigenous acts, they include no obvious Aboriginal references in their lyrics or marketing material. They do not mention Cairns in their songs, and are above all popular among non-Aboriginal audiences. Yet beyond this, Aboriginal audiences are well aware of this duo's Indigenous backgrounds, as are the performers themselves. In their short career to date, Shakaya have frequently participated in Aboriginal festivals and events, and are forthcoming in interviews about their mixed Indigenous/Pacific Islander heritage. Aboriginality is thus negotiated in different ways in different contexts, enacted by this duo when performing for certain audiences, while in other circumstances playing no part in the marketing of their music.

For Shakaya, musical links to American inspirations are clear, as Naomi Wenitong says: 'there's a lot of different styles we listen to and Simone and myself have the same tastes in music. I'm influenced by stuff my parents listen to but also groups like boy bands, TLC, Usher ... I love Destiny's Child and I'm inspired by every group, they work really hard, but I don't want to be compared. Hopefully we'll start an Australian R&B scene' (quoted in Thusi, 2002, 32). Here, the influence of black American culture is strong, but without the more overt political stances of hip-hop and rap groups. As with other Aboriginal R&B groups, such as AIM 4 MORE and Java, transnationalism apparent in music is more one of stylistic rather than lyrical influences. Yet this remains important, even though its forms of empowerment are more subtle. Shakaya and other R&B acts demonstrate how black culture re-presents itself in relation to transnational precedents, with images of professional urban Aboriginal women and men delivering classy, choreographed R&B performances in a sophisticated manner. It is in this respect, rather than in any formal political stance, that music can also act as empowerment.

Conclusion

Black transnationalism is thus both stylistic construction and social practice. As the reggae influenced songs of No Fixed Address had done twenty years earlier, contemporary Aboriginal hip-hop speaks to, and is a part of, musical expression of a global black consciousness. At times this can be overtly political – as with South West Syndicate – at other times it is appealing, danceable music with no pretence of social commentary. Hip-hop, in particular, is much more than musical text. As a subcultural practice in America, Europe and Asia, it has always been connected to social practices – graffiti, 'gang' ethos, culture, fashion and attitude. This is no different in Australia, although in Aboriginal contexts it has special importance as the source of black transnational solidarity and as a means of expression. Rather than mere absorption of American culture, or loss of Aboriginality, hip-hop and R&B have become Indigenous musical languages in their own right.

Shakaya, based in Cairns, have
become popular R&B performing
artists. The image they present is slick
and upmarket – a quite different representation of Aboriginality from those
that dominate mainstream media
reports. (Courtesy: Shakaya)

Suggested listening

Christine Anu ▲ *Stylin' Up*

George Rrurrambu ▲ *Nerbu Message*

SPIN.fx ▲ *Uluparru*

Warumpi Band ▲ *Big Name, No Blankets*

Warumpi Band ▲ *Too Much Humbug*

Warumpi Band ▲ *Warumpi Band Go Bush!*

CHAPTER 5

Sites as songs – place in the music of Warumpi Band

The closing ceremony of the 2000 Sydney Olympic Games was one of explicit pro-Indigenous sentiment. Veteran Australian rock group Midnight Oil performed their 'Beds Are Burning' wearing T-shirts that declared 'SORRY' – a reference to Australian Prime Minister John Howard's inability to apologise for Australia's history of treatment of its Indigenous peoples, most notably the 'stolen generations'. A member of boy group Savage Garden performed wearing a tank top bearing the design of the Aboriginal flag; and Torres Strait Islander musician Christine Anu performed a version of 'My Island Home', the song that had helped the success of her 1995 dance inspired CD, *Stylin' Up*.

While Anu's Olympic performance of 'My Island Home' might have been construed by listeners as a reference to Australia as an island continent, video footage of Anu's version of the song had placed it somewhere in the singer's Torres Strait background, with images of palm trees and tropical coastlines. The song had, however, originated with Warumpi Band, the pioneering Aboriginal rock group from the central Australian township of Papunya and had appeared first on the group's second album, *Warumpi Band Go Bush!* in 1987. Anu's version locates its singer 'in the city' longing for her 'island home' – the original version, however, is more explicit. Here the singer is living 'in the desert ... west of Alice Springs' from where he knows his 'island home is waiting for me'.

Song-writing credits for 'My Island Home' are attributed on both Anu's recording and *Warumpi Band Go Bush!* to non-Indigenous member of Warumpi Band, Neil Murray. Yet a later version of the song, sung in language as 'Ronu Wanga' on Warumpi Band member George Rrurrambu's 2000 solo album, *Nerbu Message*, lists Rrurrambu as its creator. According to members of the group, the song refers to Rrurrambu's origins on Elcho Island (off the northern coast of Arnhem Land) and his move to central Australia. On *Warumpi Band Go Bush!* along with 'Kintorelakutu', 'My Countryside' and 'Sad and Lonely', the song is one that emphasises attachment to place. The use of place as a theme of the group's songs on this album echoes their first album, *Warumpi Band – Big Name, No Blankets*, released in 1985. Here four songs are about place – 'Fitzroy Crossing', 'Gotta Be Strong', 'Mulga and Spinifex' and 'Warumpinya'. The last of these had already appeared on a 1983 Imparja cassette, *Rebel Voices from Black Australia*. Themes about country also recur on the group's much later album, *Too Much Humbug*, released in 1996. Here nostalgia for place is joined by explicit statements on Aboriginal land loss: 'we shall cry for our land'.

Of Warumpi Band songs based around place, 'Warumpinya' demonstrates ways in which an Aboriginal rock group uses music to state belief in a place and is symptomatic of ways through which music functions in Aboriginal communities. In effect, a place has become a song – at the same time, this song can be read as the site of contested meanings depending on how it is understood in the contexts of either Aboriginal rock music, Australian music, or the commercialised repertoire known as 'world music', one of the ways that the music of this group has been defined and marketed. Possible meanings for the song are therefore diverse. To unravel them, this chapter is organised in three sections. The first reads 'Warumpinya' as avowal of the value of a community to its members. The second analyses the song's use of structures and sounds of central Australian Aboriginal music, its relationship to roles of Aboriginal traditional songs, and implications of its use of the Aboriginal language of Luritja for its lyrics. In the third section, we question the classification by writers in the popular music industry of Warumpi Band as practitioners of the stylistic trend labelled 'world music'. This classification engenders debate over issues of ownership and intent in the song, and gives rise to tensions in meaning in a song that draws its inspiration from a place.

'Warumpinya' – affirming place

In the history of Aboriginal rock music, certain groups stand out: Adelaide-based group No Fixed Address for their role in the 1980 film, *Wrong Side of the Road*; Coloured Stone and Soft Sands for their longevity; Yolngu group Yothu Yindi for their international success; and Warumpi Band, the first Aboriginal group to be recognised for rock songs in an Aboriginal language. Warumpi Band are from Papunya in the Northern Territory, and like many Aboriginal musicians utilise country music and reggae sounds in their songs. They integrate boomerangs and didjeridu into their rock group line-up, and like other Aboriginal music groups, their songs address social issues such as cultural maintenance, alcohol abuse and the need to look after children. For many Australian listeners in the 1980s they were one of the few means of exposure to contemporary Aboriginal music; by the mid-1990s they were one of many Aboriginal groups widely accessible through recordings, videos, tours and concerts.

In a 1996 interview, group members George Rrurrambu and Neil Murray explained their backgrounds and musical influences:

> GR: we grew up with the music, listening to other bands, you know I was only a little boy, comin' up slowly; I went to college – Batchelor College – where I started learning other different languages which I'd never spoken before – I only spoke Millingimbi, Yirrkala, language on Elcho Island. I learnt different languages that I never spoke before, central languages you know? So that's kicked me out to Central Australia and I started with the band ... I used to go out to Papunya every time I used to print some papers in the language – the Warlpiri language; and after that, I heard that this guy [Neil Murray] had a band kinda going on – you know, in Papunya – there were three of them – Sammy, Gordon, and Neil Murray.

> NM: I was an outstations resource worker – I had a guitar and stuff with me 'cause I was playing music in Victoria, but I brought it up with me and just after work, I'd be sitting around and get it out on the verandah and just start playing, but young blokes just started coming up straight away, you know – and they all wanted to play you know, like a lot of the blokes are on the dole, no money, nothing to do and the settlements were boring – make your own band and it was creating excitement you know, holding concerts so people could

dance and rock and roll, all that exciting stuff ... the tastes were about ten years behind the times, there was no videos out there then, we only had films a couple of nights a week, so they were still listening to their old music from the sixties ...

GR: and Countdown

NM: ... and a lot of country and western. It wasn't until later on that people started to hear different types of music, like reggae (interview, 1996).

In another interview, when asked to explain the group's name, Neil Murray, the only non-Aboriginal member of the group, focused on the connection between the performers and a place:

[Warumpi Band is] a name that was given to us. We were just a band from Papunya and the proper name for Papunya is Warumpi. It refers to a honey ant dreaming site ... the important place there is not the buildings and the settlement, but rather the land. The most significant feature of that land to Aboriginal people is the nearest dreaming site, which is Warumpi, a small hill nearby where the honey ants come out of the ground. There's a waterhole there and there are places in the landscape people can show you that are charged with the story of the ants (interview, 1988).

In this explanation Murray used the term 'site' to refer to a place of cultural-religious significance to a person or language speaking group. This underpins much non-Aboriginal understanding of Aboriginal cultures, and is explained by Berndt & Berndt (1988, 138) in the following way:

a spiritual linkage existed/exists between a person and a specific site or part of the country by virtue of his (her) birth. This is more than an association with a piece of land ... it is rather that the land is him (her) ...

In addition to providing this rock group with their name, Warumpi is the topic of 'Warumpinya'. The lyrics, sung in Luritja, a dialect of Western Desert language, praise Warumpi:

Yuwa! Warumpinya!
Nganampa ngurra watjalpayi kuya
Nganampa ngurra watjalpayi kuya
Nganampa ngurra tjanampa wiya

Nganampa ngurra Warumpinya!
Yuwa! Warumpinya!

(Yes! Warumpi!
They always say our place is bad
They always say our home is no good
Its our place, not theirs
Its our home, Papunya!
Yes! Warumpi!).

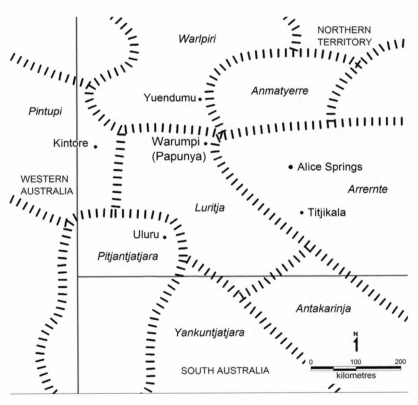

Overlaying a map of Aboriginal language regions on the state boundaries of central Australia shows how Aboriginal perceptions of territory conflict with official government ones. Unlike state boundaries, which are fixed and arbitrary, the boundaries between Aboriginal language areas are porous and fluid. The depiction of language speaking areas is not definitive. (Map: Chris Gibson)

Many Aboriginal rock groups, especially those from central Australia where links to traditional lifestyles remain, include a song about a place on an album. Such songs praise a place, express hope to return to a place, grieve about departing from a place, state familial links to a place, are nostalgic about a named place, or are about the concept of place in general (chapter 2). Such singing about place is not unique to Aboriginal rock songs. However, Aboriginal songs about place(s) assume special significance from the importance of country in defining group and individual Aboriginal identity. Often the place singled out in a song bears spiritual meaning for members of an Aboriginal rock group through sacred connotation. Sometimes this site is also the name of the community from which a band comes, and, as discussed in chapter 2, is used by the band in their name. In conjunction with the use of Luritja lyrics in this song, the naming of Warumpi Band after the Aboriginal name of a place has implications for a cultural and spatial reading of 'Warumpinya'.

As discussed in chapter 2, the Aboriginal significance of country in general, and of specific sites, stems from a complex of related concepts. This complex links a location with the ancestral beings who created it and/or performed activities there, with the language spoken in the area, the people who have lived there, those who live there today, and those who have rights to ownership and responsibility for country. The factors in this complex combine the past with the present, and link a physical location with its spiritual connotations. In a song, any one of these factors can act as a reference to the others. For example, the use of an Aboriginal language in 'Warumpinya' can imply an audience that understands the song's lyrics. This audience, speakers of Western Desert language, was estimated by Schmidt in the early 1990s as approximately 4000 (Schmidt, 1993). Rrurrambu and Murray explained the background to recording in Luritja:

> GR: We started with the covers for one year straight. We used to tour around the Kimberleys, only with the covers – everybody know though that we are rock 'n' roll band of Papunya.

> NM: We were playing Chuck Berry stuff, and Little Richard, AC/DC and Rolling Stones a sort of mixture of basic R and B and rock 'n' roll, and gradually we started working our own songs in

there, by this stage I got involved with teaching, it was a bilingual education program – teaching kids to learn to read in their own language first – and that was sort of an influence into 'oh, we've got to sing some songs in language' to make these kids think about be 'proud of their language' and that; so ... CAAMA was starting up at the same time in Alice Springs, and they wanted music, contemporary Aboriginal music to broadcast on the radio. The first song we made was 'Jailanguru Pakarnu'/'Out From Jail', in the Luritja language, and that became the first single; once we'd made the step of making our own songs ... the music became meaningful and the community started to hear it differently. It's not just for fun any more, its 'oh, you can make your own song, and it's got a message', and it suddenly became important (interview, 1996).

Language in song was thus, in an immediate sense, an educational strategy. Yet, songs in language signify more than this. As language possession is both a means of defining and naming Aboriginal nations, and of referring to the territorial extent of the use of a language, a song in an Aboriginal language or dialect makes a geographical statement about place and people and the relationships between them; such a song is a form of map. This is a cultural-spatial implication of the use of Luritja in 'Warumpinya' that asserts central Australian Aboriginal perspectives on ways of conceptualising the region, and draws attention to how these differ from those of non-Aboriginal thinking. This discrepancy can be detected in Murray's comment that 'we were just a band from Papunya *and the proper name for Papunya is Warumpi*', and can be shown by superimposing the official non-Aboriginal/state boundary map of the area around Papunya over a map based on the Aboriginal languages/ dialects spoken there. As the lyrics of the song (translated in the album notes) state: 'it's our place'. In this way 'Warumpinya' can be read as a statement of central Australian Aboriginality and a contradiction of non-Aboriginal territorialism and its agendas. The song, according to Murray, was thus written with the specific intention of refuting local attitudes to Warumpi/Papunya:

> For many years, Papunya had the reputation for being the worst settlement in the [Northern] Territory. Established in March 1960, it was chosen because it had a good supply of water ... Papunya was

a centre of enforced assimilation in which people from the surrounding tribal groups [of] Luritja, Pintupi, Warlpiri, Anmatjirra
and Aranda were expected to peacefully co-exist and develop the
standard that would allow them to assimilate into white Australian society. 'Most people', says Neil Murray, 'think it's a real hell
hole of a joint. But for a lot of people, it's their home. That's what
our song 'Warumpinya' is about. Papunya had a bad reputation; it
was always in the papers ... It's been described as like something
out of the third world; all those popular clichéd images about
being a site like a former concentration camp ...' (Macmillan, 1988,
128–29).

The title, topic and language of 'Warumpinya' all imply expressions of
Aboriginality for the song, and these can be emphasised if listeners know
that the song's creators and performers are Aboriginal. Another interpretation of the song can derive from its original recorded appearance as
the final track on *Rebel Voices from Black Australia*. The protest nature
of the songs on this cassette, which its title implies, is borne out in less
than explicit ways. The album's opening track, an anti-government
address by black activist Gary Foley, adopts a strong protest position. Following that, other songs 'protest' in less confrontational ways: they
remind, recall events, raise issues of culture and family, and state Aboriginal opinions. 'Warumpinya' – described on the album notes simply as
'sung in Luritja in defence of Papunya' – is a local protest, one intended
to state the acceptability of Papunya in contrast to non-Indigenous representations of its community as 'troubled' and 'dysfunctional'. Although
the cassette was compiled within a pan-Aboriginal cultural agenda, this
is distinct from a call for land rights, and is a demonstration of a way of
approaching national issues through discussion of local ones – something
which permeates much Aboriginal contemporary music.

'Warumpinya' – links to tradition

Another way to understand this song is to consider ways that it relates
to traditional Aboriginal music in central Australia. This requires explanation of the song's structures, the presence of an instrument of Aboriginal traditional music in its backing, and similarities between roles of
'Warumpinya' and those of central Australian Aboriginal traditional
songs.

'Warumpinya' consists of a four line verse repeated a number of times with intervening instrumental breaks: Introduction – Verse – Instrumental – Verse – Instrumental – Verse – Instrumental – Verse – Instrumental. The Introduction and the Instrumental sections are the one section of music used throughout. This means the song has only two sections repeated a number of times.

The text of 'Warumpinya' is based on a limited number of elements involving repetition and parallelism. These elements are organised into lines, each of which consists of two phrases. In turn, these lines form couplets which are arranged into the quatrain that makes up the song's text. Due to the repetition of words and phrases, each line of the verse can be analysed as two half-lines:

Nganampa ngurra / watalpayi kuya   1
Nganampa ngurra / watalpayi kuya   2
Nganampa ngurra / tjanampa wiya   3
Nganampa ngurra / Warumpinya!   4

The presence of two couplets that form a quatrain can be seen in the repetition of the first line and the subsequent later two lines. The couplets differ in their matching qualities, the first consisting of two matching (because identical) lines, the second of two contrasting lines. Poetically, this quatrain relies on repetition (*nganampa ngurra*), a formulaic statement (*nganampa ngurra* + ...), and, in line 3, antithesis:

Nganampa   ngurra / tjanampa   wiya
(our   home / theirs   it's not).

This line also has an aural and conceptual effect in which *nganampa* is balanced against *tjanampa*. Parallelism can be seen in both the form and content of the four lines.

In his work on song types among the contiguous and mutually influencing language groups of Aranda and Luritja, *Songs of Central Australia*, Strehlow (1971) analysed the structures and poetic styles found in a repertoire of traditional song texts. His conclusion was that complex 'rules' of construction could be deduced from the texts. Strehlow showed that a majority of Aranda and Luritja song texts consisted of couplets, each couplet made up of four half-lines. He also noted minimal text elements, repetition of words/phrases, a formulaic nature of lines, and the use of a series of related but seemingly unconnected statements to form a text. From his observations, Strehlow concluded that perform-ance of songs relied on repetitions of the same verse a number of times; a song performance was textually momentarily static.

His analysis of word use led him to the conclusion that poetic devices such as repetition, antithesis, parallelism, and the play on words in dif-ferent parts of couplets and half-lines were prevalent. In Luritja songs particularly, Strehlow identified a practice in which a change of rhythm or stress was made to a word at its successive appearance in the same couplet or quatrain. Finally, he could state that

> Aranda couplets tend to consist of two individual lines which, musically and rhythmically, stand in complementary relation to each other: the second line of a couplet is either identical in rhythm and construction with the first line, or it balances the first line antithetically and rounds off the couplet by a contrasting rhythm of its own (Strehlow, 1971, 109–10).

These characteristics found by Strehlow in traditional songs from central Australia can be seen in 'Warumpinya'. The song's text consists of a quatrain of two couplets, each couplet has four half-lines; the text is repeated numerous times to form the recorded version of the song; poetic devices of repetition, antithesis and parallelism are employed.

In addition to these observable links between a Warumpi Band song and the traditional music of the area from which the band originates, this song includes the use of an instrument of traditional Aboriginal music from the Warumpi/Papunya region in its accompaniment; namely, a pair of boomerangs. These are used in three ways in the song. First, for a rhythmic accent during the song's introduction and recurring instru-mental sections; second, to perform a regular beat throughout the verses of the song (aligned with the backbeat on the snare drum); third, at the song's conclusion, to perform a prolonged rattle. The latter two of these uses coincide with those ascribed to the boomerangs in the Aboriginal traditional music of this region (A Moyle, 1978).

Another level of Aboriginal implication in the song is the possibility that it transfers the site as a topic of Aboriginal traditional music (see Toyne & Vachon, 1984; R Moyle, 1986; Ellis & Barwick, 1989; Payne,

1989; Davis & Prescott, 1992; Gummow, 1995) to one of contemporary music. As Manuel (1988, vi) notes, popular music in this respect performs a vital role in maintaining continuity of cultural expression:

> we can ... observe that the unfortunate mortal blows dealt to many traditional musics and cultures have been balanced by the extraordinary proliferation of new non-Western pop genres; most of these, while borrowing Western elements, in their own way affirm modernity and express the contradictions and complexities of modern culture. In doing so they perform a social function that traditional musics can no longer fulfil.

This is an impression reinforced by the comments of Allen (1992, 16) in *Tjunguringanyi*, house journal of the Centre for Aboriginal Studies in Music, at the University of Adelaide:

> With the introduction of white man's rule and the various government policies of dispersion, segregation and assimilation ... Aboriginal people were starting to be lumped together ... As a result of this, the style of music started to change as the influences of European culture began to take more and more effect on our people. Traditionally, a lot of the music related to the land and events that changed the land ... even though the style of music was changing away from the more traditional ways, the same themes of land, events, and important occasions were still being sung about by Aboriginal people. This, as in the old days, was a way of communicating ... [about] historical events and issues of importance.

'Warumpinya' performs this function, simultaneously dispelling non-Aboriginal myths of place, and reaffirming Aboriginal links to country through language and song structures.

'Warumpinya' as world music

Another reading of 'Warumpinya' is that influenced by the activities of the record industry and ways that recorded music is classified according to commercial agendas. This presents a different view of 'Warumpinya'; as Feld (1994, 288) notes: 'once a recording is in the marketplace one has little control over how it is consumed.' When factors of this reading of the song and ways it has come about are deconstructed, they raise

Warumpi Band at the time of the
release of 'Warumpinya'.

questions over the means by which music is classified and subsequently
presented and understood. In relation to Aboriginal music as a part of
the Australian music industry, this reveals disjunctures between what
musicians might intend through their music, how local audiences
respond to songs, and what meanings are attached to Aboriginal songs
when they gain national and international exposure.

Along with those of other Aboriginal groups, Coloured Stone, Kintore Gospel Band, No Fixed Address and Scrap Metal, songs by
Warumpi Band are discussed by Sweeney (1991) in his *Directory of
World Music* as examples of world music. This classification of the group
is repeated by Breen (1994) who lists this group alongside other Aboriginal performers, Blekbala Mujik, Coloured Stone, Kev Carmody, Ruby
Hunter, Archie Roach and Yothu Yindi under the world music rubric.
'World music' is defined by Sweeney (1991, x) as a 'blend of mainstream
and indigenous styles to some extent', and by Feld (1994, 266) under
'world beat' as 'ethnic-pop mixings.' It constitutes a major late twentieth
century popular music commercial categorisation, which, as Goodwin &
Gore (1995, 123) comment, as a style of music, has its own 'sections in
record stores, its own magazines, speciality shops, and labels ... festivals ...
radio and television programs, and so on.'

The term and its origins are controversial. As 'world beat' it was in
use in the early 1980s in America to describe the blending of mainstream
rock styles and traditional musics (Goodwin & Gore, 1995). Later, at a
meeting of record company representatives in London in 1987, the term
'world music' was consciously adopted to label and market the global
prevalence of the integration of rock and indigenous musics (Sweeney,
1991).

Syntactically, 'Warumpinya' is an 'ethnic-pop mix', and thus adheres
to both Sweeney's and Feld's definitions of 'world music/beat'. This classification would represent for many listeners the context through which
music by Warumpi Band is marketed and received. It is a context with
implications, among them that the inclusion of Indigenous musical
instruments and sounds can reference aspects of Indigenous traditions.
How these sounds are interpreted by listeners may vary. Feld (1994,
266–67) lists three possibilities:

> a Western gaze toward the exotic and erotic ... other or oppressed
> people's party music commercially appropriated ... [or] a new, pop-
> ulist, honest, commercially viable form of dialogue or equalization
> between musics and musicians in different cultural spaces.

Other possibilities for interpretations of songs by Warumpi Band
include a sense of black consciousness, even solidarity, suggested by the
topics of many of their songs (for example, *Koori Man*: 'I'm black and I'm

hard, And I'm better than ever before'). The invitation to the band to perform in Port Moresby at the 1985 celebrations marking the first decade of Papua New Guinea's independence from Australian rule implies a level of international support for other indigenous peoples. In Australia since the mid 1980s, during a decade in which Aboriginal issues were at the forefront of political debate, the promotion and reception of recordings by an Aboriginal rock group for many implied alignment with a variety of left-wing political causes. Specifically for Warumpi Band, this was particularly the case, given their relationship to Midnight Oil, a non-Aboriginal rock group of publicly expressed left-wing opinion, which resulted in the joint EP release 'The Dead Heart' (1986), concerts, and the two rock groups performing to Aboriginal communities during a combined tour of central Australia in 1986.

Categorising music and musicians is always problematic, and categorising Warumpi Band as a world music group raises a number of issues. Among these is the chronology of world music in relation to the release of *Big Name, No Blankets*, and the problem of labelling an indigenous music from a non-indigenous perspective. Comparison of the recording date of *Big Name, No Blankets* (1985) with the date given by Sweeney for the coining of the world music classification (1987) makes it clear that, with Warumpi Band, categorisation was imposed on a musical practice that existed before the commercial branding of that practice took place. While members of the band admit to the influence of Chuck Berry and the Rolling Stones (Pollak, 1984) and country and western and reggae musicians (interview with Neil Murray, 1988; interview with Neil Murray and George Rrurrambu, 1996), their comments show no intention to be placed within the world music genre. Whether Murray in 1988 was conscious of the world music trend or not, comments of the band show that they had clear agendas of their own as far as their repertoire was concerned. At the same time, reception of the band, as indicated by rock music critics in the press, was more inclined to revolve around their representation of social issues rather than membership of any emerging popular music trend such as 'world music'. For example, Pollak (1984) writing in the *Sydney Morning Herald*, commented that Warumpi Band was a group 'whose songs have some social relevance. They tackle issues that affect black people – the law, violence, alcoholism – without turgid sentimentality.' Alongside Creswell (1985), Stapleton

(1985) also interpreted the invitation to the group to perform at Papua New Guinea's celebrations of a decade of independence as a sign of perceptions of the band as representing black people, commenting that the group was 'specifically requested by [Papua New Guinea's] Prime Minister Michael Somare as being the Australian group most appropriate to help mark his country's independence'. Aboriginal musical texts like those of Warumpi Band are both connected to traditional practices and circulate in national and global cultural economies, where their reception can be quite different, and where non-indigenous perceptions are shaped by commercial strategies or the political stances of reviewers and listeners.

Labelling a song about Warumpi/Papunya as world music presents another problem, that of a category being used to denote a range of musical practices as if they were unified and global. The unification implicit in the term overrides the extent to which various 'ethnic' musics are rooted in specific social practices and cultural meanings – world music deterritorialises music as it amalgamates diversity within its boundaries (Connell & Gibson, forthcoming). 'World music' is thus positioned as a collection of 'others', in opposition to European and American musics, the ethnicity of which – whiteness – is contradictorily under-emphasised. More simply, global implications are contradicted by the clearly local focus of songs such as 'Warumpinya'.

In addition, there is a distinction to be drawn here between music by Western musicians who supplement their musical profiles, for whatever reason, with indigenous sounds (Paul Simon's *Graceland* album is perhaps the best known example), and indigenous musicians who incorporate Western rock sounds into their own evolving musical traditions. Classification of songs by Warumpi Band as world music makes no distinction between types of musical combinations and their implicit agendas, suggesting a musical commonality. This commonality carries with it a lessening of the aesthetic position of the music so named, in this case by disassociation of songs by Warumpi Band from their Aboriginal settings. This deterritorialisation ignores the historical development of Aboriginal music, a development on its own trajectory with little or no points of intentional intersection with world music.

The use of Aboriginal languages by the group, somewhat of a rarity for non-Aboriginal listeners in the 1980s before the success of groups such as Yothu Yindi, was picked up by critics and noted as significant. Murray was quoted by Creswell (1985) as commenting that

> We're aware that Warumpi Band is becoming something bigger than just us ... in terms of singing songs in Aboriginal languages and just helping Aboriginal people generally. If they see us as being successful, everyone gets a lift out of that.

Stapleton (1985) also commented on the use of an Aboriginal language in some songs:

> although there is a good deal of novelty in their use [of an Aboriginal language] Warumpi Band believes there is value in reinforcing these languages, which are slowly dying, and in educating wider audiences that they are legitimate.

The band's status as positive role models for other Aboriginal people was noted in 1993 when the group performed for prisoners at Goulburn (NSW) jail, where 10 per cent of inmates at the time were Aborigines (Elder, 1993). The impression that accrues from these comments is of a band more concerned with presenting an Indigenous perspective on issues affecting Aborigines than of one concerned with popular music marketing categories. Despite these criticisms, for many listeners the marketing of Warumpi Band as world music was perhaps the only way the band was known, the issues of their songs exposed, or listeners were able to have contact with an Aboriginal culture. This draws attention to the contradictory nature of the world music category. While such classification may be out of line with band members' agendas, it acts nevertheless as the means through which issues they seek to raise are mediated into the community. This may suit Aboriginal musicians who, despite world music appropriation of output and intent, understand that in this way the messages of their songs will be heard by a wider listening public.

Conclusion – after 'Warumpinya'

Fifteen years after their first releases and regional tours, Warumpi Band have dispersed geographically, and altered their intentions, as Neil Murray explained:

The people at Papunya used to claim us as theirs, when we were still based there but we're not based there anymore, and the band's kind of grown up and moved on; we're doing a lot of songs in language, talking about the places in [Arrernte] country as well, but even so they're relevant to everyone, especially Aboriginal people all over Australia, they understand the themes behind those songs, you know? [it's] the kind of material that will work for us, and we have this sort of indigenous world view, that we channel stuff through, you know what I mean? 'Cause I've been influenced by ... I've learnt stuff, the whole philosophy just by hanging around with people and I have an affinity for those ideas, those ideas are mine too, I believe in them too, so ... that's what we do (interview, 1996).

Despite the winding down of the group's career, Warumpi Band remain seminal to the position of Aboriginal rock music within broader Australian culture, both Aboriginal and non-Aboriginal. The place they sang about in 'Warumpinya' also remains active as the inspiration for song – in 2002 it reappeared as the topic of a song by another Papunya group, SPIN.fx. As the final track on their album, *Uluparru*, their 'Warumpinya' is 'a song about Papunya, a community of about 200 people 250 klms NW of Alice Springs. The birthplace of dot painting and nice hospitality' (*Uluparru*, album notes). Singing not only about Papunya but the sites there also appears on this album – in the album's title track, SPIN.fx sing about 'the big hill in Papunya. It is very important to everyone and people always talk of that hill when they are away from home' (*Uluparru*, album notes). In these ways, as with the songs of Warumpi Band, a place and its importance to a local community are affirmed and continued.

Suggested listening

Gudju Gudju ▲ *Follow One Track*

David Hudson ▲ *Didgeridoo Spirit*

David Hudson ▲ *Gudju Gudju – Songs Inspired by the Djabugay Language*

David Hudson ▲ *Woolunda – Ten Solos for Didgeridoo*

Tjapukai ▲ *Storywaters*

Tjapukai Dancers ▲ *Proud to be Aborigine*

CHAPTER 6

Djabugay – language, education, tourism, music

In 1989 the Tjapukai Dancers, musicians from a theatre troupe in Kuranda (Qld), released the album *Proud to be Aborigine*. In the imme-diate post-bicentenary period, such a title resonated with the ethos of numerous Aboriginal rock musicians keen to gain acknowledgment of Indigenous cultural identity and survival – to make the point that mem-bers of Indigenous cultures would not accept a back seat when it came to avowing their place in the Australian social and political landscape.

The lyrics of the album's title song refer directly to the events of 1788:

Two hundred years ago the whitefella found
A land he thought that no-one owned

Like the songs of other Aboriginal rock groups such as Blekbala Mujik, Yothu Yindi and Warumpi Band, the lyrics of this song went on to raise hopes for reconciliation:

Together we can live in harmony
Be as brothers in the land down under.

Beyond the pan-Aboriginal tone of this song's lyrics is reference in the word 'Tjapukai' (Djabugay, Djabuganydji) to intentions of members of the Djabugay speaking community to further their own agendas of revival necessary to reverse the effects of cultural dispossession since the beginnings of Djabugay/white contact in the 1870s. These agendas revolve around and utilise four factors: language, education, tourism and music.

It is significant that the song 'Proud to be Aborigine' was the closing number of a musical performance first staged in 1987 for tourists in the Kuranda rainforest area, as it summed up the overall message of the show. Moreover, the song included sections sung in Djabugay language. Here, music was a vehicle for expression of a number of simultaneous agendas. It was most likely the case that listeners to those first performances would not have realised that what they were watching was more than entertainment, that the Djabugay language was under severe threat, and that the performance was part of a strategy to provide employment for members of the Djabugay community. This chapter discusses the cultural politics of creating songs with Djabugay lyrics as a tactic for cultural revival. It links these songs to debates about the efficacy of Indigenous involvement in Australia's tourism industry, and reveals tensions between economic benefits and cultural compromises that such engagements entail.

Djabugay culture

Aboriginal presence has been dated back beyond 5000 years in the Djabugay area, the coastal and adjoining region around the town of Cairns (Bottoms, 1999, 2). According to Djabugay creation histories, local land formations are the results of the activities of Gudju Gudju, the Rainbow Serpent. Djabugay and neighbouring Aboriginal existence was disrupted by the seizure of their lands by white settlers in the 1870s, and establishment of Cairns in 1876 on the site of a Djabugay water source (Bottoms, 1999, 18). Discovery of gold in the area, construction of a railway linking Cairns to the inland (completed in 1891), and in 1893 government approval for the opening up of the area for logging and farming, signalled the beginning of contestation of Djabugay sovereignty. From the early 1890s, some Djabugay were removed to the nearby (Anglican) Yarrabah Mission. Between 1913 and 1962 Djabugay and members of other neighbouring language groups were also housed at the (Seventh Day Adventist) Mona Mona Mission, where, as at Yarrabah, their language was suppressed (see Johnson, 1994; Kidd, 1997). By 1962 Djabugay was spoken by only approximately fifty people. Moved away from Mona Mona Mission on its unannounced closure, Djabugay gravi-tated to the town of Kuranda and into the living conditions usual for many dispossessed Aboriginal communities: 'fringe dwellers on the edge of white Australian society, unemployed and unconnected to their tradi-tions' (*Storywaters*, album notes). In 1987, two and a half decades after the closure of the Mona Mona Mission, the writing of a show about Djabugay culture, and establishment of the Tjapukai Dancers could be seen as something that

> launched the Djabugay on the road to international recognition. Employment opportunities and the recognition of the value of Djabugay cultural heritage has contributed to a resurgence of pride in the community (Bottoms, 1999, 93).

Since 1987, performances by the Tjapukai Dancers (also sometimes referred to as the Tjapukai Dance Theatre, and more recently, Tjapukai) have become standard tourist fare. The group has recorded several albums, toured internationally, and won a number of tourist industry awards.

The success of this contemporary music group does not occur in isolation from other local Indigenous activities, or from events affecting Indigenous peoples on a national level. Nor should the work of Djabugay musicians other than the Tjapukai Dancers be ignored in these processes – musicians such as the rock groups Gudju Gudju, Mantaka Band and Lance Riley and Friends, singer-songwriter and teacher, Ashley Galgam Coleman, and the didjeridu player and entrepreneur David Hudson. Bottoms (1999) positions the setting up of the Tjapukai Dancers as one component of rebuilding of Djabugay cultural identity alongside other local initiatives. These include formation of the Mona Mona Corporation to rebuild the defunct Seventh Day Adventist mis-sion as a Djabugay enterprise; setting up in 1992 of the Djabugay Tribal Aboriginal Corporation to oversee Djabugay culture and to handle nego-tiations with governments; and founding of the Tjapukai Cultural Park as a venue for Tjapukai Dancers' performances and as a focus for Indige-nous cultural tourism in the area.

Nationally, the Mabo decision, in 1992, and the levels of debate over

Indigenous land ownership that it engendered, acted to strengthen the Djabugay in activities to refashion their cultural identity. Moves by the Queensland state government to allow some Indigenous ownership of traditional lands also acted as an impetus in the groundswell of Djabugay cultural renaissance. Rowse (2002) links the recognition of native title that flowed from the Mabo decision to successful Indigenous cultural

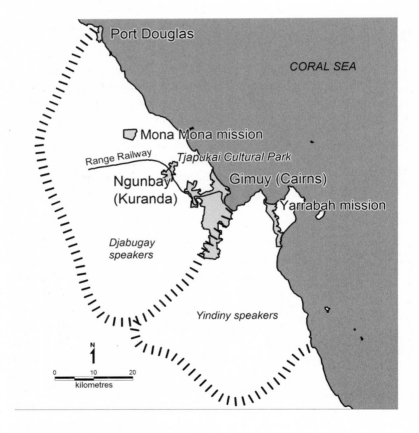

The original extent of Djabugay language surrounds the commercially valuable port of modern day Cairns. Language speaking areas depicted here are not definitive. (Map: Chris Gibson)

tourism through its ability to reinforce cultural identity and traditional links to country. He quotes a study of the Tjapukai Dance Theatre that demonstrated how the success of this troupe had led to 'more confident participation in current debates about land ... [and] Indigenous commercial interest in tourism thus developed into an Indigenous political interest in regional land use planning' (Finlayson, in Rowse, 2002, 90). In effect, 'native title legislation has given the Djabugay people hope that their participation in tourism will eventually be based not only on the attractiveness of their culture to tourists, but also on their rights to land that the tourist industry requires' (Rowse, 2002, 90).

Among other ways this refashioning of Djabugay identity was taking place was commencement of the teaching of Djabugay language in local schools (Johnson, 1994). Recordings of songs by Djabugay musicians have been an important element of this teaching project. In this way the practices of Djabugay musicians work at a local level for Djabugay needs. At the same time they reflect a national use of music by Indigenous musicians in which recordings of contemporary songs are seen as an important means of preserving and teaching Indigenous languages, thus of reinforcing Indigenous cultural survival.

Contemporary music and Aboriginal languages

Ngawu ngirrma waygany. Ngawu buwal bugang djabugay bibun-bayngunda. Ngawu dagil maying. Ngawu djabi dja: ngawu galing.

[Now that I found my language, I'm teaching Djabugay to the kids. I am getting stronger. I know where I am going.] (Ashley Galgam Coleman, in *Alive and Deadly: Reviving and Maintaining Australian Indigenous Languages*, Department of Employment, Education and Training, 1995, 7).

Linguists estimate that at the time of British invasion of Australia in 1788 there were between 200 and 250 mutually incomprehensible Aboriginal languages in use. Of these, many had different versions or dialects (Dixon, 1980; Schmidt, 1993; Walsh & Yallop, 1993; Nettle & Romaine, 2000). In the early 1990s, Schmidt noted that only ninety of these were still in existence. Of these ninety, twenty were in a 'relatively healthy state' and 'the total number of surviving languages is expected to diminish to less than ten within the next thirty to forty years. Only ten percent of the Australian Aboriginal people still speak their indigenous languages' (Schmidt, 1993, Executive Summary).

This wholesale loss of Aboriginal languages is the result of numerous influences, some actively deployed by white colonisers, others the unsurprising result of social and cultural change. The proscription of Indigenous languages by government officials, teachers and missionaries, as the Djabugay experienced in Yarrabah and Mona Mona missions, was one of the main ways through which this was engineered. Dyer et al. (2003, 90), for instance, mention that Djabugay on Mona Mona Mission were flogged when using traditional languages. The removal of Aboriginal children from their families, and the forcing together onto reservations of different language speaking groups were other ways through which this was achieved. Disregard for Aboriginal linguistic variety was aided by colonial thinking about Australian Aborigines. The misconception by colonisers that all Aborigines would speak the same language, or that Aboriginal 'language' was incapable of expressing complex thought is clear from colonial writings. Running alongside such thinking was the attitude prevalent in the nineteenth and early twentieth centuries that Australian Aborigines were a 'dying race', and that preserving aspects of Aboriginal culture would be a fruitless undertaking.

Across Australia, various strategies have been undertaken to maintain, revive and teach Indigenous languages. In a controversial and partially successful practice, some schools teach bilingually (Harris, 1990; Hartman & Henderson, 1994; Rhydwen, 1996). In these schools, various aspects of teaching are carried out in an Indigenous language, others in English. Other means of maintaining levels of Aboriginal language use include documentation of them by linguists, their use by Aboriginal authors, and radio and television programs in Aboriginal languages.

Among strategies such as these, rock songs with lyrics in Aboriginal languages are an important way of preserving and teaching language. Such preservation is a means of recording vocabularies, grammars and sounds, and provides tangible objects for audible expression of group identity. As discussed in the previous chapter, Warumpi Band were the first group to receive widespread acknowledgment for rock songs in Aboriginal languages (in their case, Luritja and Gumatj). Warumpi

Band members George Rrurrambu and Neil Murray explained the impact such actions had throughout other Aboriginal communities:

> CG: So the community at Papunya started to feel a pride in you as a band and the songs in language?

> GR: Oh, yeah.

> NM: Yeah, everywhere, not just Papunya, it started to go outwards wherever we toured.

> GR: It started at Papunya, and started spreading out slowly you know? Today you see round Kimberley now they're singing in their own language, I heard them singing in their own language because we spread the word around from the centre, and they went to south, east, west, north, southeast, Top End, right up all around; it spread right up to Groote [Eyelandt] – many people started singing in their own language, because we give them the idea, with our own lyrics, for 'Jailanguru Pakarnu' (interview, 1996).

This, and the emergence of other bands singing and recording in language around the country, was also borne out by the experience of the speakers of Djabugay:

> in recent years there has been a resurgence of interest in the Djabugay language and culture by Aboriginal people in [the town of] Kuranda. It is the younger members of the Aboriginal community in particular who have a positive attitude and keenness in all aspects of Aboriginal language and culture [and] within the community, more and more Aboriginal people are becoming involved in learning and using the language. The Tjapukai [Djabugay] Dance Theatre ... incorporates culture, corroboree and language into a show that tells a Djabugay story. Other local groups, including the Mantaka Band and Lance Riley and Friends, now write and sing songs in the Djabugay language. These groups have had a great influence on both Aboriginal and non-Aboriginal people's interest and desire to learn more about the Djabugay language and culture (Johnson, 1994, 40–41).

Various government reports have been written on Aboriginal language loss, and mention of the role of rock songs as a means of assisting in language preservation and revival features in a number of them. For example, in a 1992 Australian federal government report, *Language and Culture – A Matter of Survival: Report of the Inquiry into Aboriginal and Torres Strait Islander Language Maintenance*, this role of rock songs was acknowledged:

> Another objective of language maintenance is to reduce unneces-sary pressure destructive of language. This involves maintaining pride in the language and maximising the use of language within the community ... The production of books, videos and conte-mporary songs in language are ... useful in maintaining pride in language. The recent success of Yothu Yindi and other Aboriginal bands ... while using traditional language in songs has raised the awareness of Aboriginal and Torres Strait Islander languages. It has also helped make traditional languages less 'old-fashioned' to ... teenagers (House of Representatives Standing Committee on Aboriginal and Torres Strait Islander Affairs, 1992, 39–40).

Three years later, in 1995, another government report, *Alive and Deadly: Reviving and Maintaining Australian Indigenous Languages*, quoted Ashley Galgam Coleman, from Djabugay band, Gudju Gudju, explaining his group's use of Djabugay language in songs as 'for the kids so they could pick up the language' (Department of Employment, Educa-tion and Training, 1995, 7). This is reinforced by the album notes on Gudju Gudju's *Follow One Track*: 'many of the songs sung by Gudju Gudju [are] specially for the purpose of teaching the [Djabugay] language to Djabuganydji descendants'.

The significance of Aboriginal rock songs 'in language' does not escape the policy direction of the Alice Springs based Central Australian Aboriginal Media Association (CAAMA), as the album notes accompa-nying the CAAMA album, *In Language* make clear. The intention to instruct non-Aboriginal people about the diversity of Aboriginal cul-tures through the example of the diversity of Aboriginal languages is also evident here:

In Aboriginal ... is the first in a series of compilation albums which feature Aboriginal language with eleven bands and two soloists singing in Warlpiri from the Tanami Desert, Pitjantjatjara from the southern desert lands, Gapapunyngu from the top end, Gumnadga from the Gulf country, and Arrente from the centre. Our languages are alive and vibrant, our peoples and our cultures are diverse and growing. The 'In Aboriginal' series can help all Australians to understand that we are not all the same but we are all Aboriginal (*In Aboriginal*, album notes).

The proactivity of Djabugay musicians in the use of recordings of rock songs in language as a strategy for language learning clearly aligns with a national Indigenous use of contemporary music, and this is made explicit in numerous ways. Notes accompanying albums by Djabugay musicians state, for example, that 'like other Indigenous languages of Australia, Djabugay/Tjapukai was in danger of becoming extinct and members of this band have been working in local schools to help preserve the language ...' (*Gudju Gudju – Songs Inspired by the Djabugay Language*, album notes). The power of language ability to strengthen school children, and also their teachers, as members of Djabugay culture, was noted by Ashley Galgam Coleman, who teaches at Kuranda State High School:

I find that language is picked up more easily through songs and rhythm. Now that I found my language and I'm teaching it to the kids, I feel stronger, and I know where I'm going. The Bama [Djabugay] kids are also stronger from learning it. They are doing much better at school (Department of Employment, Education and Training, 1995, 7).

Often the explicitness of Djabugay language use in songs is linked to other aspects of a recording, intensifying the expression of Djabugay identity. The presence of didjeridus in rock groups, references in songs to the totemic symbols of band members, album and song titles that refer to Djabugay imagery and cosmology, and songs which praise places special to Djabugay sensibilities – all of these reinforce Djabugay cultural revival through music. This overlayering of symbols of Djabugay cultural representation can be heard on the 2000 CD, *Storywaters*, by Tjapukai. Here the album title, 'Storywater', refers to the histories of the Djabugay past;

listeners are encouraged to 'Hear the voice of the Bama' [Djabugay for a Djabugay person]; traditional chant is interspersed with contemporary rock sounds; song lyrics name totemic ancestor figures; didjeridu is integrated across the album. As with Tjapukai Dancers' original album of 1989, expression of so many symbols of Djabugay identity seem linked to the ongoing expression of pride in being Djabugay:

> My people, my pride
> Look into me
> See the spirit inside
> Tjapukai, the spirit's alive ...

The revival of Djabugay culture through music and dance resulted in one of the most significant Aboriginal economic ventures in the country – the Tjapukai Aboriginal Cultural Park, built near Kuranda, to cater to rapidly growing domestic and international tourism markets. Cultural tactics thus became economic strategy. With this, however, came a raft of ethical, cultural and political issues which implicate contemporary Djabugay musical expression in other, more complex fields.

Culture, commodification and compromise

For all its gains, Djabugay cultural revival needs to be understood in a wider context. As with many other Indigenous communities, problems of discrimination, racism and structural inequality have historically prevented access to mainstream employment opportunities for Djabugay, while they have been dispossessed of their traditional means of survival through links to country. Socioeconomic disadvantage has thus exacerbated dispossession, cultural loss and emotional trauma.

In recent years, government initiatives have sought to redress socioeconomic disadvantage though promoting Aboriginal cultural tourism and cultural industries. The most significant of these initiatives was the joint release, in 1997, of ATSIC's National Aboriginal and Torres Strait Islander Tourism and Cultural Industry Strategies (Aboriginal and Torres Strait Islander Commission 1997b; 1997c). These were in response to the 1991 Royal Commission into Aboriginal Deaths in Custody, which identified tourism as one means to economic empowerment for Aboriginal communities. Also during the 1990s, Australian state and territory governments began to develop Aboriginal tourism strategies

Beyond music and dance, the depiction of
Aboriginality for tourist purposes relies heavily
on visual appearance. Here, Tjapukai Dance
Theatre appear in 'traditional' garb. (Courtesy:
Tjapukai Dance Theatre)

that include references to Aboriginal participation and perspectives
(such as ecotourism). The Howard Government has been criticised for
not supporting ATSIC's tourism and cultural industries strategies with
sufficient funding, instead promoting 'market-based' mechanisms as trig-
gers of economic growth (Zeppel, 2001; Gibson & Connell, 2002). To
date these have not resulted in many tangible returns. Instead, state-
based tourism authorities and Indigenous organisations have tended to
underwrite Aboriginal enterprises such as cultural centres (at which
tourists hear stories, see performances and purchase souvenirs); Aboriginal cultural tours (often within national parks); and Aboriginal-owned
accommodation facilities and other tourism-related joint ventures.

Currently, the estimated income from Aboriginal-owned/controlled
cultural tourism in Australia is A$5 million per year, with a further
A$20–30 million generated from diversified Aboriginal tourism enter-

prises (Zeppel, 2001), although these figures certainly underestimate returns, as the Tjapukai Cultural Park alone is reputed to have a A$7 million annual turnover. Nonetheless, these figures are low given the emphasis placed on tourism in government strategies for Aboriginal economic development. While there is much institutional support for Indigenous cultural tourism, very few enterprises have become sustainable or have made significant returns – a reflection of the lack of federal funding provided to develop longer-term sustainable enterprises, but also variable and questionable demand (Ryan & Huyton, 2000), transport problems, and issues of remoteness and cultural appropriateness (Altman, 1989). In contrast, sales of souvenirs, art and craft (including didjeridus) forms a much larger market for tourists, approximately A$100 million per annum (Zeppel, 2001). Non-Aboriginal owned companies largely satisfy this market, with appropriation of Indigenous designs and traditions that are often ethically suspect, resulting in legal action in order to protect Indigenous intellectual property, although this itself is poorly articulated or protected in the Western legal system (Janke, 1999). Aboriginal providers have, however, made important inroads into the visual art and didjeridu markets (Wright, 1999; Wright & Morphy, 2000).

In contrast to this story of unfulfilled demand, structural problems, lack of capital and lost opportunities, the Tjapukai Cultural Park has been widely perceived as an exception to the rule. It operates as a joint partnership between Aboriginal and non-Aboriginal owners/managers, a private sector business with no ongoing public funding support. It 'offers Aboriginal people employment options in the tourism and hospitality industry, as well as the opportunity to develop specific technical and retail skills' (Finlayson, 1995, 5). Tjapukai performances began in the late 1980s as a partnership between a local non-Aboriginal couple and Aboriginal didjeridu player David Hudson. The initial venture employed ten people, seven male Aboriginal dancers and three production staff, with performances held in rented space in a shopping centre.

The original Tjapukai Dance Theatre was superseded by the 10 hectare Tjapukai Aboriginal Cultural Park, effectively an Indigenous theme park, built at a cost of A$9 million, and opened in 1996. The Park includes the Magic Space Museum, featuring Djabugay artefacts returned to the community from Brisbane's Queensland Museum; the Creation Theatre, which explores Djabugay spirituality in language; the History Theatre, subtitled 'A Survival Story', which retells Aboriginal histories of the area; a traditional camp; and a Cultural Village, with retail outlets and an art gallery. Finlayson (1995, 15) argued that Tjapukai tourism ventures

> constitute a watershed in the politics of identity formation in the Kuranda Aboriginal community. Employment in the Theatre has provided not simply a basis of income equality with non-Aboriginal people in Kuranda, but a forum for the emergence of a specific Aboriginality ... The employment and wages provided ... certainly developed the self-esteem of Aboriginal people and their ability for dealing with the burgeoning tourism which was increasingly part of daily life in Kuranda during the 1980s.

However, over time, criticisms that Tjapukai Dancers were not authentically representing Djabugay culture and that they too heavily borrowed from other Queensland Aboriginal groups became more frequent. Thus,

> wholly identifying the Tjapukai Dance Theatre with Djabugay culture and Djabugay personhood is seen as problematic. There are now two ways of spelling the local language reflecting distinct political positions; Tjapukai refers only to the Dance Theatre, while Djabugay is the cultural, as opposed to theatrical identity (Finlayson, 1995, 16).

Use of the didjeridu illustrates the extent to which inter-Aboriginal borrowings were incorporated into Tjapukai performances: this instrument was used to provide a musical accompaniment for the dancers, and tourists were taught how to play it. Yet the Djabugay people were very clear that traditionally their people neither made nor played the didgeridu as it 'belonged only to one tribe ever, but not Djabugay' (Dyer et al., 2003, 90). Performances were adjusted in line with visitor feedback surveys, so that they better conformed with tourists' expectations of Aboriginal culture, despite Djabugay concerns about authenticity and control of representation.

Beyond issues of cultural representation, the politics of economic power, management practices and financial control limited benefits accruing to the Djabugay community. A recent study of Djabugay partic-ipation in the Park revealed 'confusion concerning participation and equity, authenticity and control, [and] access to resources and services' (Dyer et al., 2003, 86). When the new park was built, an agreement was signed between Djabugay elders and the Park, in order to ensure that Djabugay people would benefit economically and socially, without exploitation (Holden & Duffin, 1998). This included the establishment of the Djabugay Cultural Co-ordinating Committee to 'ensure cultural appropriateness and authenticity' (Dyer et al., 2003, 86). Intentions of establishing the Park were for it to eventually become 100 per cent owned by Djabugay over a period of time. Since its opening, much pub-licity has been made of the Park's 50 per cent Aboriginal ownership. Dyer et al. (2003), however, reveal that actual Aboriginal interest is more likely to be only around 25 per cent of total equity, and that this is split between Djabugay and Yirrganydji peoples from Kuranda and Cairns, while a range of other interests, including the parties originally estab-lishing Tjapukai Dance Theatre as well as non-Aboriginal companies and ATSIC's Commercial Devlopment Corporation, hold the other major stakes in the company.

Decision-making powers remained confused, with uncertainty over the roles of management, Djabugay elders, and other Aboriginal and non-Aboriginal people employed at the Park; thus 'unless the Park's man-agers recognise which of their employees are Djabugay, they are not able to recognise the custodians of Djabugay culture' (Dyer et al., 2003, 88). Djabugay staff raised concerns that a formally recorded affirmative action principle, in the original agreement between elders and the Park, was not being adhered to. Despite Djabugay employment as dancers, front office staff, sales assistants and caretakers, less than 50 per cent of the Park's workers were Djabugay, and few Aboriginal people had climbed the ranks into management positions, contrary to stated objectives to improve employment and career options for locals employed in the Park. Tensions were present between elders, Djabugay employees and (non-Indigenous) Park management, and also between Djabugay and other Aboriginal groups whose families were forced into the area and onto Mona Mona Mission by colonial administrators. Tensions also revolved around issues of rights to own, perform and benefit from the Park: 'Djabugay employees mentioned continuing divisions between the various departments at the Park, occasional arguments, and their dislike of supervisors telling them what to do and how to do it. They had a resentment of, and disregard for, managers who determined how to present Djabugay culture' (Dyer et al., 2003, 90). Issues included the truncation of performances and disagreements over presentation of dancing styles. More disconcerting, the Deed of Partnership between Djabugay elders and the Park 'prohibits cultural activities that compete with the Park. The only business activity specified by the Deed as not restricted was the design and marketing of clothing'. Elders had traded away these rights in exchange for ongoing royalty payments that had not materialised when expected; hence, understandably, there was much mistrust of Park management, and resentment about 'lack of respect for protocol' (Dyer et al., 2003, 92).

There were also difficulties of maintaining a hectic schedule of performances for the constant tourist market, particularly in relation to practices as they would have otherwise been undertaken in non-tourist contexts:

> A Djabugay employee argued that everything had to be done to schedule, for example, making boomerangs and spears and painting bodies quickly in preparation for dance performances. Yet, the time required for preparation and performance in a traditional manner was incompatible with short-term tourist itineraries (Dyer et al., 2003, 90).

On the other hand, there was still much to celebrate about the Park, and its imperatives. While tension between commercial and non-commercial desires was constantly present, Djabugay employees emphasised that 'you can feel the spirit around when you dance', that 'knowing and understanding culture makes us aware of who we are', and 'we're still proud of our culture even though living in today's world' (Dyer et al., 2003, 91). More modestly, the Park challenged misrepresentations of Aboriginal people, because it showed Djabugay in employment, proud of their culture and as active participants in a contemporary tourist economy, in contrast to mainstream perceptions of welfare dependency and cultural loss.

Conclusion – negotiating cultural and economic identities

Revival of Djabugay cultural expression, including music and dance, embodies a series of contradictions apparent in contemporary attempts to implement Aboriginal self-determination (Gibson, 1999). Across Australia, music has played a key part in the revival of Indigenous languages, in education programs, as an appeal to youth of the relevance of language, and as texts reproduced in everyday use through the act of singing. A range of Djabugay bands and solo artists has released recordings in language as part of this effort, while at the Tjapukai Cultural Park, this principle is 'writ-large' in an economic venture that seeks to preserve and celebrate culture, maximise economic independence and reduce welfare dependency through tourism revenues.

The operation of the Tjapukai Cultural Park illustrates a range of problems that occur when Aboriginal cultural expression forms the basis of commercial, private sector enterprise. These include control over decision-making, distribution of benefits, and implementation of affirmative action principles for Djabugay employment. Even so, the Park remains a unique space for the reproduction of Djabugay cultural forms, a means for community pride and articulation of 'survival' in a region heavily influenced by white invasion, globalisation and cultural change. The Tjapukai/Djabugay case illustrates elements of the political economy and representational politics involved in cultural revival, and shows how both economic and cultural issues are intertwined in Aboriginal cultural tourism ventures. There are policy implications of Djabugay/Tjapukai experiences, as Dyer et al. (2003, 94) argue,

> The relatively limited benefits of the Park for the Djabugay people serve as a warning for those indigenous communities and tourism enterprise operators contemplating new cultural tourism ventures. Because of the range and complexities of tourism impacts, the gap between capitalist corporate culture and traditional indigenous culture needs to be addressed openly and honestly. Reciprocity, timelines and contingencies should be in place so that cultural and intellectual property remains in the hands and control of the rightful owners.

Cultural revival is thus not all 'smooth sailing'; however, given the devastating impacts of colonialism and enduring colonial relationships enacted through academic writing about Aboriginal people and issues, it would be wrong to expect Aboriginal cultural revivals to be unproblematic. This case study demonstrates how 'Aboriginal agency' operates in 'both participating in and resisting structures of state bureaucratic practice, and representations of cultural authenticity' (Henry, 2000, 322). That cultural revivals are both supported and contested from within demonstrates that Aboriginality is fluid and negotiated, and highlights the extent to which there are various interests – commercial as much as traditional – in the tourism industry, in the workplace and within a community, involved in creating contemporary Aboriginal identities.

Rather than 'take sides' or pass judgement over the success of the Tjapukai Cultural Park or Djabugay tactics for cultural revival more generally, this chapter has sought to discuss these issues as an inherent juxtaposition of culture and economy, as tensions apparent within capitalist forms of production. As alluded to in the introduction to this book, there are ethical problems in assessing Aboriginal cultural expressions within a framework developed and imposed by others, within already existing frames of reference and political worldviews. The success of Djabugay cultural revival and the Tjapukai Cultural Park will not be determined by us, but ultimately by Djabugay themselves, in the legitimacy and trust (or otherwise) they continue to place in particular activities, sites and musical texts.

Suggested listening

CAAMA ▲ *How Could I Know – The AIDS Album*

CAAMA ▲ *In Aboriginal*

CAAMA ▲ *From the Bush*

CAAMA ▲ *Wama Wanti – Drink Little Bit*

Kintore Gospel Band & Mt Liebig Band ▲ *Western Desert Gospel*

Nokturnl ▲ *Haterz*

Nokturnl ▲ *Neva Mend*

Josh Thomas ▲ *Thylacine*

Ulpanyali Band ▲ *Ulpanyali Band*

Bart Willoughby ▲ *Pathways*

Frank Yamma and Piranpa ▲ *Playing with Fire – Warungku Inkanyi*

CHAPTER 7

Recording and cultural tourism in Alice Springs

Many Aboriginal musicians and music groups, such as Kev Carmody, Ruby Hunter, Leah Purcell, Archie Roach, Tiddas, Bart Willoughby and Yothu Yindi are recognised within Australia and internationally. At the same time, other Aboriginal musicians are largely unknown to the wider listening public. One grouping of such musicians is that from the less urbanised central and northern parts of Australia. It includes the groups Fitzroy Xpress, Ilkari Maru, Irwin Inkamala and the Country Lads, Lazy Late Boys, Letterstick, North Tanami Band, the Pigram Brothers, Titjikala Desert Oaks Band, Wairuk, Wedgetail Eagle Band, Wirrinyga Band, and singer-songwriters Kevin Gunn, Herbie Laughton, Bob Randall, Bill Wellington and Frank Yamma. The music of these Aboriginal musicians would remain largely unnoticed if it were not for the work of recording companies that specialise in the production and dissemination of Indigenous music. The most significant of these, by reference to amount of releases, spatial origins of the musicians it records, and size of its artist roster, is the Central Australian Aboriginal Media Association (CAAMA), based in Alice Springs (NT).

Most Aboriginal musicians from the major Australian cities, even though their songs are unambiguous as comment about Indigenous and other social and political issues, rarely use Indigenous languages in their lyrics. Unlike songs by their counterparts in central and northern

Australia, the recordings of these artists are not dominated by country music sounds and influences. Ideologically their songs are often best described as pan-Aboriginal, while those of many musicians from central and northern Australia are more inclined to address issues relevant to local Indigenous communities, often to the point of close specficity. The work of CAAMA in recording this second set of Aboriginal musicians, therefore, constitutes a significant aspect of the contemporary Aboriginal music landscape, providing a substantial corpus of contemporary music since the early 1980s, one which can be thought of as a discrete repertoire for various reasons. These reasons derive from CAAMA's policies to foreground recordings of Aboriginal musicians as a strategy to strengthen central Australian Aboriginal cultures. Through these policies, music is positioned within Aboriginal-controlled agendas of representation and survival. Due to this publicly enunciated involvement in cultural politics, and because of its extensive production facilities, CAAMA's location in Alice Springs helps define that town as an important site of contemporary Aboriginal music activity. Added to this aspect of the town's musical identity is another dimension, that of Alice Springs as a centre of Aboriginal cultural tourism in which music plays a role. This chapter explores these two facets of Aboriginal music in the heart of the Australian continent, first through explanation of the scope and intention of the work of CAAMA, second by analysis of music as an element of Aboriginal cultural tourism in the town.

The Central Australian Aboriginal Media Association

CAAMA began radio broadcasting in 1980, its early work also included recording of albums of songs by Aboriginal singer-songwriters released under the Imparja label. Video recording commenced in 1983, and television broadcasting (through Imparja Television) in 1988. CAAMA is one of a number of broadcast and recording companies overseen by the National Indigenous Media Association of Australia (NIMAA), a network of over one hundred Indigenous owned and run facilities serving the broadcast and communication needs of Aborigines and Torres Strait Islanders (National Indigenous Media Association of Australia, nd). These media associations are partly financed through the federal government's Broadcasting for Remote Aboriginal Communities Scheme (BRACS), set up to service the media needs of Indigenous communities in 1988, well after Aboriginal communities had begun to establish their own media outlets and networks. Recording Aboriginal musicians is an important aspect of CAAMA's work. The musicians involved, with a few exceptions, are from the Northern Territory, the northern areas of South Australia, and the northeastern fringes of Western Australia.

Inherent in this description of CAAMA's responsibilities to a large area of central and northern Australia are problems of access and equity. This area covers regions of differing language and cultural specificity; any media facility attempting to provide services to it is automatically required to negotiate multiple languages and community expectations. Indeed the matter of choice of languages for broadcasting was an early cause for concern among CAAMA's Aboriginal listeners, as only three major languages were initially to be used: Arrente, from the Alice Springs area; Pitjantjatjara, used to the south of Alice Springs; and Warlpiri, spoken to the north. The choice of these languages led to accusations of inequity by communities, and speakers of smaller languages voiced the concern that their languages 'will get swallowed up if we maintain these big languages all the time' (Bowden, 1990, 30). CAAMA's recordings of Aboriginal rock musicians respond to these concerns in various ways and act as a means of linguistic and cultural maintenance. However, by attending closely to local issues and concerns, CAAMA may be limited in its potential to appeal to broader audiences. A tension thus develops between a desire to work successfully as a focus for the work of central Australian musicians, and an expressed company objective of disseminating the work of these musicians to audiences across Australia and beyond that, internationally.

CAAMA – policies and output

CAAMA produces, markets and broadcasts Aboriginal material through Imparja Television, CAAMA Shop, and CAAMA Productions. In 1980, the company was run by three volunteers, with a second-hand car, some donated equipment and a typewriter. Its office was provided rent free, and donations funded activities. By 1988 the staff numbered over one hundred and fifty, and CAAMA was operating eighteen radio and television transmitters and maintaining five production studios. This level of activity was a measure of its initial success

Postcards advertising CAAMA broadcasting and
recordings. The use of local languages (as well
as a map of broadcast area) emphasises the
intention to attract Aboriginal audiences. These
services were among the first of their type in
Australia. (Courtesy: Central Australian Aboriginal Media Association)

alone. The corporate and administrative structures of CAAMA ensure that the group is owned and run by Aboriginal people.

CAAMA has specific objectives that relate directly to its role as a recorder and distributor of Aboriginal music. The social nature of these objectives and the ways in which popular music is used as a means of spreading information, reviving and maintaining Aboriginal cultures, and addressing specific problems in Aboriginal communities are made explicit in documents released by the organisation. These documents also make explicit an agenda of informing all Australians about Aboriginal cultures, and of recognising Aboriginal music as a component of wider Australian imagery. For example, in an undated press release about the range of CAAMA's activities:

> The objectives contained in the CAAMA charter were to provide full media service to Aboriginal people by arresting cultural disintegration through broadcasting educational material in language and song. Specifically, the CAAMA charter aims to alleviate problems ... in areas of health, law, social services and literacy experienced by Aboriginal people ... [and] to promote knowledge and understanding by the Australian community of Aboriginal culture and traditions. [This] is carried out through specific campaigns such as preventing alcohol abuse and recording and distributing the work of many Aboriginal artists through CAAMA's recording facilities. (CAAMA, nd.d)

CAAMA's production of recordings of Aboriginal contemporary music groups fulfils a number of agendas. First, it is a means of preserving Aboriginal oral history and music. Second, CAAMA provides training for Aboriginal musicians and the technical personnel to record, produce and promote them. At the time of his appointment to establish and head CAAMA's record label in 1984, Richard Micallef singled out the potential contribution of CAAMA to Australian music in general:

> Australia has its own black music – Aboriginal music – which, given the chance, can make a huge social and economic impact on Australian culture. Just as contemporary American music reflects and respects its black roots, the time has come for Aboriginal music to take its place in the mainstream of Australian culture. If

we can absorb the influences of Aboriginal music, it would mark
the dawning of a new era, as Australian music would at last have
an identifiable Australian sound (CAAMA, nd.c).

CAAMA is bound by its charter to provide an educational service to
help produce and distribute information on 'social disintegration and
other special problems in areas of health, law, social services and literacy'
(CAAMA, nd.h). Because of this, the topics of songs reflect Aboriginal
needs and wants, and songs are 'situational ... about appalling conditions,
general environment problems leading to bad health, the continual battle
with the grog affecting communities, the apocalyptic effect [of] AIDS'
(CAAMA, 1990). Specific albums target individual social problems:
HIV/AIDS on *How Could I Know – The AIDS Album*; health on *UPK
– A Strategy for Life*; alcohol on *Wama Wanti – Drink Little Bit*. Information provided by CAAMA about these recordings makes the proactive part played by CAAMA in the writing, recording and release of
songs clear. For example:

> In the very early days CAAMA staff could be found in a dry
> creekbed recording traditional singers with only a single microphone
> plugged into a reel to reel tape recorder. This is still an effective way
> to capture the timeless sound of clap sticks and voice, but contempo-
> rary black musicians, utilising the electric guitars and drum kits of a
> modern rock and roll line up, demand full mixing and engineering ...
> Despite the pressure to function as a small business, the Unit has not
> lost sight of its original goals – the development of Aboriginal music.
> Workshops such as the Hamilton Downs music camp in March 1988
> have proven that Aboriginal musicians respond readily to the oppor-
> tunity to write and record their own music. At Hamilton Downs
> 25 Aboriginal musicians from all over the Centre were paid a small
> fee to write songs on AIDS and the changes likely to lifestyle which
> it requires people to make. Over one week four new songs were
> written and recorded. One of the songs, 'AIDS – It's a Killer' by the
> Areyonga Desert Tigers, has become a local hit and is used as backing
> music to community announcements promoting the use of condoms
> in the wake of the AIDS pandemic ... This was one of many local ini-
> tiatives which have led public health authorities to point to Aborig-
> inal Australians as leaders in AIDS education among indigenous

people. But the exercise was also testament to the innate ability of local musicians who are at the forefront of the development of a unique contemporary Aboriginal music (CAAMA, 1989, 16–17).

Also in relation to songs about HIV/AIDS, CAAMA's role in raising public awareness of the problem was noted:

> AIDS out here was not talked about and because there was hysteria in silence, Aboriginal organisations together with CAAMA decided to throw their weight behind a priority. A priority if not addressed that would have immeasurable costs and losses coupled with other health problems (CAAMA, nd.e).

Beyond health and social issues, other CAAMA recordings act as references to central Australian Aboriginal contact history. Albums such as *Aboriginal Choirs of Central Australia* and *Western Desert Gospel*, of church choirs and religious rock bands, recall the history of central Australian Christian missionisation and the prevalence of campfire gospel sing-alongs on missions as a regular form of entertainment. According to CAAMA, musical mixtures of pre-contact and contemporary styles resulting from the presence of missionaries has produced 'an interesting crosscultural, indigenous Christianity, even Creole Christianity, where in some communities (in particular the Warlpiri community of Yuendumu) traditional *inma* (corroboree) is mixed with Christian ceremony' (CAAMA, nd.a).

In addition to social issues targeted through the release of albums, CAAMA attends to matters of cultural maintenance through recordings. Songs and albums 'in language' are positioned by CAAMA as a means to 'help keep Aboriginal cultures and languages strong and fresh in the minds of Aboriginal people young and old' (CAAMA, nd.f), while a recording of traditional songs from east Arnhem Land, *Andhanaggi – Walker River Clan Songs*, was undertaken by CAAMA at the request of the songs' owners 'in order to preserve their heritage for future generations of the Walker River people' (CAAMA, nd.g). Moreover, CAAMA's policies include the expectation that the association act as a means of broadcasting information about Aboriginal cultures to the general population and thus encourage understanding of Indigenous Australians. The adoption of a new company slogan, 'CAAMA music – Aboriginal music for the world', that appeared on CAAMA recordings around 2000, indicates

CAAMA's intention to distribute its product on an international level.

A number of points significant to contemporary Aboriginal music in this context emerge from these positions on and activities in recording. It is clear, for example, that contemporary Aboriginal music is seen as a significant means of distributing information, often about health, lifestyle and family responsibility. It is also clear that CAAMA has firm policies in place for supporting Aboriginal musicians in the production of repertoire. There is indication of control of Aboriginal cultural objects by and within the Aboriginal community. This is in line with the observations of Michaels (1986) in his work with the introduction of film-making and television broadcasting in the Warlpiri community of Yuendumu in the early 1980s, at the same time that CAAMA was establishing itself in Alice Springs. Michaels noted that the Yuendumu community, having gained access to equipment for video-taping and local broadcasting, exercised control of technology for their own ends in two ways. They developed their own, culturally appropriate ways of filming and editing materials, and they assumed the 'authority to vet, alter and redistribute any and all incoming signals as essential to cultural and linguistic maintenance' (Michaels, 1986, 127). This resonates with the comment of Freda Glynn, first managing director of CAAMA, that 'it is important that Aboriginal communities become involved in using new technologies, or they risk being used by them' (in Breen, 1989, 105). The opposite view, that by utilising technologies such as TV, Aboriginal people run the risk of losing 'grassroots culture', has been levelled at Aboriginal rock music. Chester Schultz (in Breen, 1989, 105–106) explains this with the comment that:

> There is the risk also in using them [modern technologies]. Fighting modern technological culture by 'participation' in its own methods, you may find that you have given in on the main issues, which are issues of means. You cannot keep grassroots culture alive by giving lots of money and TV exposure. Grassroots culture can be maintained only by pursuing it in local life ... that which depends on TV becomes part of TV culture. CAAMA and other organisations will have to battle to change TV culture itself, to keep it in its place, make it less necessary, and more amenable to non-standard arts. This is a cruel dilemma, familiar to tribal people: salvage what you can by compromising what you must – or else lose the lot.

Schultz continues his criticism of the wholesale adoption of modern technology in the representation of Aboriginal cultures by pointing out that
rock music is cost intensive, and this may lead some Aboriginal bands into
dependence on white financial support. The result of this, he maintains, is
loss of artistic integrity, and 'of course, the music changes'. Specifically he
worried in the late 1980s that country music, a mainstay of Aboriginal
rock group musical styles up to that point, would become less popular.
This in turn may cause a split between different generations in Aboriginal
communities. While recordings released through CAAMA in the late
1990s/early 2000s of Red Sunset (*Nangu*), Josh Thomas (*Thylacine*,
Nightmare Dreaming) Bart Willoughby (*Pathways*) and Frank Yamma
and the group, Piranpa (*Playing with Fire – Warungku Inkanyi*) demonstrate stylistic developments among Aboriginal rock musicians, including
increased dependence on heavier, grungier sounds and virtuosic guitar
breaks not heard on earlier recordings and a more studio driven finished
sound, it is still possible to hear country songs and the influence of
country music in these and many other Aboriginal albums.

   While country sounds still surface in Aboriginal rock music from central Australia, more recently other musical scenes and styles that veer
from the CAAMA/country sound have emerged in Alice Springs. These
expressions are similarly influenced by the reach of global communications technologies, but are created through adoption of youth subcultural styles that flow to remote communities through popular television
shows and radio broadcasts. Nokturnl, described by Triple J radio in
1998 as 'the Public Enemy of Australia', combine metal guitar and
techno rhythm backing with confrontational lyrics, delivered in hip-hop
and thrash styles – what they describe as 'rip rock', 'hard hitting music
with groove that challenges ignorance' (Nokturnl, 2003). Their music
displays influences from American groups such as Rage Against the
Machine, Pantera and Metallica. Vocalist and lead guitarist, Craig
T(ilmouth) formed Alice Springs' first metal band, Nemesis, in the late
1980s, then, influenced by, among others, Michael Franti's Disposable
Heroes of Hiphoprisy absorbed the sounds and ethos of hip-hop. Nokturnl see themselves as decidedly urban in sound and attitude: 'as youth
growing up in Alice Springs, the members of Nokturnl were not drawn
into the local Aboriginal country music scene so prevalent in Central
Australia. Instead, the lads grew up on a varied diet of heavy metal,

rhythm and blues, hip-hop, jazz and progressive rock 'n' roll' (Condie, 2000b, 45). According to Craig T, 'one of the reasons we got together as a band was because we were all listening to very different music to what was popular locally. We come from a different school of thought in rela-tion to local music, so we like playing distorted guitar and heavy riffs' (in Condie, 2000b, 45). Nokturnl gained popular support among youth audiences in Australia after gaining significant airplay on Triple J and undertaking a national tour with Spiderbait and Nitocris in 1997. They have since released CDs through Mushroom, won Deadly Awards for Band of the Year and been nominated for numerous ARIA awards.

Nokturnl radically recast meanings for Alice Springs, musically and politically. They distance themselves from the country sound of other Aboriginal bands from the central Australian area, and stylistically and lyrically unsettle images of a desert paradise and the romantic colonial nos-talgia that surrounds Alice Springs when marketed to tourists. Instead, interpreting their lyrics, Alice Springs is a dystopia, plagued by similar problems as urban America or Europe – frustration, addiction, disillusion-ment. Also distinct from Aboriginal country and rock bands from central Australia, Nokturnl downplay an emphasis on overt Aboriginality in their music, preferring instead to write political songs that appeal to both Abo-riginal and non-Aboriginal audiences: 'Obviously [Aboriginality] comes out here and there when we write about our lives and what we think ... but we don't feel we should make our music more "Aboriginal sounding" or make it obvious we are talking about Aboriginal issues ... I guess you could say we are trying to raise some issues in a way that is not so blatant' (in Condie, 2000b, 45). At the same time that Nokturnl do not fit into a tradition of music making in Alice Springs, when appealing to national audiences the band does not sit comfortably within the urban metal scene either. As guitarist Damien Armstrong has put it, 'because we come from Alice Springs a lot of people think that we must be aliens. You know, that tin shed next to Ayers Rock? Yeah, that's where we come from.' (in Hall, 2000, 3). Other metal bands from Alice Springs (with both Aboriginal and non-Aboriginal members) have taken inspiration from Notkurnl, including Chronic Fatigue, Kinderflip and Dead Famous People, although none has achieved the same success. The emergence of a nascent metal scene in Alice Springs nonetheless diversifies the town's musical output and provides a challenge to its musical and social status quo.

photo: K Blackwell

by Simon Moore

Nokturnl, based in Alice Springs, combine hip-hop and metal to create a confrontational, political sound. Nokturnl are performing here at the 2001 Deadly Aboriginal Music Awards in Sydney. (Courtesy: Katherine Blackwell and Simon Moore)

Tourism and music in Alice Springs

Over time Alice Springs has become a crucial destination for national and international visitors, initially because of its symbolic position as the his- torical and geographical 'heart' of Australian pastoral expansion and fron- tier exploration, and more recently through its relative proximity to Uluru-Kata Tjuta National Park (some 400 kilometres south). Tourism has proved to be crucial in a restructured central Australian economy, a point acknowledged by local councillors and Territory tourism authorities (Alice Springs Town Council, 1998; Northern Territory Government, 1999). The central Australian region (which includes Alice Springs and Uluru-Kata Tjuta) now receives over 40 per cent of tourist expenditure for the Northern Territory; and while there has been a steady drop in domestic tourists over the last ten years, this has been made up for by increases in international visitors and a more diversified tourism market, including many backpackers, international retirees and ecotourists.

Since the increased popularity of Aboriginal art and music in the 1990s, Alice Springs has also become a site of cultural tourism – a 'gateway' for vis- itors keen to access a range of attractions and Aboriginal experiences throughout central Australia. Through cultural tourism and the marketing of Aboriginal cultural products to tourists, parts of Alice Springs have been transformed into 'Aboriginalised' urban spaces, in similar ways that have occurred in other tourist centres where Aboriginality is a drawcard, such as Broome, Katherine and Darwin. The most prominent of these spaces in Alice Springs is Todd Street Mall, a pedestrianised streetscape in the centre of the town, originally designed in 'colonial' style when it was built in the 1980s, but since transformed around images of Aboriginality and the com- mercial availability of Aboriginal cultural products. Businesses there include art galleries, music performance theatres and didjeridu and souvenir shops selling ubiquitous souvenirs and a range of 'Aboriginalia' (Neuenfeldt, 1997, 107), including didjeridus, paintings, T-shirts, string bags and necklaces.

Music has played a significant role in this 'Aboriginalising' of tourist land- scapes: art shops play music as accompaniment to works on display, affirming the authenticity of objects for sale; buskers play didjeridus in the mall; live per- formance of non-Aboriginal bush music takes place in tourist-oriented pubs; and more 'serious' Aboriginal performances occur at tourist resorts and in specialised venues – such as (non-Aboriginal performer) Andrew Langford's Sounds of Starlight Theatre, where tourists are taken on, a musical journey through the ancient landforms, history, light and space of Australia's heartland ... Andrew Langford demonstrates his mastery of the didgeridoo to evoke a vibrant wilderness of sandy deserts, mountain ranges, deep gorges and icy waterholes. He captures the contrasting power of Ancestral Beings and the rhythmic march of honey ants (Sounds of Starlight Theatre flyer).

Alongside quasi-Aboriginal themes, this show takes in diverse musical influences and notions of exotica: 'Andrew is supported by guest artists using an array of world instruments including the Aztec hum drum, spirit catcher and shamanic drums used by American Indians and the qweeka of Latin America' (Sounds of Starlight Theatre flyer).

With some exceptions, Aboriginal cultural producers have only sparsely profited from the Aboriginal cultural tourism industry in Alice Springs. This has been less so for Aboriginal visual artists, whose paintings are on sale in many outlets around the town, although what artists are paid can vary significantly from the market price of paintings (see Wright, 1999), but more the case for musicians, who on the whole do not receive substantial incomes from the cultural tourism market. Aboriginal attempts to reclaim shares of the tourist market for Aboriginal cultural products include art co-operatives establishing outlets for distribution, such as Warumpi Arts and Jukurrpa Artists Aboriginal Art Gallery. Paul Ah Chee, previously a member of the Alice Springs based rock group Amunda, now manages the Aboriginal Art and Culture Centre in Todd Street on behalf of the Pwerte Marnte Aboriginal Corporation. It features, among other things, a 'did-jeridu university', talks, performances and artefact sales. Their Red Centre Dreaming show is described as 'high quality Aboriginal performance by tra-ditional and contemporary artists, [featuring] traditional dancing, weaponry, didgeridoo playing and fireside storytelling' (flyer).

There is an extensive market for didjeridus in Alice Springs, with spe-cialist shops and art galleries stocking comprehensive collections. How-ever, these artefacts are generally not produced in the region and the didjeridu is not originally from this area. Thus, there are few local pro-ducers to profit from these sales. Art and crafts represent socially consti-tuted economies of Aboriginal cultural production, often characterised by small-scale production, distribution based on social and historical con-nections between retailers, distributors and craftspersons, and 'enmeshed in degrees of dependence' (Neuenfeldt, 1997, 112). What are considered 'authentic' didjeridus (those created by Aboriginal people in remote communities where didjeridus were traditionally produced and played) are increasingly competing with mass-produced ones manufactured by interstate and overseas companies. In the Top End and in Far North Queensland, where the instrument is traditionally produced from the hollowed out trunks of trees eaten by termites, there has been dissent surrounding the mass production and importation of bamboo didjeridus, and disquiet over the environmental impacts of the demand for didjeridus, with many now carved (inappropriately) from solid wood, while existing supplies of hollowed trunks have become more scarce. The demand for hollow trunks has led to vegetation loss in the Top End, and has made it more difficult for those who wish to produce didjeridus for ceremonial, rather than commercial use. According to Roy Morris, an Aboriginal artist:

> A plain didge can sell for $150, and if painted it can bring anything from $250 to $700 or more. Yet sadly the designs painted on the didgeridoos are often done by non-indigenous people. Not only are they rip-offs and fakes, they are an insult to Aboriginal culture as the original design is often altered. A real didgeridoo occurs in nature. Termites get in and eat out a tree's inside, leaving a hollow log. Didge dealers are not even giving the termites time to eat out the inside of the tree. They're just cutting down healthy young saplings of yellow box, stringy bark and bloodwood, leaving the land dry (in Ajuria, 1997, 11).

Josh Fornea, who has researched the environmental impacts of didjeridu harvesting in Jawoyn country in the Northern Territory, has estimated that, even though permits are issued by the NT government parks and wildlife office for a maximum harvest of 3000 didjeridus per annum across the whole territory, more than 9000 are sold each year in Darwin and Alice Springs (*Koori Mail*, 13 Jun 2001, 38). Estimates of total national didjeridu production are in the hundreds of thousands, illustrating the potential both for ecological damage and for a 'flooding' of the market for souvenirs that potentially threatens prices and the share of the market controlled by Aboriginal artists and organisations.

CDs and cassettes are also popular souvenir items purchased in Alice Springs, although despite the presence of CAAMA in the town, these are rarely of local artists or groups. Aboriginal sounds and images that are purchased tend to be those recorded by artists from elsewhere and sold as part of national distribution chains by metropolitan compa-nies such as Holborne Music Interactive, based in Sydney, who sell music in souvenir shops, airports and newsagents via interactive systems in which a consumer presses a button to hear snippets from a small range of CDs. According to CAAMA representatives, Holborne currently con-trol 90 per cent of the tourist market for Aboriginal music (interview with Chris Ross, 2000) through their releases of CDs by David Hudson, Tony O'Connor and others.

Some of these recordings are fusions of traditional and contemporary musical styles. They mobilise 'traditional' sounds in technologically altered settings, using genres such as ambient music, with synthesizers and the sounds of bird calls and whale songs. For David Hudson, co-founder of the Tjapukai Dance Theatre in Kuranda (see chapter 6), his *Guardians of the Reef* album is described as 'an enchanting and melodic sound of guitar and didgeridoo, enticing you through the sparse outback countryside. Let this music take you to another frontier of Australia and into another dawning' (*Guardians of the Reef*, album notes). Mean-while, (non-Aboriginal) Tony O'Connor's range of recordings, marketed alongside postcards, calendars and posters, features titles such as *Bush-land Dreaming: Kakadu*: 'Tony journeyed through Kakadu, recording with astounding clarity the sounds of nature and didgeridoo – and has reproduced them here on this amazing album. Then, inspired by the magic of this ancient landscape, he composed seven pieces of musical wonder and blended his own creations with the music of nature' (*Bush-land Dreaming: Kakadu*, album notes). His *Uluru* album 'features a hint of rhythm and percussion and will evoke the sensational experience that is Uluru. Vast and majestic landscapes of music, didgeridoo, clap sticks and sounds from the Red Centre complete this very special recording' (*Uluru*, album notes). Semantically, such releases appeal to tourists through imagery of Aboriginality and landscape, a potentially dangerous combination that constructs indigenous people in relation to 'ancient', unchanging pasts and nature (Waitt, 1997, 1999). Such imagery is in danger of rendering indigenous people 'exotic' but silent objects of neo-Darwinian landscapes (Neuenfeldt, 1994), and, despite musical fusions contained in the recordings themselves, downplays the dynamism and

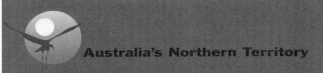
Australia's Northern Territory

Central Australia
Holiday Guide
ALICE SPRINGS • ULURU/AYERS ROCK • TENNANT CREEK
2001/2002

You'll never never know if you never never go

Aboriginal musical performance, incorporating the didjeridu (not originally from this area) is now a regular component of tourism promotional material in Central Australia. Brochures featured here are from both government tourism campaigns and Aboriginal-controlled performances. (Courtesy: Northern Territory Tourism Commission and Aurora Resorts) hybrid nature of contemporary indigenous lifestyles and expressions.

At the same time that such products dominate the tourist souvenir market for music, there are very few links between the tourism industry, the market for Aboriginal cultural products, and contemporary Aboriginal musicians in Alice Springs – the artists that CAAMA records. This is in part because tourist demand is for 'exotic' or 'tribal' representations of culture, rather than syncretic or modern styles. There is a lack of knowledge or understanding among backpackers and other tourists that Aboriginal people play anything but didjeridu-based 'ceremonial' styles of music (Gibson & Connell, 2004). In one sense, this is to be expected, as tourists' perceptions of 'authentic' Aboriginal music have often already been mediated through advertising of Aboriginal Australia as 'ancient' and 'timeless' (Waitt, 1999). Tourists are perhaps not made aware of the existence of Aboriginal reggae, rock or country music. It is, however, a missed opportunity, particularly within the backpacker market, as elsewhere backpackers are more likely to consume local expressions of popular music, for example, at Byron Bay and Cairns, rather than uncritically absorb imported sounds. On the other hand, appealing to tourists' demands may not, ultimately, be a goal of CAAMA and other Aboriginal labels. This is in contrast to experiences at Tjapukai Cultural Park in North Queensland (chapter 6), where 'authenticity' and integrity have been seen to be compromised (or at least transformed) by the encroachment of the tourist industry. That some Aboriginal expressions remain beyond the ambit of tourists may not be considered a negative thing.

What results in relation to Aboriginal culture in places such as Alice Springs is a bizarre, almost tragic set of ironies. Tourists flock to central Australia to, among other things, experience 'authentic' Aboriginal culture, to see and purchase art, hear Aboriginal music and see Aboriginal dance. The 'Aboriginalised' spaces, including 'staged' venues such as the Sounds of Starlight Theatre that have sprung up to cater for this market, depict Aboriginality in ways that may confirm stereotypes often out of touch with the exigencies of contemporary Aboriginal life. Furthermore, such spaces are situated only a few hundred metres from pubs and clubs frequented by Aboriginal people and occasionally featuring Aboriginal country music or rock bands, where active, negotiated, contested and celebrated contemporary cultures are produced. Few connections with this sphere tend to be made. Aboriginal music fills the streetscape of Todd

Street Mall, authenticating the objects on sale inside shops, however, local contemporary Aboriginal musicians as yet do not profit from tourism in any comprehensive manner.

Conclusion

Alice Springs is a symbolic centre in Australian geography, in many ways. It is literally at the heart of the Aboriginal recording industry in Australia, with CAAMA well established as the country's premier Aboriginal-controlled music label and central Australia's main media institution. Alice Springs is also symbolic within the Australian tourism industry – from its origins as an archetypal colonial place in the 1960s and 1970s, when the tourism industry emerged in 'a town like Alice', to a desert hub for adventure, ecotourism and Aboriginal cultural tourism. Alice Springs and its surrounding areas are where most tourists, particularly international ones, go in order to find 'real' Australia, yet these myths are reproduced in particular ways. Alice Springs is emblematic of a political economy of cultural production, where symbols of the exotic and ancient create tourist markets, distinct from the cultural forms and expressions that are popular in everyday life among local Aboriginal people. The town's articulation as a cultural/Aboriginal tourism site is thus quite different from that at Tjapukai, discussed in chapter 6, where Aboriginal involvement in a major tourism venture raised questions about control, representation and employment. Here, more deeply entrenched schisms persist between a well-organised but largely non-Aboriginal tourism industry, and a range of music scenes, from country to hip-hop, that are vibrant in Arrente, Pitjantjatjara, Luritja and Warlpiri communities.

Suggested listening

Letterstick Band ▲ *An-Barra Clan*

Meinmuk – Music from the Top End

Wirrinyga Band ▲ *Dreamtime Shadow*

Wirrinyga Band ▲ *Dreamtime Wisdom,
Modern Time Vision*

Yothu Yindi ▲ *Birrkuta – Wild Honey*

Yothu Yindi ▲ *Freedom*

Yothu Yindi ▲ *Garma*

Yothu Yindi ▲ *Homeland Movement*

Yothu Yindi ▲ *One Blood*

Yothu Yindi ▲ *Tribal Voice*

CHAPTER 8

Meinmuk mujik
– the Top End sound

(Meinmuk: Gumatj – good; Mujik: *Kriol* – music)

In this chapter we present an investigation of music in a specific region, the Top End, the area of the Northern Territory to the north of the town of Katherine. In a similar manner to contemporary Aboriginal music in central Australia (chapter 7) and the Kimberley (chapter 10), some similarities in the music of Aboriginal rock bands in the Top End allow a degree of collective interpretation – although it is important to stress that there are also individualisms at work and that we do not intend to imply that musicians automatically conform to patterns of musical practice.

Aspects of songs and albums which emerge as characteristic of contemporary Aboriginal music in the Top End are the focus of the opening section of this chapter. We interpret these as symptomatic of ways in which elements of Top End Aboriginal cultures are embedded in forms of contemporary musical expression. In the second part of the chapter, we narrow our focus to investigate how the songs of Yolngu group Yothu Yindi exemplify aspects of the Top End sound and function as expressions of Yolngu relationships to land.

Our unpacking of the music/place relationship in this chapter, therefore, takes a number of forms. The chapter is a summary reading of contemporary music within a region; it acknowledges the work of individual groups/performers as arising from lives lived in specific places; it proposes that these specificities are reflected in songs through references to factors of Aboriginal life, both past and present; and it investigates the hypothesis that songs and albums by Yothu Yindi can be understood as articulations through music of social structures as those structures reflect land ownership and land-based beliefs.

Meinmuk – music from the Top End

In 1997, ABC Music/Triple J released a compilation album of songs by Aboriginal musicians from the Top End, *Meinmuk – Music from the Top End*. This album presents twenty-four tracks from fourteen bands/solo performers in nine languages. It provides access to the work of performers who have had little exposure outside of Top End Aboriginal contexts, despite releases of music by some of them through various recording companies, for example, Broken English (Skinnyfish Records), Letterstick (CAAMA), Marrugeku Company (Maningrida Media) and Soft Sands (Imparja).

Meinmuk typifies the contemporary Aboriginal music soundscape in a number of ways. It covers a range of musical styles: hard and soft rock, gospel influences, adaptations of reggae, mixtures of traditional singing and rock group backings. There is regular use of didjeridu and clapsticks; Dreamtime imagery suffuses songs. The multilingual nature of the album is reflected in individual songs at the sectional level. Other features of *Meinmuk*, however, are more prevalent in the recordings of Top End bands than in those from other parts of Australia. The presence on albums of tracks in purely traditional style performed by the standard Arnhem Land ensemble of didjeridu, clapsticks and male singer/s, alongside tracks in which these sounds are mixed with contemporary musical instruments and technologies, is more a practice of Top End groups than of others. The didjeridu, heard in much contemporary Aboriginal music across Australia, is more prominent here, and is presented in a more sustained way with a wider range of uses. This may reflect the didjeridu's origins and uses in traditional music in the northern parts of the Australian continent. These factors of Top End recordings index high levels of connection between Top End rock groups and maintenance of Aboriginal cultures. As Corn (2002, 89) notes in discussing one of the groups on *Meinmuk*, Letterstick (from Maningrida): 'Letterstick Band is but one of many bands in contemporary Arnhem Land with a repertoire that embodies the continuation of traditions in a period of radical sociocultural change'.

The case for situating *Meinmuk* as representative of the Top End sound is supported when recordings by groups not on this album are considered. For example, links between tradition and contemporary ways of figuring and handling it that can be heard on *Meinmuk* resurface in the work of Broken English, Blekbala Mujik, Mimi Band, Sunrize Band,

ABC Music/Triple J's graphic for their CD, *Meinmuk – Music from the Top End*, uses the painting 'Hunters with Falling Cabbage Palm' by Bardjarray 'Bobby' Nganjmirra.

Nabarlek. Wirrinyga Band and Yothu Yindi. Songs by Broken English are 'reflections on the past with a medium of the electric age ... [the group] respected the past and remained solid in the modern world' (*Broken English – The Studio Sessions*, album notes). Nabarlek and Wirrinyga Band state that their songs are modern versions of Dream-time/Dreaming stories, while Sunrize Band recorded two versions of 'Wak Wak (Black Crow)' as contiguous tracks on their 1993 album, *Lunggurrma*, making the musical relationships between them clear. Here, an upbeat 'bluesy' version of 'Wak Wak' is followed by a traditonal ren-dition by *manakay* (singing), *bilma* (clapsticks) and *yidaki* (didjeridu). As discussion of the work of Blekbala Mujik in chapter 9 and of songs by Yothu Yindi later in this chapter demonstrates, explicit connections between traditional songs and contemporary ones, such as in 'Wak Wak', can readily be heard on albums from this region.

For one Top End group, Wirrinyga Band (from Milingimbi), the Dreaming is openly acknowledged as an ideological reference point in their songs. Titles of two albums by this group refer to the Dreamtime (*Dreamtime Shadow*; *Dreamtime Wisdom, Modern Time Vision*), and it provides personnel for song topics (for example in 'Thunderman', 'Black Evil Woman'). It also appears as a conceptual site from which knowledge for handling life can be gained. The setting up of a Dreaming/modern time opposition by Wirrinyga Band is explained by them on their first album, released in 1990, as: '[Wirrinyga Band's] music is inspired by the strength of their connections to their cultural background and deals with a number of issues encountered by living in the modern world as people strong in their Aboriginal identity' (*Dreamtime Shadow*, album notes). For this group, the Dreamtime also occupies a place that can be conflated with the reality of a specific location:

Take me back to the Dreamtime
Far away into Yolngu land ...

This conversion of Dreaming imagery into the topics of contemporary songs also appears in the work of Nabarlek (from Manmoyi), for example in rock songs about devil people who prey on *Bininj* (Aboriginal people). Like Wirrinyga Band, this group makes the modernisation of Dreaming materials explicit with a proactivity linked to cultural maintenance: 'the reason we live here is because it's our fathers' and our grandfathers' and our great grandfathers' land. The songs are dreamtime stories done in a modern way ... we want to teach our children what the old people taught us, so our kids still have our culture' (*Munwurrk – Bushfire*, album notes).

Listing of the Dreaming in this way on the notes accompanying recordings implies an ideological stance among Top End bands that information accompanying an album be uncompromising in reference to cultural factors. Sunrize Band's listing of *manakay, bilma* and *yidaki* rather than singing, clapsticks and didjeridu (above), demonstrates one of the ways through which this is achieved. An implicit agenda of using songs or an album to educate the listening public about aspects of Aboriginality occurs in this region in the ways that the language affiliations of performers and/or the communities from which they come are indicated. Wild Water, from Darwin, and Sunrize Band, from Maningrida, state that they use the Brarra (Burarra) language; Kunwinku (Gunwinggu) language is noted for songs by Nabarlek, Ngalkbon for songs by Blekbala Mujik from Gulin Gulin; didjeridu player Ash Dargan is noted as 'of the Larrikia tribe, Northern Territory'; Broken English describe their origins in Ngukurr, on the Roper River; Yothu Yindi list Gumatj as a language used on their recordings; all Aboriginal languages on *Meinmuk* are named. The topics of songs sung in Aboriginal languages are also indicated by Top End groups. On *Meinmuk* these are invariably about natural events or aspects of local Aboriginal life – 'Guyularri' by My Boys Are Good Boys is about brolga and their second track on the album, 'Djutarra', is about Gumatj women; Harry Yalungani's 'Mamarika' treats the east wind; Letterstick's 'Bartpa' is about waves, their 'Yirrana' about sunset; Marrugeko Company sing about yam in 'Karrparra', and about the stringybark tree in 'Munborookork'. In line with a practice found among a considerable number of Aboriginal rock groups and solo performers nationally, *Meinmuk* contains Christian rock songs – a musical reference to a Top End past of missionisation. Particularly important in this respect is the song 'Promised Land' by Soft Sands, from Galiwinku on Elcho Island. Soft Sands are the dedicatees of *Meinmuk*, and the album notes make special mention of them as 'one of the very first Aboriginal bands ... [who have performed] in remote communities since 1962' (Djirrimbilpilwuy, 1997). As Leonard Amagula's song 'Home Sweet Home – Amarranga' demonstrates, the topic of land as a home to which the singer expresses spiritual attachment, a regular trope of Aboriginal songs nationally, appears on this album:

And my memory's comin' back
To the place I left behind
Amarranga, the place I love the most.

It is also one sung about by other Top End musicians, from Wild Water's 'Arnhem Land Blues', which 'is about missing your homeland and about the background of the land and the people' (*Baltpa*, album notes) to Sunrize Band's 'Lem Bana Mani Mani' (about Maningrida), Broken English's 'Ngukurr Sunrise' and Wirrinyga Band's 'My Sweet Takarrina' (about Galiwinku).

Levels of proactivity in providing details of cultural factors on *Meinmuk* can be observed in reference to more complex concepts of personal and group identity on other recordings. This is in the listing of the ownership of songs by clans or by people from specific locations, indicating links between songs and places. Sunrize Band attribute ownership of songs on their *Lunggurrma* album to the Marrangu, Warra Warra and Balngarra clans, taking pains to show the provenance of each clan. On Blekbala Mujik's *Comen Dance*, origins of traditional material are given. Songs on the albums of Yothu Yindi are heavily noted as belonging to or deriving from named Yolngu clans from northeast Arnhem Land. Letterstick name an album, *An Barra Clan*, from the name of a clan. As Corn (2002) demonstrates, songs by this rock group rely on implications of connections between songs, ancestors and estates. There is an implication in this that where a song is from or who owns it are important and require notification. By doing this, not only are the topographical origins of songs indicated, but connotations deriving from songs' links to place-related definitions of personal and group identity and the significance of specific sites are brought into play.

These indications of information about songs and performers, whether minimal or to the extent used by Yothu Yindi, reinforce the sense of Top End songs as articulations of Aboriginal music/place interdependence. In many cases, through explanations of the origin/s, meaning/s and painter/s of designs, the artwork on an album cover draws attention to this practice of stating cultural factors significant for understanding recordings. That some album cover designs relate to the topics of songs or albums emphasises the impression of songs and albums as statements of Top End Aboriginalities. Moreover, accrual of these forms of reference to facets of Top End Aboriginal cultures across a number of recordings creates a sense of intention to broadcast information about local Aboriginalities, and to indicate that in this part of Australia Aboriginal cultures are strong. Mandawuy Yunupingu implies as much when he describes music by Yothu Yindi as 'a cultural fusion of the contemporary elements of 200 years and the traditional ones of 40,000 years' (Chryssides, 1993, 248).

The amount of detail entered into in explaining the cultural backgrounds of Top End songs and albums is read here as an indication through contemporary music of the strength of continuing Aboriginal cultures in this region in comparison with those in other parts of Australia. Researchers agree on the relative lateness of full-scale Aboriginal contact with non-Aboriginal peoples in the Top End, and on the vibrancy and diversity of the cultures they studied there (A. Moyle, 1974; Stubington, 1979; Clunies Ross, 1983; Morphy, 1991). Morphy (1984, 1–2) notes, for example, that for the Yolngu of northeast Arnhem Land, 'intensive contact with Europeans began in the 1920s' and that 'until the early 1960s northeast Arnhem Land remained fairly isolated from the rest of Australia', while Heath (1978, 1) states that his research into Yolngu languages, conducted between 1973 and 1977, was assisted by the fact that 'Aboriginal languages and cultures have generally survived in this area longer than in

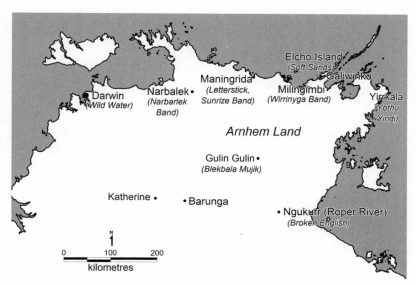

The Top End Aboriginal music scene takes in bands from several scattered communities, from Darwin to Yirrkala. (Map: Chris Gibson)

other parts of Australia'. Yothu Yindi also make reference to this on their website: 'the people of the region [northeast Arnhem Land] have had contact with Balanda [Europeans] only over the past sixty years or so. Consequently, their traditional cultural, religious, artistic and ceremonial activities are still among the strongest in the country' (Yothu Yindi, 2003).

This rock group provides more cultural background information to accompany their albums than other Top End performers do. What they provide is also at a higher level of intricacy and complexity than that on other Top End albums, and reifies stated objectives of the group's leader to 'give others an understanding of Aboriginal life and an idea of where we're coming from' (M Yunupingu, in Thompson, 1990, 103). For these reasons it is worth considering music by Yothu Yindi as a separate case study of the Top End sound, and as a means for understanding how a specific repertoire of songs expresses land-based belief systems.

Yothu Yindi

Yothu Yindi's output has attracted widespread attention since this Yolngu band began their career in 1986. This is both among writers in the popular music press and from academic researchers working on contemporary Aboriginal cultures, communication studies, popular music and cultural anthropology (Thompson, 1990; Mitchell, 1992, 1993; Muecke, 1992; Chryssides, 1993; Hayward, 1993; Neuenfeldt, 1993a; Nicol, 1993; Smith & Dunbar-Hall, 1993; *Bulletin of Immigration and Population Research*, 1994; Dunbar-Hall, 1994; Magowan, 1994; Stubington & Dunbar-Hall, 1994; Magowan, 1996; Dunbar-Hall, 1997a, 1997b; Knopoff, 1997; Gibson, 1998; Neuenfeldt, 1998; Hayward & Neuenfeldt, 1998; Corn, 1999; McFarlane, 2000; Smith, 2000; Dunbar-Hall & Gibson, 2000). This interest in Yothu Yindi mirrors investigations of Yolngu society and culture by a wide range of researchers (*inter alia*: Warner, 1937; Hiatt, 1965; A Moyle, 1974; Heath, 1978; Stubington, 1978; Wells, 1982; Morphy, 1984, 1991; Williams, 1986; Watson et al., 1989; Davis & Prescott, 1992; Turnbull, 1993; Christie, 1994; Keen, 1994; Trudgen, 2000). Discussion of the work of Yothu Yindi often overlaps with the work of anthropologists, sociologists and/or linguists who have studied the Yolngu. At times, therefore, analysis of the music of this group can be positioned as one component of broad-ranging Yolngu studies which date back over a number of decades (Williams, 1986, and Keen, 1994, both provide succinct summaries of interactions between Yolngu and researchers).

Despite the disciplinary direction from which researchers approach their work on the Yolngu, land-based perspectives of Yolngu society and culture continually resurface in their work. This is not surprising, as Yolngu social structure is organised around an ideology of ownership and responsibility for country traceable back to the Dreaming. Yolngu cultural representations, such as song, dance, story and design, focus on articulating this through metaphorical and/or symbolic means. As various writers have noted, attempts by non-Yolngu to unravel the multiplicity of meanings in Yolngu place-based cultural artefacts is complex and can only ever be partially successful. To this must be added the caveat that what we present here is our interpretation of the ways in which we hear songs by Yothu Yindi acting as mediation of aspects of Yolngu society.

Our reading of these songs addresses land in two broad ways. First, we discuss songs which make overt statements about land and the history of Yolngu/non-Yolngu land related confrontations. This is an area of fact, relying on reference to legal and political struggles undertaken by Yolngu, recalling of these in Yothu Yindi songs, and the long-term outcomes of these struggles for Aboriginal peoples in general. Our second area of discussion is more inscrutable and propositional. In it we investigate how acknowledgment of Yolngu social structures, made explicit through song lyrics, music, album notes and publicity materials, maps Yolngu land based cosmology into this group's albums.

Land-related events in Yothu Yindi songs

Yothu Yindi's first album, *Homeland Movement*, issued the year after the 1988 bicentenial celebrations, concludes with a tongue-in-cheek song about the 1788 loss to British invaders of Australia as an Aboriginally owned place, 'Luku-Wängawuy Manikay (1788)'. Mention of Yirrkala, one of the communities from which Yothu Yindi members come, is worked into the song's opening line:

> My boy said the old Yirrkala man
> I've a very sad tale to relate
> The *Balanda* say we lost our land in seventeen eighty eight.
> (*balanda* - non-Yolngu/white people)

The main topic of this album celebrates the establishment of Yolngu homeland stations (outstations) in the early 1970s, 'a move pioneered in

north east Arnhem Land [which saw] Aboriginal people returning to
their traditional lands and ... relying ... more on traditional activities such
as hunting, fishing and cultural and ceremonial education' (Yothu Yindi,
2003). Emphasising concepts of cultural strength associated with the
homeland movement, other rock songs on this album are about Yolngu
people: 'Yolngu Woman' and 'Yolngu Boy'. Moreover, traditional songs
on the album that relay information about the actions of Dreaming ancestors are indicated as referring to specific sites of significance to Yolngu
people. Thus through rock songs and traditional songs, individual song
topics, and references to events in both the Dreamtime and the more
recent past, the album has a collective undertext of reference to places
meaningful to Yolngu in various ways.

On their second album, *Tribal Voice* (1992), 'My Kind of Life' echoes
the sentiment of 'Luku-Wängawuy Manikay (1788)' on *Homeland Movement*: 'we have lived here now for a long, long time'. Also on this album,
'Treaty' makes a clear statement about the Aboriginal position on invasion: 'this land was never given up, this land was never bought and sold'.
The original video clip of 'Treaty' makes specific visual reference to Yolngu
loss of rights to their lands on the Gove Penninsula to Nabalco, who introduced mining for bauxite there in the early 1960s. It includes footage of
then Prime Minister Bob Hawke (who in 1988 at the Barunga Festival
had promised to conclude a treaty between Aboriginal and non-
Aboriginal Australia) and Minister for Aboriginal and Torres Strait
Islander Affairs, Robert Tickner, implying a Yolngu position on the
inability of the Australian federal government to fulfil Hawke's promise.
Voicing calls for such a treaty alongside images of mining and the ambit of
Yolngu coastal territory, makes the original video version of 'Treaty' a multivalent text on land rights through the combination of lyrics, history, personnel, music, visual effects and place. A later video version of 'Treaty'
removed footage of Hawke and Tickner on the grounds that the images of
Australian politicians would not be understood by international audiences (Mitchell, 1996, 181). Less easily recognised on *Tribal Voice* are
oblique references to the area of Yothu Yindi's origins in coastal locations.
References to estuarine interactions between salt water and fresh water,
to driftwood, to animals found in water, to water imagery as a metaphor
for ways of living – all of these infuse the album with imagery of Yolngu
coastal places and help situate this album in the Yolngu landscape.

Yothu Yindi's third album, *Freedom*, released in 1993, presents a different perspective of land as a focus of song. In 'Mabo', this album includes the group's response to the Mabo decision of the High Court of Australia in the previous year. Here Yothu Yindi flaunt the Aboriginal position on the doctrine of *terra nullius*:

> We were right that we were here
> They were wrong that we weren't here.

On this album there are also references, in 'Baywara', to the activities of Dreaming personnel who created the land and the songs through which Dreaming events were to act as the basis of rules for living, and were to be recalled:

> Maker of the land, maker of the song
> Maker of the constitution ...

As on *Homeland Movement*, traditional clan songs on this album are noted as about places and the activities that define them for local Yolngu people.

On *Birrkuta – Wild Honey* (1996) place related songs are not in evidence in the same way that can be found on Yothu Yindi's first three albums. Here a broader place referent issue is broached. In 'Timor', Yothu Yindi liken the struggle of the Timorese for independence from Indonesia to similar struggles by Yolngu, Chechens and West Irianese. However, on Yothu Yindi's fifth album, *One Blood* (1999) there is a return to material that can be read as direct reference to events involving Yolngu in actions to assert their rights to land in the Gove Penninsula of northeast Arnhem Land. This is in the song, 'Written on a Bark', which recalls an important moment in Yolngu history, one which subsequently affected Aboriginal/non-Aboriginal interactions over recognition of Aboriginal rights to land.

The discovery in 1950 of bauxite in the islands off the Yolngu coast, and commencement of mining there in 1954, signalled the beginnings of a period of land-based struggle for Yolngu from the Gove Penninsula. In the early 1960s, mining began to encroach onto land closer to the Yolngu community at Yirrkala; the town of Nulunbuy was established nearby to service the mining industry, and in 1963 Yolngu lands were excised from the Arnhem Land Reserve to allow mining to expand. In August 1963, local reaction to these events coalesced in a petition from the Yolngu at

Yirrkala to the Australian federal parliament. This petition, a typed document stuck onto a bark board and surrounded by Yolngu painted designs, stated that Yolngu country had been appropriated without explanation to the Yolngu, that this decision was taken without their approval, and that Yolngu disapproval had not been properly relayed to the Australian government when this had occured. In the words of the petition, the land in question had been 'hunting and food gathering land for the Yirrkala tribes since time immemorial' (Wells, 1982, 127), and included land sacred to Yolngu. Through this petition, the Yirrkala Yolngu requested that their interests be acknowledged, that a government committee be appointed to 'hear the views of the Yirrkala people before permitting the excision of this land ... [and] that no arrangements be entered into with any company which will destroy the livelihood and independence of the Yirrkala people' (Wells, 1982, 127). In response, later in 1963 the Australian government initiated a report into the Yirrkala situation. Five years later, members of the Yirrkala Yolngu mounted a legal case in the federal court to assert ownership of their country. This was the first Aboriginal land rights case to be pursued in an Australian court (Williams, 1986), and although the Yolngu lost this case, 'they were correct in believing subsequently that the case contributed to the enactment of legislation at the end of 1976 which gave Aborigines title to Aboriginal Reserves in the Northern Territory through the statutory creation of 'Aboriginal land' and enabled Aborigines to claim crown land. That legislation was the *Aboriginal Land Rights (Northern Territory) Act 1976*' (Williams, 1986, 19).

Like 'Luku-Wängawuy Manikay (1788)' and 'Treaty', 'Written on a Bark' relies on Yolngu readings of history to remind us that little changes in non-Aboriginal treatment of Aborigines. In a tone similar to that of 'Treaty', this song makes the point that: 'you mine the land, you turn it to steel, but you still don't have a deal'. In concert with these earlier songs, 'Written on a Bark' contributes to recurring appearance in Yothu Yindi's songs of events through which the Yirrkala Yolngu position on treatment of them in relation to ownership and use of their lands is put forward.

These ideas – ownership of places, links to places, retelling of events at places, mining as the instrument of dispossession – recur on the group's most recent album, *Garma* (2000), in song lyrics such as 'lakes of salt, hills of sand, burning bush, this is our land' and 'gone is the land, to the man in the mine.' Through these continual references to land related topics across their six albums between 1989 and 2000, Yothu Yindi put their position on land as an aspect of Yolngu life and belief, managing alongside the specificity of Yolngu land topics to give a level of pan-Aboriginality to their songs. These songs are a form of history – a Yolngu retelling of events from Yolngu perspectives – and embody a period of Yolngu legal action to have their tenure to land recognised. They provide an example of what Attwood (1996) calls 'the new Australian history', one that challenges non-Aboriginal recounting of events. They do this partly by positioning Yolngu as the centre of discourse, rather than using them as mere attendant figures. In this way, these songs contribute to the reshaping of the narratives through which Australia is defined as an acting out of the contrasting agendas of Aborigines and non-Aborigines as distinct groups of people with differing interests in and understandings of country.

References to Yolngu land

Songs that mention events of Yolngu land ownership related struggles are only one dimension of place as a trope of songs by this group. As we saw in the previous section, at times this can be traced in references to historical events; at other times, place is implicated through references to aspects of the location of Yolngu coastal communities, for example, through the use of water imagery symbolic of lives lived near and at times dependent on rivers and the sea. Further, through Dreaming events and personnel in song topics, there are references to places of importance to Yolngu. A more opaque level at which land exists in the songs of this group is in the practice of Yothu Yindi of indicating the clan origins of material on their albums. To understand how we intrepret songs and albums by Yothu Yindi as statements of territoriality through this, it is necessary to explain elements of Yolngu social organisation and how that organisation acts as a matrix for land ownership and responsibility. Three separate components of Yolngu cosmology require explanation at this point: the Yolngu moiety system; Yolngu clans; and links between clans and land.

Among researchers into Yolngu society and cultures, the significance of a moiety system is regularly discussed (for example, Morphy, 1984, 1991; Williams, 1986; Keen, 1994). As a principle of Aboriginal social organisation, Berndt & Berndt (1987, 44) explain moiety as 'the system of classifying everyone ... and in fact all natural phenonmena in two distinct divisions, or moieties. Moiety simply means half ... this system of dual organisation ... provides a clear cut division for social and ceremonial purposes.' The Yolngu moieties are called *Dhuwa* and *Yirritja*.

Already this fact can be used to illuminate the significance of the name, Yothu Yindi. In Yolngu society, each person belongs to one of the moieties; protocols governing marriage require that a person marry outside her/his moiety – a *Dhuwa* person must marry a *Yirritja* person and vice versa. Moiety descent (the moiety a newborn person inherits) is that of her/his father – Yolngu society is therefore patrilineal. This means that a child and her/his mother will always be of opposite moieties – thus the child–mother relationship reflects the world as a duality expressed through the moieties. This concept is encapsulated in the Yolngu words for child (*yothu*) and mother (*yindi*) when they are combined in the phrase, *yothu yindi*. Synec-dochically, this phrase symbolises the overriding system of the world as the side-by-side existence of a duality: 'the name Yothu Yindi conjures up the idea of balance ... for us, when Yirritja and Dhuwa are working in harmony, the land and its people are one.' (M Yunupingu, in M Yunupingu et al., 1994, 1). When applied to ownership of and responsibility for land, the moiety system causes Dhuwa-owned and Yirritja-owned tracts of land to alternate. If drawn, or shown in a painted design, a chequerboard effect results which maps the moiety system onto the landscape on a quotidian basis. In Watson et al.'s (1989, 37) explanation, 'the most important func-tion of the system is the orderliness it imposes on the relations of individuals and groups to each other, to the land and to all things in the Yolngu world.' Yolngu *Dhuwa* and *Yirritja* moieties, and ways they interact through Yothu Yindi, are discussed by Mandawuy Yunupingu in the following way:

> ... every Dhuwa child has Yirritja mothers and Dhuwa fathers, and every Yirritja child has Dhuwa mothers and Yirritja fathers. Every Yolngu child has responsibilities both to mother's people and places and to father's people and places. Hence every Yolngu person has responsibilities both to Yirritja and Dhuwa. In our band, Yothu Yindi we have a balance between Yirritja and Dhuwa. But we also have another balance, one between black and white, or Yolngu and Balanda. Among the Yirritja members of our band there are both black and white, and among the Dhuwa members of our band there are both black and white (M Yunupingu, in M Yunupingu et al., 1994, 2).

A related concept, through which duality can be seen in other applications, is the Yolngu ideology of *ganma*. Through water-based imagery, Mandawuy Yunupingu explains *ganma* as:

> the talk of *ganma* brings another image to my mind. A deep pool of brackish water, fresh water and salt water mixed. The pool is a balance between two natural patterns, the pattern of the tidal flow, salt water moving in through the mangrove channels, and the pattern of the fresh water streams varying in their flow across the wet and dry seasons ... for us the sight and smell of brackish water expresses a profound foundation of useful knowledge – balance. For Yolngu Aboriginal people brackish water is a source of inspiration. In each of the sources of flowing water there is ebb and flow. The deep pool of bracksh water is a complex dynamic balance ... Ganma is metaphor ... Ganma is social theory. It is our traditional profound and detailed model of how what Europeans call 'society' works (M Yunupingu, in *M Yunupingu* et al., 1994, 8–9).

Balance, or *ganma*, between different types of expression and sets of ideas can be heard throughout the songs of Yothu Yindi. Their albums mix songs in traditional style with rock songs. Sometimes these mixtures are between contiguous songs, at other times the two genres are mixed within a song. Specifically, they sing and adapt *djatpangarri*, a genre of Yolngu song noted by Moyle (1974) in her northeast Arnhem Land fieldwork where she shows *djatpangarri* as a regional category of song. Yothu Yindi make their use of this genre explicit on *Tribal Voice* through the album's dedication: 'This album is dedicated to the following masters of *djatpangarri*, popular Yolngu song – Balun Yunupingu, Dhambutjawa Burrwanga and Rirkin Burarrwanga.' (*Tribal Voice*, album notes). Balance appears in the way songs counterpose topics that deal with events of the Dreaming, the more recent Yolngu past and the current situations of Yolngu life. Songs with clan specificity address both Dhuwa and Yirritja moieties. Languages in song lyrics alternate between Gumatj and English – between songs and within songs. The sounds of *yidaki* (didjeridu) and *bilma* (clapsticks) integrate with those of electric guitars, keyboard and drumkit.

The element which combines these aspects of Yolngu social organisation to make Yothu Yindi's songs and albums statements of the Yolngu system of land tenure, thus to function as notification of Yolngu land ideology, is the way in which clan membership relates to land ownership.

This is an aspect of Yolngu society explained by various writers, among them Morphy (1984, 1991), Williams (1986) and Keen (1994). The description of the system that follows is based on that of Morphy (1984) and Williams (1986).

The main form of Yolngu social organisation is the clan. Each clan speaks a dialect of Yolngu, although 'differences between some of the clan dialects are minimal' (Morphy, 1984, 5). Each clan owns lands; associated cultural artefacts, such as songs, 'belong' to each area of land. To perform these is an indication of clan, and following that, by implication, of the land a clan owns and the people involved. As songs and dances retell events through which the land was created and shaped, they can be place specific. Williams (1986, 1) defines the Yolngu clan/land system as a 'jural structure for Yolngu relations to land', indicating its legal nature. She further notes that 'this system continues to govern Yolngu relations to land. The Yolngu have not yet expressed any desire to alter the system ... whenever changes have been imposed by external agents, the Yolngu have attempted to deal with them in terms of their own law' (Williams, 1986, 19). She goes on to explain how the system is a reification of 'sacred endowment':

> ... during the mythic past spirit-beings bestowed land on the first ancestors; rights to land now inhere in their living descendants who expect the right to continue in future generations ... The rights inhere in groups that Yolngu define and symbolise in a number of ways ... but which they define primarily ... in terms that we call kinship ... the rights [to land] include those of ownership, occupation, and use (Williams, 1986, 20).

The high levels of indication of clan sources for songs by Yothu Yindi make points about Yolngu lands. Naming a clan indicates a group of people and their clan estates. Mention of a clan name references the clan system, calling up ways in which the system attests continuity of land ownership since the ancestral past. Referring to the Yolngu clan system brings into play Yolngu ways of conceptualising, dividing up and naming people and country through reference to Dreaming creation activity and its resultant topographical features, such as rivers, swamps and hills. That this differs from non-Yolngu ways of understanding country and governing its use is an added implication of the system, especially when songs that speak out against the mining of Yolngu lands are considered.

Mandawuy Yunupingu provides a succinct way of explaining the relationships between Yolngu, the past, kinship and land: 'Yolngu people relate to
one another in the kinship terms that were laid down by our ancestors in
the beginning and which are embedded in the land itself' (M Yunupingu,
1996, 3). Naming the clans who own songs, therefore, carries with it
implications for calling up Yolngu land tenure and the history of fights
over it. One song in particular makes its point through a listing of the
names of Yolngu clans – 'Tribal Voice', the title track of Yothu Yindi's
second album, an album already noted for its multiple mediations of
Yolngu references to country. In this song the summons, 'you better listen
to your tribal voice', is followed by listing of Yolngu 'tribes' and 'voices':

> You better listen to your *gumatj* voice
> You better listen to your *rirratjingu* voice
> You better listen to your *wangurri* voice ...

Yothu Yindi are not unique in the way their songs can be compre-
hended through explanation of aspects of Yolngu social organisation, the
inclusion within songs and on albums of continuing song traditions, and
the unravelling of clues, in the form of the names of clans and moieties,
to possible meanings. In his analysis of songs and albums by Top End
band Letterstick, Corn (2002) discusses how this group's contemporary
songs, like those of Yothu Yindi, reflect genres of local, continuing traditions of song. He demonstrates that this group's 'Bartpa', a song 'deriva-
tive of mainstream popular musics' (Corn, 2002, 80), in fact 'possesses
formal elements that are structurally and aesthetically characteristic of
the northeast Arnhem Land *manakay* genre' (Corn, 2002, 86). Similarly
he shows how 'An-Barra Clan', the title track of Letterstick's first album,
utilises musical elements of *borrk* in a reggae setting. *Borrk* (also *kunbork*)
is discussed by A Moyle (spelt *gunborg*), and is shown in her regionalisation of song styles as belonging to the northwest Arnhem Land region
(A Moyle, 1974). Summarising his interpretation of this group's musical
aesthetic stance, and also the stylistic languages of other contemporary
Arnhem Land bands, Corn notes the 'concrete influence of local song
genres' on musicians from this region, also stating that through such
strategies 'musicians from Arnhem Land ... deliberately imbue their
popular-song repertoires with traditional meanings and materials' (Corn,
2002, 77).

Corn links these musical strategies of referencing continuing traditions of genres of local song to ideologies through which the expression of personal and group relationships to land are made: 'much of Letterstick Band's repertoire is steeped in the conceptual frameworks of local kinship and beliefs that inform its members' hereditary ownership of estates' (Corn, 2002, 81). He also provides clues to how the name 'An-Barra' exemplifies a music/place/people nexus which we position as traceable in contemporary songs by other Top End groups. As Corn (2002, 81) explains, *An-barra* can be translated from Burrara as 'mouth of the river'; An-Barra estates are at the mouth of the Blyth River. The term refers to a type of place, the lands of a named clan, and the clan itself. 'An-Barra Clan' is the title of a song – a song which utilises a *borrk* melody, invoking implications of a regionally defined song style – and of an album. The simultaneous use of the term *An-barra* in a number of different but related senses produces a complex of ideas stemming from and deriving meaning from a place specific concept at the same time that a specific place is recalled in song. As discussed in relation to Yothu Yindi's listing of clan names in songs and in explanatory notes about songs, naming a clan intertextually references other factors a clan name summons up – its members, its language and its sites.

Conclusion

In this chapter we have presented ways that we hear music from the Top End acting to reveal some of the richness of Aboriginal cultures from that region. That these cultures are based on worldviews in which land figures as the prominent element imbues Top End contemporary Aboriginal music with a continual pivotal theme – even if at times this theme is not always overt. While examples of songs about land hand-back and redress of government and industry appropriation of country, such as appear nationally, are heard in this region, mediation of land-based cosmology through references to aspects of social organisation in songs from the Top End define contemporary Aboriginal music from this region in ways not always observable to the same extent in other parts of Australia. The at times explicit utilisation of music genres originating in earlier periods, as could be observed in Letterstick's adaptations of *borrk* and *manakay* and Yothi Yindi's recording and rearrangement of *djatpangarri*, acts to reinforce in sound the ideology of stating Top End Aboriginal cultures and through that statement avowing their vibrancy and continuation.

Like Yothu Yindi, Letterstick Band sing about
contemporary lives that rely on Aboriginal
perspectives of country. (Courtesy: CAAMA)

CHAPTER 9

Nitmiluk! – place and post-colonialism

The word '*Nitmiluk*' signifies a series of spectacular gorges and chasms stretching for 12 kilometres down the Katherine River in Australia's Northern Territory, to the north of the town of Katherine. On official, non-Aboriginal maps, this site is shown as Katherine Gorge. As a symbolic feature in the natural landscape, Nitmiluk reflects divergent histories of conquest and colonialism, and more recently, Indigenous rights struggles. For the Jawoyn people, traditional owners of Nitmiluk, it forms a nexus of cultural and spiritual practices central to political strategies towards self-determination and economic independence from Australian governments. The traditional country of the Jawoyn surrounds the series of sites known as Nitmiluk, covering a vast expanse of what is now known as the Top End of the Northern Territory. As the Jawoyn develop models of community management for their lands, the sites delineated by tribal boundaries have become known collectively as the Jawoyn Nation.

In this chapter, as in chapter 5, we provide a close reading of one song, in this case 'Nitmiluk!' by Top End group, Blekbala Mujik. Our discussion of this song focuses on Nitmiluk as a physical location central to the process of an Indigenous (re)construction of post-colonial space. This involves discussing Nitmiluk as a complex site of cultural and political discourse. First, we outline the project to reclaim and reinscribe Aboriginal spaces after colonial experiences of appropriation and contempt, as read through the expressions of Indigenous musical recordings – in particular the text of Blekbala Mujik's song. Second, we examine how this cultural discourse has been used by a Jawoyn representative organisation to assert its own presence in the Katherine region of the Northern Territory and to resolve competing Indigenous and non-Indigenous interests. In this sense, we point to the importance of popular music as mediator of geographical and political conflict, and as an accessible tool of education, communication and identity construction.

Nitmiluk – creation and colonialism

Nitmiluk continues to be central to Jawoyn tradition and law. Jawoyn sovereignty has governed over country through complex and holistic systems of responsibility and social organisation for at least an estimated 50 000 years. In Jawoyn mythology, creation beings including the *Bolong* (Rainbow Serpent) and *Barraya* (Kookaburra) have continuously occupied the gorges that make up Nitmiluk, inscribing the country with physical features, social responsibilities and cultural meaning since the *Burr* period (roughly translated as 'the Dreaming'). Jawoyn naming of the gorge is attributed to a particular *Burr*-figure, Nabilil, who 'camped at the entrance to the Katherine Gorge where he heard the song of the cicada [*Nitmi* in Jawoyn language] and called this place Nitmiluk' (Jawoyn Association, 1993a, 5). Traditional songs and dances that communicate these stories continue to be practised as part of Jawoyn oral culture as exercises in naming and owning. More recently, the musical practice of naming and owning a site in a song has resurfaced in Aboriginal rock music. Blekbala Mujik's 'Nitmiluk' can be interpreted in this way.

The spectacular geomorphological features of Nitmiluk did not escape the colonising gaze of non-Indigenous settlers and authorities. The expansion of pastoral and mining activities in the late nineteenth century had tragic consequences for Aboriginal groups throughout the Northern Territory, including the Jawoyn. Jawoyn indigenous sovereignty over country was disregarded in the often violent process of asserting European sovereignty over land. Jawoyn people no longer had free access and mobility over their country, pastoral stock polluted water sources, and traditional lands became populated by strangers. Jawoyn people were, by the turn of the century, 'experiencing the violence and culture shock of colonisation' (Jawoyn Association, 1993a, 9).

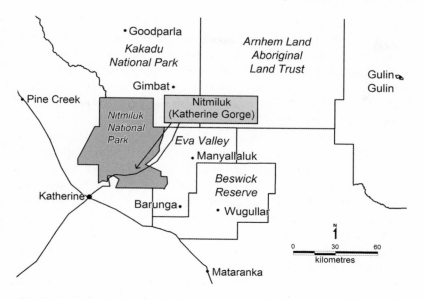

Nitmiluk is a physical landscape with a number of layered meanings. At one level, it is a Jawoyn site of deep spiritual significance. At another, it is a major tourist destination. It is surrounded by national park, and other important sites, including Barunga, home to a popular music and sports festival, and Eva Valley, where a statement on post-Mabo reconciliation was forged between Aboriginal leaders from across Australia. (Map: Chris Gibson)

Colonial histories by non-Indigenous writers as recently as the 1980s reflect the denial of the Jawoyn and other local Indigenous voices (such as the Wardaman and Warlpiri), mapping physical sites without Aboriginal referents, for the purpose of legitimising non-Aboriginal rule. According to Forrest (1985, 6), for example, 'the survey, construction, and operation of the telegraph line *brought people* to the Territory. Alfred Giles, pioneer of Springvale, *was one of the first*' (emphasis added). The conspicuous exclusion of Indigenous peoples from these narratives, and absence of Aboriginal places on maps, stems from the naming practices of frontier settlers and planners. Sites such as Nitmiluk and Wurliwurliyn-jang (now covered by the Katherine Town Council chambers) were overwritten with European names. This colonial strategy demonstrates the centrality of naming and mapping to acts of disposses-sion, furthering the doctrine of *terra nullius* (empty land) through which British sovereignty over Australia was enacted. In effect, Australian landscapes were 'emptied' of competing indigenous meanings (Harley, 1988; Huggan, 1989; Ferrier, 1990; Jacobs, 1993).

Nitmiluk has been central to attempts by Aboriginal people to reclaim these colonised spaces within wider Australian arenas (both cul-tural and legal). This includes the role Nitmiluk has played in strategies to reclaim land tenure within Australian land rights mechanisms (the Jawoyn [Katherine Area] Land Claim); formal projects to develop Indige-nous employment and training opportunities (through the Jawoyn Asso-ciation); and its symbolic role within cultural expressions of local artists and performers, notably musicians such as Blekbala Mujik. In this con-text, popular music forms a site of expression and empowerment which intersects with wider Australian institutions, polities and audiences in complex ways. Perhaps more effectively than formal political avenues, Aboriginal musicians are able to promote mainstream engagement with themes of Aboriginality and sovereignty. As Blekbala Mujik's principal singer-songwriter Apaak Jupurrula argued:

> Music is perhaps one of the few positive ways to communicate a message to the wider community. Take, for example, politicians. They address an issue but people will only listen if they share those partic-ular political views. Music has universal appeal. Even if you have your critics, people will still give you a hearing (in McCabe, 1995).

Accordingly, the expressions enabled through music remain sensitive to shifts in government policy and the wider atmosphere of Australian race relations. In this sense, music becomes a means for understanding issues of social and political change. As demonstrated in a range of recent writings on the subject, music not only reflects political and cultural shifts, but is also bound up in the processes through which these shifts occur and in the ways in which communities perceive and understand place (Lipsitz, 1994; Leyshon et al., 1995; Kong, 1995; Feld & Basso, 1996). Indigenous organ-isations such as the Jawoyn Association continue to provide challenges to the nation-state with demands for new, fluid spaces of co-existence, such as

Blekbala Mujik performed at the hand-back
ceremony for Nitmiluk in 1989. Behind the band
is a banner celebrating the event, and depicting
Bolong, using the same artwork as the cassette
cover for Nitmiluk.

on National Park land and pastoral lease-holdings. As this occurs, Indigenous popular musicians are becoming increasingly important as mediators in the national 'mediascape', writing and singing about 'Aboriginal methods for melding the disparate worlds of Aboriginal and non-Aboriginal Australians' (Neuenfeldt 1993b, 1). The sociopolitical concerns of these songwriters and performers are articulated in ways that symbolically reclaim space, inscribe interpretations of Indigeneity upon a popular cultural landscape, and delineate material empowerment strategies.

The song 'Nitmiluk' was first performed in public on 10 September 1989, at the hand-back ceremony of the site to its traditional owners as a commemoration of the Jawoyn's successful land rights claim. By examining 'Nitmiluk' as a musical text, we can begin to understand how an Indigenous rock group has transferred traditional Aboriginal ways of expressing history (that is, orally, through song) into a contemporary music genre. In this way, Blekbala Mujik mobilised diverse strategies to signify, re-map, and gain influence over, traditional country.

Blekbala Mujik's 'Nitmiluk'

In a similar manner to that employed by other Aboriginal rock groups, Blekbala Mujik combine elements of traditional and contemporary musical styles, incorporate multilingualism in the texts of their songs, and consciously use pre-contact music to raise awareness about Aboriginal cultures. As Apaak Jupurrula stated: 'We enjoy different feels, different genres ... What I do as a songwriter is base new works around what we already have in the way of traditional music. I tend to build around that and we come up with new ideas ... we want to provide some kind of information to the audience that we are strong within our cultural beliefs, that we still maintain our traditional ideology and understanding of a world view, and we would like to share that with the public' (in Smith, 1996a, np).

Writing of the song involved a particular set of cultural practices in the build-up to the hand-back of Nitmiluk to its owners. Accompanied by senior Jawoyn elders, members of the group camped in the area for two weeks, learning about the role of Nitmiluk in local law/lore. At a crucial point in this process, the song emerged, in ways resonant with the creative processes apparent in music considered 'traditional' (Ellis, 1985). As explained by Apaak Jupurrula: 'We slept on that earth and it protected us. Our lifestyle revolved around that place and old people came telling us of

Cassette cover for *Nitmiluk!* (Courtesy: CAAMA Music)

its importance. One night we were strumming around the camp fire and the song and words came from the wind into our collective mind' (CAAMA, nd.b, 2). As this suggests, there is more to the song than commemoration of the hand-back of land to its owners, as a study of the musical and textual profiles of this song reveals. In the reading presented here, the song is interpreted through references to country and identity, and linked to this, agendas of Jawoyn cultural revival and self-determination.

Recognition for Blekbala Mujik (Kriol for 'blackfella music') has come from a number of sources, including the 1996 Deadly Sounds Album of the Year, nomination for an Australian Record Industry Association (ARIA) award, extensive touring within Australia and internationally, and the use of their song 'Walking Together' as the signature tune of the Australian Council for Aboriginal Reconciliation. To date, this group has issued five albums: *Nitmiluk!* (1990), *Midnait Mujik* (1990), *Come-n-Dance* (1993), the self-titled *Blekbala Mujik* (1995), and *Walking Together* (1995). These releases have received wide critical acclaim. They have been variously described as 'an exuberant concoction' (Eliezer, 1996); 'catchy, airplay friendly Aboriginal pop'; 'decidedly deadly Arnhem grooves' (Jordan, 1995, 90); while the group has 'musical sophistication, diversity and innovation which pushes them beyond the usual recipes of Aboriginal reggae, Aboriginal country and Aboriginal rock' (Elder, 1995, np).

The songs on these albums address topics pertinent both to aspects of Australian pan-Aboriginality and to local communities of the Jawoyn speaking area. In its music and text, 'Nitmiluk' reflects this ability to signify on different levels, exhibiting characteristics common to the music of numerous Aboriginal rock groups across Australia, as well as some specific to Jawoyn culture. It is through the second of these contexts, music that can be understood as Jawoyn, that the role of a rock song as an expression of current agendas and activities of cultural revival can be interpreted.

'Nitmiluk' employs the integration of two types of music in an overall three-part structure: an opening traditional section of west Arnhem Land song with didjeridu and clapsticks accompaniment gives way to a rock section, performed with electrified guitars and drumkit. This rock section is followed by the return of the opening traditional section. The traditional sections of 'Nitmiluk' can be identified as 'White Cockatoo' by the appearance of that song as the track immediately preceding 'Nitmiluk' on the album *Nitmiluk!* The readily identifiable musical differences between traditional and rock sections of the song are further delineated by the use of different languages for each: the traditional sections are sung in a local Aboriginal language, the rock section in English.

This diachronic use of two styles of music, a feature of recordings by other Top End Aboriginal rock groups such as Sunrize Band and Yothu Yindi, occurs alongside a synchronic use when the descending melody of the framing traditional sections is heard as the basis of the melody of the rock section. In common with a large proportion of Aboriginal rock music, 'Nitmiluk' relies heavily on a country and western feel, especially in its use of a repeated guitar lick as a 'break' between vocal sections of the song.

A further characteristic of 'Nitmiluk' found in much Aboriginal rock music is the inclusion in its inner rock section of didjeridu and clapsticks as members of the rock group line-up. Both are integrated into the rhythmic profile of the song through a one-bar repeated pattern that constitutes the basis of the song's accompaniment. Two didjeridu playing styles can be identified in 'Nitmiluk'. In the opening and closing traditional sections, the didjeridu provides a rhythmic drone. This is the playing style identified by researchers as that found in west Arnhem Land traditional music – one that only employs the instrument's fundamental pitch. This is in contrast to that heard in the traditional music of east Arnhem Land, where in addition to the instrument's fundamental sound, hooted upper partials and unpitched 'spats' are used (A Moyle, 1974; 1978; Stubington, 1979). In the rock sections of 'Nitmiluk', it is the upper partial that is used in rhythmic interplay with the drumkit. Through this, 'Nitmiluk' demonstrates that despite Blekbala Mujik's west Arnhem Land origins, the distinction between west and east Arnhem Land traditional playing styles does not adhere in contemporary uses of the instrument. In this analysis, uses of the didjeridu in 'Nitmiluk' refer both to specific Jawoyn musical cultures and to contemporary, national Aboriginal ones.

These four aspects of 'Nitmiluk' (presence and integration of traditional and rock styles; multilingualism; influence of country music style; and use of clapsticks and didjeridu as rock instruments) are also found in songs by numerous Aboriginal rock groups across Australia. These may be responsible for giving the song an Aboriginal 'feel' – a pan-Aboriginality that assists in creating relevance for listeners from other Aboriginal cultures, and increasingly, wider non-Aboriginal audiences. A fifth aspect of the song, its topic, is also one used by many Aboriginal rock groups, but it is here that more specific references to Jawoyn culture are made.

'Nitmiluk' as map of Jawoyn country

The song topics used by Blekbala Mujik favour issues significant to Abo-riginal communities: Aboriginal life ('Blackman's School'), invitations to understand and enjoy Aboriginal cultures ('Come-n-dance with Blekbala Mujik', 'Walking Together'), the problems of alcohol abuse ('Drangkin-bala'), references to Dreamtime personalities ('Dreamtime Dancer'), local events ('Barunga Festival'), the disastrous effects of British nuclear testing on Aboriginal lands ('Ngukliya Fiya'), and celebrations of place ('Kakadu', 'Nitmiluk', 'Uluru'). Including a song about a place on an Abo-riginal rock album is common among many Aboriginal rock groups and can be heard on recordings by groups such as Amunda, Kulumindini Band, Mixed Relations, North Tanami Band, Sunrize Band, Western Desert Band, Warumpi Band, Wedgetail Eagle Band and Yartulu Yartulu Band. Although based around a place, such songs can have dif-ferent purposes. Some celebrate sites, others express longing for a lost site, describe a tract of land, call for the restitution of country to Aborig-inal people, or, as in this case, commemorate the return of country to its owners.

Analysis of the ideas presented in 'Nitmiluk' demonstrates how ele-ments of place, history, language and ownership are linked in a musical statement about a site, acting as a signifier of identity and the implica-tions of that identity in current policies of Jawoyn cultural revival. It should also be borne in mind that *singing about a place* is *singing a place*. By performing a song about a place, the events of the past, through which that place came into being, are re-created in the present; through the performance of an Aboriginal rock song about a place, that place is in a state of continual (re)creation. Here, 'Nitmiluk' connotes the coming into existence of Nitmiluk, at the same time that it references the gorge's more recent past of dispossession and reclamation. In this way, the song not only writes a Jawoyn *Burr* history, it refers to colonial attitudes and activities in relation to Jawoyn country. Levels of past and present on which the song relies can be read into the song, not only through these textual references but also in the song's use of distinct musical styles, while the dependence of the present and the past on each other can be heard in the ways that musical styles interact with each other throughout the song.

The text of the rock section of 'Nitmiluk' is:

Verse 1

In the beginning
There was nothing on this land
An echo came from the past
Gandayala breathed the fire of life   [*Burr* figure]
Whistling sounds were heard
Bolong made the waters flow   [*Burr* figure]
In the distance land formations stirred
It turned into life

Chorus

Nitmiluk! Nitmiluk!
You're the father of the land
Break the chains and help to set me free
Nitmiluk! Nitmiluk!
You're there for one and all for one
We honour you – we depart in harmony

Verse 2

Mungana's taken you   [Ab. Eng. = white man]
There was nothin' we could do
A fight took place in court
It seemed that we had won
The *bunggul's* been revived   [trad. song and dance]
People praise your mighty name
A jury gave the answer
You're free for everyone

Chorus

Nitmiluk! Nitmiluk! ...

Verse 3

Forgive the white man
They're our brothers and our sisters
Let's join hands together
Share one earth forever
Teach the young our culture
Be happy and be peaceful
This land's for you
This land's for me
Take pride, it is yours, it is ours

Chorus

Nitmiluk! Nitmiluk! ...

The three verses present a storyline which involves the creation of Nitmiluk; dispossession; land rights claim/court action; return of country and cultural revival; followed by hopes for the future. The specific events/factors of this storyline are the elements that combine to create the nexus of associations through which land ownership and identity are expressed. These elements, their exemplifications and locations within 'Nitmiluk' are listed in the following table.

Thematic elements in 'Nitmiluk'

Element	Example	Location in song
Aboriginal language	White Cockatoo	traditional sections
location	Nitmiluk	chorus
Burr beings	*Gandalaya*	v1
	Bolong	v1
past	history of site	v1
	dispossession	v2
	land claim	v3
present	return of land (1989)/ownership	end v2
	position of land in reconciliation	v3

The generalised themes of local Aboriginal identity and attachments to land which pervade Blekbala Mujik's 'Nitmiluk' also signify another field of Aboriginal politics – Jawoyn strategies to 'rebuild the Jawoyn Nation', formulated by traditional owners and their own representative, non-government organisation, the Jawoyn Association (Jawoyn Association, 1994a). These have been enacted through land use agreements and negotiated sovereignties based on the recognition of Jawoyn native title rights over traditional lands. In this sense, the song contributes to inscription of Nitmiluk as a physical space of profound importance, mythologising its position at the cutting edge of Aboriginal struggles for their lands.

The Jawoyn land claim for Nitmiluk

The significance of the song 'Nitmiluk' must be appreciated in the context of Indigenous land rights struggles in Australia that accelerated

during the 1970s with the growth of pan-Aboriginal political consciousness and the drive for formal recognition of Indigenous rights to self-
determination. Under land rights legislation passed by the Commonwealth
Government in 1976 in respect to the Northern Territory, Jawoyn tradi-
tional owners submitted, on 31 March 1978, the *Katherine Area Land
Claim* over a wide stretch of their homelands, including Nitmiluk.
Despite the stated intentions of traditional owners not to exclude non-
Jawoyn people's access to Nitmiluk in the event of a successful land
hand-back (recognising its importance as a tourist drawcard for the
Katherine region), the *Katherine Area Land Claim* met with fierce oppo-
sition from local non-Indigenous people (Jawoyn Association, 1993a).
The amplification of intense racism, fears of separatism and exclusion in
the non-Aboriginal community, particularly in the township of
Katherine, was no doubt exacerbated by the lengthy process of delibera-
tion on the claim (initial hearings were not held with the Aboriginal
Land Commissioner until 1983–84).

During this time, opposition to the claim was articulated through both
formal and informal means. The incumbent Northern Territory Government actively opposed the claim, supporting the funding of oppositional
challenges in the court of the Aboriginal Land Commissioner, while the
then speaker of the Northern Territory Legislative Assembly led a street
rally against land rights (Northern Territory Government, 1989; Jawoyn
Association, 1993b). Katherine Town Council attempted to reinvoke
nineteenth-century colonial cartographic strategies in order to halt the
claims process. In response to the claim, the town's official boundaries
were expanded to increase its official area from 33 square kilometres to
nearly 4700 square kilometres, incorporating Nitmiluk into town council
jurisdiction, and potentially nullifying indigenous land rights. Once again,
the map was employed as a device to legitimise and exclude. This act of
twentieth-century colonialism was rejected by the Aboriginal Land Commissioner in his final report on the Jawoyn (Katherine Area) Land Claim,
as an unnecessary expansion of the town's boundaries given all projections of growth in the foreseeable future (Kearney, 1987, 51).

Many local non-Aboriginal residents deployed their own racist strategies, including the formation of anti-land rights lobby groups such as
'Rights for Whites', and the adornment of suburban front gardens with
mocking 'sacred sites' signs (Crough, 1993). While opposition to the

claim was generally not violent, at one stage shots were fired by an oppo-
nent of the Jawoyn claim over the head of a senior elder implicated in the
hearings (Jawoyn Association, 1993b). A survey of local residents in
1983, conducted by the Katherine Town Council, captures the extent of
the sensitivity surrounding the Katherine Area Land Claim at the time.
Over 60 per cent of local respondents voiced opposition to the potential
for Jawoyn ownership of Nitmiluk, citing arguments such as 'Aboriginal's [sic] claims not necessary – they have enough land already'; 'country –
especially National Park, is for everybody – land shouldn't belong to one
section of the community'; and 'whites had to pay for land – so should
Aborigines' (Katherine Town Council, 1983, 36–38). These comments
demonstrate not only non-Aboriginal misunderstanding of the continuing practical sovereignty being exercised by Jawoyn (even if not legally
recognised), but also the extent to which Jawoyn intentions to keep
access to Nitmiluk open after a successful claim were ignored. Many non-
Aboriginal locals seemed incapable of accepting that Jawoyn rights to
country stemmed from cultural practices established millennia prior to
European colonisation and the imposition of market-based systems of
property ownership. Consequently, the conflict surrounding the site of
Nitmiluk was emblematic of wider political struggles and debates concerning the rights of indigenous peoples in the Australian polity.

The hearings for the Jawoyn land claim were protracted, the final Land
Commissioner's report, recommending the return of Nitmiluk to traditional owners, not being released until 1988. Even then, less than half of
the original area claimed (approximately 5000 square kilometres), was recommended for hand-back to Jawoyn owners (Jawoyn Association, 1994a).
However, the 2032 square kilometres to be handed back did include Nitmiluk and surrounding areas, allowing the Jawoyn Association Aboriginal
Corporation (hereafter referred to as 'The Jawoyn Association'), to negotiate with the Northern Territory's Conservation Commission the terms of
a lease-back arrangement and management plan for the site. This would
become a financial and symbolic platform for the development of the
Jawoyn's formal strategies for self-determination and economic independence, captured in the use of the phrase 'Rebuilding the Jawoyn Nation'.

Given this set of circumstances, the performance of the song 'Nitmiluk'
by Blekbala Mujik at the hand-back ceremony on 10 September 1989, sig-
nified much more than an affirmation of Aboriginal cultural identity

and connections to place (which a purely text-based analysis suggests). The themes of sharing country, reconciliation and pride in land in the song reacted to a tangible set of local circumstances, challenging the misinformed narratives of exclusion and economic ruin which dominated opposition to the Jawoyn land claim. The song declared the Jawoyn's intention to rejoice in the return of traditional lands, while retaining access for both Aboriginal and non-Aboriginal populations to the National Park. While many of the song's themes could be seen as expressions of pan-Aboriginality, they occupied another layer of meaning for Jawoyn people, given the background of racism and division which preceded the Jawoyn's land rights victory. As Blekbala Mujik sang 'This land's for you/This land's for me/Take pride, it is yours, it is ours', they were simultaneously answering local critics of Aboriginal land rights who appealed to narratives of separatism, and pointing to further directions which Jawoyn empowerment and regional development strategies could take. The performance of the song at the hand-back ceremony for Nitmiluk, under the banner 'Mamgun Mungguy-wun lerr-nyarrang Nitmiluk' ('Sharing our Country'), occurred at a significant moment in indigenous struggles, and at a turning point in local political relations between the Jawoyn and non-Aboriginal residents of the Katherine region.

'Rebuilding the Jawoyn Nation'

Since the hand-back of Nitmiluk, the Jawoyn Association have signed a Nitmiluk Tours joint venture with local tourist operators, providing further community income and securing control over potential employment opportunities for the Jawoyn (Pritchard & Gibson, 1996). Nitmiluk has therefore been (and continues to be) a central part of the Jawoyn's strategies for empowerment and autonomy from government welfare funding.

The most recent developments in Jawoyn politics are the formation of strategies to 'rebuild the Jawoyn Nation', which also capitalise on the tangible gains secured through the hand-back and management of Nitmiluk National Park, and recapture the themes of 'sharing our country' that pervade Blekbala Mujik's recordings. By the use of the term 'Jawoyn Nation', the Association aims to crystallise the broad spectrum of its political claims and its assertions of indigenous rights. The Jawoyn Association has employed the term 'nation' in a multivalent sense, to represent a whole people, a language, and areas of traditional country (Gibson,

1999), and to suggest the rights of the Jawoyn to govern traditional lands, to 'care for country' in a region in which they are greatly outnumbered by both the non-Aboriginal population and the diversity of other Aboriginal groups who have been dispossessed from their country further afield. It represents the attempt of the Jawoyn to assert their distinct status as indigenous guardians over much of the region. The term 'Jawoyn Nation' does not, however, represent Jawoyn claims for a 'separate nationhood' in a Western political sense. The Jawoyn, in line with principles to 'share our country', suggest a concept of sovereignty which recognises their indigenous rights to negotiation and decision-making, without implying a parallel monolithic and monopolistic sense of land ownership as that entrenched in Western, capitalist forms of land tenure (Jawoyn Association, 1994; Patton, 1995). Thus, the Jawoyn are able to assert political strategies for autonomy that avert the implication of long-term secession from the Australian nation-state and the narratives of separatism espoused by local opponents of land rights.

These new concepts of multiple sovereignty and discourses of Indigenous nationhood are suggested throughout Aboriginal popular music recordings, and specifically in Blekbala Mujik's 'Nitmiluk'. The phrase 'Sharing our Country', expressed in the song 'Nitmiluk' and emblazoned across the stage at the hand-back ceremony, refers simultaneously to generalised approaches to reconciliation which apply across Australia and to expression of highly local, specific, and material narratives of nationhood. Regev (1997, 128) argues with regard to popular music that the 'nation' is itself a field of meaning, a contested term, a concept which provides the basis for debates about cultural difference, uniqueness and attachments to territory:

> Local culture becomes, in this regard, a field in which different versions of the 'nation' struggle to gain recognition, legitimacy, dominance – or separation. Each position in the field formulates a version of the nation's history, invents traditions and produces specific artworks that express its different identity. But the idea of 'the nation' dominates and underlies the existence of the field – it is its doxa.

In 'Nitmiluk' such assertions are articulated in ways that suggest the accommodation of these claims within the Australian nation-state. The solution to tensions between the local and the national is one of reconciliation ('This land's for you/This land's for me/Take pride, it is yours, it is ours'), a topic common to Blekbala Mujik's wider repertoire. As Apaak Jupurrula explains:

> The underlying feature ... is about being one, of Australia's people being one, being together in various aspects of what we do, particularly having to live in this part of the world as a collective group, I guess. The concept is actually reconciliation. It's not only a concept that's been emphasized within the political world, but people are beginning to think of it as a very important issue socially as well (in Smith, 1996a).

Thus 'Nitmiluk' utilises symbols of Jawoyn nationhood to assert regional identity, to contextualise Indigenous strategies for empowerment, and to refer to the position of Indigenous Australians within the Australian nation.

Conclusion

The construction of Jawoyn nationhood and the narratives of survival and celebration in the song 'Nitmiluk' represent significant attempts to generate new post-colonial spaces. The Jawoyn Association's political strategies and the song by Blekbala Mujik signify fluid, negotiated approaches to land tenure in areas where separatist agendas are both unrealistic and unwelcome. Themes that resonate throughout these formal political and popular cultural texts involve going beyond the strict individualistic undercurrents of Western land ownership, about reinscribing space with indigenous meaning but not resorting to a non-indigenous discourse of inclusion and exclusion. The song 'Nitmiluk', alongside activities such as the Barunga Sports and Cultural Festival held annually on Jawoyn country, is part of this process of reinscribing Aboriginality on the landscape of the Katherine region. The physical space of Nitmiluk therefore occupies the focal point of various meanings: through music, in formal political strategies of indigenous nationhood, and as a contrast to non-Aboriginal cartographic representations. With Blekbala Mujik's 'Nitmiluk', to sing the song is in many ways to re-sing the place.

Suggested listening

All this Spirit in the Land

Jimmy Chi and Kuckles ▲ *Bran Nue Dae*

Jimmy Chi and Kuckles ▲ *Corrugation Road*

Kerrianne Cox ▲ *Just Wanna Move*

Fitzroy Xpress ▲ *Little Bit Country, Little Bit Rock 'n' Roll*

Pigram Brothers ▲ *Saltwater Country*

Singing up the Country

Walking along the Edge

CHAPTER 10

Mapping the Kimberley – music and regionalism

This chapter considers contemporary Aboriginal music in the Kimberley region, in the northwestern part of the Australian continent. Much of what has been discussed in the music of Blekbala Mujik, Tjapukai Dancers, Warumpi Band and Yothu Yindi in earlier chapters applies here – songs are often about places, appeals are made through them to language speaking communities and their identities, and music is used to voice Aboriginal opinion. What distinguishes Aboriginal contemporary music in the Kimberley from that in other parts of Australia, however, is an underlying sense of regionalism. This is expressed in various ways – through songs and albums, music production companies, festivals, and links to regional political agendas. To show this, we approach Kimberley contemporary Aboriginal music through a number of focal points. First, we place it within the national context to draw out ways in which it aligns with or differs from similar repertoires in other parts of Australia. This is followed by two explanations of music at specific places – charting of the historical dimensions of Aboriginal music in the town of Broome, and the roles of music in the dispute over mining on sacred sites at Noonkanbah in the south Kimberley. An analysis of emergent regional politics and coincidental burgeoning of music activity in the Kimberley concludes the chapter.

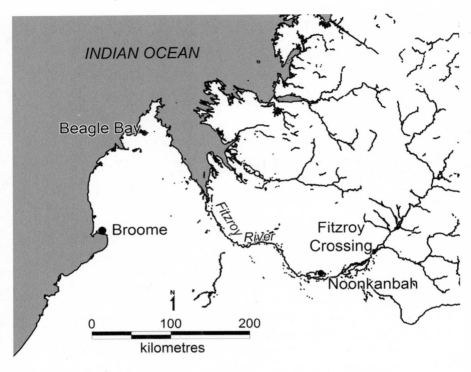

Locations discussed in this chapter.
(Map: Chris Gibson)

Kimberley Aboriginal music

As early as the late 1960s, Alice Moyle identified the Kimberley as a separate area in her survey-style work on Australian Aboriginal music, with
the release of an LP of field recordings from the region in 1968 (see A
Moyle, 1977). The appearance since then of some literature on the music
of the Kimberley (for example, Keogh, 1989, 1990, 1995) and texts such
as *Reading the Country: Introduction to Nomadology* (Benterrak et al.,

1984/1996) contribute to acknowledgment of the musical activity of this region. This includes continuing traditions of music creation and per-formance, high levels of contemporary music production, secure media presence, and support for musicians through radio, TV, recording and uses of information technology.

Taking the recorded repertoire of contemporary Aboriginal music from the Kimberley as a collective object and reading it as part of a national body of Indigenous music, a number of factors correlate between the local and the national. As in Aboriginal music groups across Australia, in the Kimberley musical instruments associated with pre-contact music (in this region, pairs of boomerangs, didjeridu, clapsticks and shell rattles) are integrated into rock groups. In the texts of songs, multilingualism (and implied agendas of reflection of contemporary Abo-riginal life, expressions of identity, sense of community, and language preservation) appears in a number of ways. For example, songs mix Abo-riginal languages with other languages, both at the sectional/verse level where languages alternate, and throughout songs at the individual word level. Stylistically, country music and reggae sounds are popular among Kimberley musicians. As with many Aboriginal music groups, member-ships are often family or community based. Through their names, the lan-guages of their lyrics or the topics of songs, music groups 'represent' communities. Membership between groups is flexible, with musicians appearing not only with their own groups, but also as backing artists on other musicians' recordings. A strong dependence on Aboriginal owned and operated media outlets (for example, Broome Aboriginal Media Association [BAMA]; Goolarri Media), and the support of a limited number of independent recording studios (for example, Moondog Records [Fremantle]; Troppo Studios [Broome]) reflects a similar situa-tion throughout Aboriginal Australia in the ways music is recorded and disseminated. Regular Indigenous controlled and run festivals and song-writing workshops support the music activity of the region.

In the Kimberley, song topics of a political nature align with those found throughout Aboriginal contemporary music as a whole. Songs address the removal of children from their families, the role and influence of the Church in post-contact Aboriginal history, disputes over ownership and custodianship of land, political battles over specific sites earmarked by governments and businesses for industrialisation, issues of health, and the importance of sites to Aboriginal people – as Kimberley singer-songwriter Kerrianne Cox sings in her 'Beagle Bay Dreaming' (on *Just Wanna Move*): 'no matter how far I go, my feet will carry me home ... Beagle Bay dreaming ... ' In relation to this last song topic, due to the large number of songs from the Kimberley about places and the meanings attached to them, it is not difficult to read contemporary Aboriginal music from this region as a composite text on country and Aboriginal relationships to it. This is from a number of perspectives – a pre-colonial one in songs that affirm attachment to sites; in songs created since colonisation, expression of feelings for places at which Aboriginal workers were employed or lived (for example, in the stations of the Kimberley cattle industry), or at ones which have been the locations of confrontation between Aborigines and non-Aborigines. Such a reading based around land constructs this repertoire as an oral text through which past events in the Kimberley can be studied from an Aboriginal perspective. This assists in redressing what John Watson, former chairperson of the Kimberley Land Council, notes as a lack of Aboriginal 'input into books recounting the history of the Kimberley' (in Marshall, 1989, x). As Muecke (1992) notes, a major problem in the recounting of Aboriginal history is authentication of discourse. In our interpretation, songs by Aboriginal musicians are more than recounting of events that the term 'history' often implies. They are also a form of mediation of Aboriginal concerns, and a means through which Aboriginal voices are heard, both literally and figuratively.

Broome

Broome is the major town of the Kimberley. The main venue for tourism in the region, it is also a significant centre of Aboriginal music activity. The location of two recording studios patronised by Indigenous musicians and responsible for much of the dissemination of Aboriginal music from this region (Goolarri Media; Troppo Studios) and support networks such as the Broome Musicians Aboriginal Corporation, home of numerous performing groups, scene of various music festivals, and source of the musicals *Bran Nue Dae* and *Corrugation Road*, it features as the topic of numerous songs and albums (for example, the CDs *Dreaming in Broome* by the Little Piggies, and *Full Moon Over Broome* by Michael Torres).

While the Broome area has links to its Aboriginal pre-contact past as the home of the Bardi people, the town's history sets it apart from other parts of Australia in many ways. Broome was gazetted officially in 1883, although the waters of the area had been the location of pearl shell diving since the 1870s. The pearl shell industry relied on Aboriginal divers and imported Asian divers; this had resulted in the multicultural nature of the town – something which resurfaces in Aboriginal songs from there today. When Little Piggies, a children's rock group from Broome, sing:

> Shuffling on from Chinatown in his squeaky orange cart
> Like a paperboy who's doing his rounds he knows just where to
> start
> Olanji, Olanji, one shilling, one shilling one, hiding in the shade
> from the midday sun
> Mr Chinaman don't turn your back on me, might take your olanji
> for free.

the intermingling of Asian people into Broome's profile is referenced (see Edwards, 1984; Bailey, 2001; Crawford, 2001). Similar multicultural influences appear in other songs from and about the town. For example, the Pigram Brothers use multilingualism representative of the workers in the diving industry in their song 'Saltwater Cowboy' on their 1997 album, *Saltwater Country*:

> Stand back you shallow water man
> Let a deep sea diver through
> *Selamat tingal, nakula jarndu*
> *Sayonara, slo'n', gallow nyundu ...*

By locating Aboriginal music in Broome within a national Aboriginal music context, Lawe Davies (1993b) relies on a local/national paradigm to give meaning to musical activity in the town. His interpretation of Aboriginal music in Broome relies on seeing it historically in three periods. He defines the first of these as the time before the 1980s – during which, due to higher levels of arts funding and increasing acknowledgment of Aboriginal issues in the press and the general national consciousness, 'the 70s in Broome was a highly productive [musical] gestation period ... [and] dozens of bands sprang up doing covers and even writing original material – quite unusual for those times' (Lawe Davies, 1993b, 51–52). Groups from this period include the

Broome Beats (since c. 1971), a reggae group described by Robertson (1983, 26) as playing with a 'Broome sound' and the basis after 1981 of Kuckles; and Cross-fire (founded in the late 1970s), which became Sunburn, and in 1980 metamorphosed into Scrap Metal.

Lawe Davies' second period is the 1980s, which he identifies as one of local development and greater connection between Broome and the rest of Australia through completion of the sealed highway from Perth, the arrival of ABC TV and the beginnings of Lord McAlpine's development of commercial interests in the area. What he fails to mention is the effect of the 1978–1980 nearby Noonkanbah dispute on the town and its music, and the concomitant drawing of the Broome region of the Kimberley into the national consciousness which the dispute engendered.

To Lawe Davies, this is the period of the growth of 'the Broome sound' and he positions Indigenous music there at this time as a reflection of wider acknowledgment of contemporary Aboriginal popular culture, citing the example of Warumpi Band from Papunya (NT) as rising to national notice in the early 1980s. Music activity in Broome in the 1980s includes performances there on tours by Warumpi Band and by Coloured Stone; formation of local groups, Kuckles and Scrap Metal; Kuckles' tour to Germany in 1982 to perform at the Third International Cologne Song Festival (Breen, 1989), and to Perth in 1983 for an Aboriginal Arts Festival; the setting up of the Broome Musicians Aboriginal Corporation; in 1985 the recording of local musicians by the Central Australian Aboriginal Media Association; founding of a new group, Bingurr, from members of Kuckles; and travel by Broome musicians Jimmy Chi, members of Kuckles, and Arnold 'Puddin' ' Smith, to study at the Centre for Aboriginal Studies in Music, in Adelaide.

Lawe Davies predicted that the 1990s would be 'Broome's third musical phase' (Lawe Davies, 1993b, 53), one to be exemplified by national interest in Broome musicians, established record production in the town, and the success of musicians such as Jimmy Chi. Recognition of Broome musicians has flowed from events such as the 1993 appearances of Broome Beats, Bingurr, Kuckles, Local Land, No Name, New Image, and Scrap Metal at the Media and Aboriginal Australia National Conference in Brisbane. The national success of two musicals originating in Broome, *Bran Nue Dae* and *Corrugation Road*, adds to this recognition. Indigenous music production in Broome is readily accessible

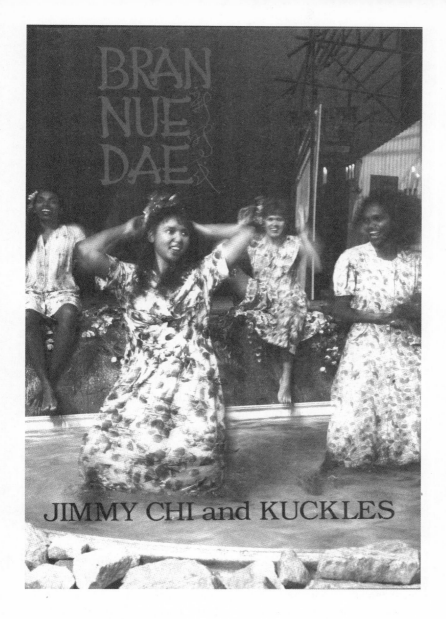

The musical *Bran Nue Dae*, by Jimmy
Chi and Kuckles, toured Australia during the
early 1990s, and helped identify the Kimberley
region as an important location of contemporary Aboriginal music activity.

through the availability of recordings by, among others, John Albert, Kerriane Cox, Kuckles, The Little Piggies, The Pigram Brothers, Scrap Metal, and Michael Torres, and albums of *Bran Nue Dae* and *Corruga-tion Road*. Moreover, Broome's position as the site since 1992 of a series of Stompen Ground Festivals contributes to the town's position on the map of Aboriginal music.

Mining at Noonkanbah

Noonkanbah station, in the south Kimberley, was purchased by the Abo-riginal Land Fund Commission for Nyikina and Walmatjeri people in 1976. Re-ownership of their lands was a significant factor in affirming these groups' identities. They had spent the years from 1971 to 1976 dis-possessed from their traditional country as fringe dwellers in the nearby town of Fitzroy Crossing after walking off Noonkanbah because of poor treatment by its white 'owners' and managers and disputes over pay and conditions. As part of their strategies for reinforcing their own cultures once back on their traditional lands, they established a school on Noonkanbah and funded its teaching positions without government assistance. Learning their Aboriginal languages was considered a central part of this agenda, as when 'our children began to learn the language, they began to belong to the land again' (Dicky Cox in Smith & Plater, 2000, 112). The role of music in this process was also important: 'some of the old men and women sat around the fire singing songs of their country. The children ... hummed along. The sound of loud country music from a cassette player drifted over from one of the camps "We want the children to learn about the old ways ... We teach them the songs and the dances" ' (Smith & Plater, 2000, 112).

Return to their lands on Noonkanbah station was a short-lived period of security of land tenure for its Aboriginal owners. In 1978 Amax Cor-poration, with the assistance of the West Australian government, began mining for oil at a sacred site on the property. This precipitated the Noonkanbah dispute, one in which music played an important role. At least three locally written songs became associated with the dispute: 'Bran Nue Dae' by Broome musician Jimmy Chi; a rock song, 'Noonkanbah Blues' (Breen, 1989, 56); and another song, 'Nguyipinya Marnalunya' ('We hunted them out') by George Manyanji Bell about specific events of the dispute (Hawke & Gallagher, 1989, 214–19).

Broome musicians Jimmy Chi and Steve Pigram commented about music and Noonkanbah in the following ways:

> JIMMY CHI: Noonkanbah was the turning point in people's identi-fication of themselves – they realised you couldn't be half this or half that – you had to make a stand about where you stood and I think it brought out a lot of people to realise that they were no different from any other black fella in Australia ...

> STEVE PIGRAM: in the mid 70s ... I ran into a guy called Jimmy Chi who was starting to write his own music in them days. We started to get together to write original songs, and a lot of the songs that we were writing were about issues that were happening around us ... I guess the first big social issue that was effecting people in the Kimberley here was the Noonkanbah issue where a company called Amax wanted to mine on sacred sites out at Noonkanbah station just north-east [sic] of Broome. A lot of the songs that Jimmy and I were writing then been prompted by them sort of issues that were happening in them days (Bran Nue Dae Productions, 1991).

The contribution of Chi's music to statement of the Aboriginal position over Noonkanbah, and the effect that this also had on other Broome musi-cians as their songs became increasingly politicised, is also commented on in Smith & Plater's biographical text about life in the Broome region:

> Many managed to overcome their fear of conflict and trouble to take part in the protest at the Broome turn-off waiting for the oil rig that was headed for Noonkanbah in mid-1980. A group of the town's musicians performed on the back of a truck. They sang 'Bran Nue Dae', Jimmy Chi's song that had become Broome's anthem. Many had matured in their political thinking. Their songs reflected this, as they gradually added words with a political influ-ence to a mixture of West Indian reggae beat and Aboriginal tra-ditional rhythms, to their repertoire of country and western and rock love songs (Smith & Plater, 2000, 139).

The Noonkanbah dispute lasted for approximately two years, from 1978 to 1980 (see McLeod, 1984; Davey & Dixon, 1987; Kolig, 1987, 1990; Hawke and Gallagher, 1989). Occurring at a time when development of the Argyle diamond mine in the northwest Kimberley region was creating its own confrontations between Aborigines, governments and developers (Dillon, 1991), the Noonkanbah dispute had a musical profile, aspects of which continue to the present day. Apart from the three songs mentioned above, this includes the use by the Noonkanbah mob, and their neighbouring language speaking groups, of corroboree songs and dances in an all-night performance which was unequivocally intended to achieve a number of agendas: to affirm ownership of the Noonkanbah site identified for drilling; at a point in the dispute when the government and miners seemed to be setting the agenda, for the elders of the Noonkanbah mob to reassert control of the situation; to move the dispute onto a different, more spiritual, level than had been prevalent to that point; and to protest about treatment of Aborigines and their relationship to the land through expression of and appeals to Aboriginal Law:

> ... the dancing was for the benefit of the Amax camp. They had no choice but to listen ... Not a word was said to them, hardly a look cast in their direction. But the dancing continued with hardly a pause for more than six hours ... it was a masterly piece of psychological warfare ... by one-thirty [the next day] they [the miners] were gone. The Lawmen had won through (Hawke & Gallagher, 1989, 208–13).

Sometime after the dispute a cassette, *Corroboree: Australian Aborigines of Noonkenbah* (sic), and consisting of songs about Noonkanbah Dreaming sites was released – seemingly as a tribute to the Noonkanbah mob:

> the Aborigines of Noonkenbah [sic] made world headlines in August 1980 when they tried to prevent oil companies drilling on their sacred sites by lying down on the road in front of the rigs, but they were forcibly removed by the police. They consist mainly of Walmatjeri people from the Great Sandy Desert (*Corroboree: Australian Aborigines of Noonkenbah*, album notes).

Twenty years after the dispute, it and the people who fought in it remain both the creators and the topics of songs. This can be heard in 'Tribute to Noonkanbah People', on the album of the same name, 'written by Malcolm

Skinner and Troy Laurel for the twentieth anniversary celebrations of the stand taken by Noonkanbah people to have a say in the protection and use of their homelands' (*Tribute to Noonkanbah People*, album notes).

Commenting on Aboriginal reactions to the Argyle diamond mine in the northeast Kimberley and grouping it with Noonkanbah at a macro-level in Aboriginal struggles over land, Dillon (1991, 149) comments that Kimberley Aborigines 'are yet to fully develop the capacity to define their interests in a broader regional or national sense.' Given Dillon's comment, it is apposite that the Noonkanbah dispute, which brought together Aborigines from approximately thirty communities to protest at the site, is cited in documents of the Kimberley Land Council as seminal to the formation of that body. Since the time of Dillon's text (1991), and propelled by the activities and agendas of the Kimberley Land Council, a definable Aboriginal regionalist ethos has developed in the Kimberley, one which is reflected in music, and in which music plays a role. This provides a third context for investigating Aboriginal music activity in this region.

Music and politics – regionalism and Kimberley music

Reasons for the evolution of an identifiable Aboriginal regional agenda in the Kimberley are various, symbiotic, and not always transparent. However, appeals to the need to present a proactive combined Indigenous front to politicians at both state and federal levels, Indigenous responses to the Mabo and Wik decisions of 1992 and 1996 respectively, a concerted effort by Kimberley Aborigines to preserve culture and relationships to country, and the work of the Kimberley Land Council as the representative body for all Indigenous groups in the area can be cited as contributing factors. Regionalism surfaces as the basis of much Indigenous activity in the area in various documents. For example, the *Report of the Conference on Resource Development and Kimberley Land Control* (usually referred to as the *Crocodile Hole Report*, Kimberley Land Council & Waringarri Resource Centre, 1991) documents the establishment of a regionally based group to represent Kimberley Aboriginal positions on land in negotiations with governments. The conference reported in this publication was a response to research activity by Aboriginal communities in the east Kimberley in the early 1980s and a 1989 report (*Land of Promises*) edited by Dr H C Coombs et al., which analysed Indigenous 'concerns and aspirations ... in relation to development ... While *Land of Promises* focused on the east Kimberley ... it was obvious that the issues identified were applicable across the whole of the Kimberley' (Kimberley Land Council & Waringatti Resource Centre, 1991, 9–10).

The role of the Kimberley Land Council (KLC, founded in 1979) as the driving force in regionalist direction can be seen as a thread in that body's reports. For example, the Introduction to the KLC 1992–1993 annual report states that: 'the Kimberley Land Council grew directly out of the struggle of Aboriginal people to protect their land from mining companies backed by the Western Australian Government. In May 1978 people from more than 30 communities came together at Noonkanbah station in what was then the biggest gathering of Kimberley Aboriginal people in recent history' (Kimberley Land Council, 1993, 3).

The development of Indigenous regionalism is explained in the introductory comments to a report initiated by the KLC in 1991 – *Aboriginal People in the Economy of the Kimberley Region* (Crough & Christophersen, 1993). According to the report's authors, the 1991 Crocodile Hole meeting, a series of documents which impinged on Aboriginal existence in the Kimberley (viz. a 1989 study of Aboriginal contributions to the economy of Central Australia; a 1990 regional report by the West Australian government; the 1991 report into Aboriginal deaths in custody), and the 1992 Mabo decision of the High Court of Australia, are all acknowledged as impetus for this study and as contributing to a sense of regional rather than local community ethos. The report had a number of intentions, but overall its focus was regional, and based on the specific situation of Kimberley Aborigines. For example, in it information was to be 'aggregated on a Kimberley regional basis' (xi); the document itself was to be seen as a response to increasing federal and state government regionalisation of affairs of state; it was intended to redress a lack of consideration of Aboriginal people in government reports and policies; it advocated proactive means of applying results of the Mabo decision to the Kimberley situation; above all it set out to acknowledge and seek acceptance of the level of Aboriginal contribution to the Kimberley economy (Crough & Christophersen, 1993, 1–18 passim). Five years later another initiative of the KLC, a 1998 conference, *The Kimberley: Our Place – Our*

Future was clearly organised with the aim of furthering attention to regional issues by providing 'an opportunity to identify issues of imme-diate and long term concern to the peoples of the Kimberley, faced as we are, by an accelerating pace of change and powerful external forces' (Kimberley Land Council, 1998, Foreword). As Kurijinpi McPhee, Chairman of the KLC at that time stated, 'we want to live together and work together in the Kimberleys – our place' (Kimberley Land Council, 1998, 25).

These documents are not the only sources to put forward an Abo-riginal regional agenda in the Kimberley. Others which reinforce this perspective can be cited. In 'Multilateral agreements: a new accounta-bility in Aboriginal affairs', Peter Yu, one time Chairman of the Kim-berley Land Council, also clearly enunciates the needs and benefits of an Aboriginal Kimberley regional ethos with statements such as: 'regional control of decision making on community infrastructure development, health and education services, land ownership and man-agement, and economic development is essential' (Yu, 1997, 168–69).

In a more anecdotal form, many older Aboriginal people have pre-sented their life stories in publications which collectively present a pic-ture of the Kimberley. These publications, for example, *Raparapa Kularr Martuwarra: Stories from the Fitzroy River Drovers* (Marshall, 1989), *When the Dust Come in Between: Aboriginal Viewpoints in the East Kimberley Prior to 1982* (Shaw, 1992) and *Nyibayarri: Kimberley Tracker* (Bohemia & McGregor, 1995), while restricted to east or west Kimberley contexts, cover the whole region by the fact that stories in them range over the region through travel, work and inter-marriage. Rather than concentrate on individual locales, these books present Aboriginal life in the past from a Kimberley perspective. As noted above, they appeal to another regional aspiration by redressing a lack of Aboriginal contribution to the telling of the region's history.

It is significant that documentation which identifies and puts for-ward a defined regional perspective for the Kimberley dates from the early 1990s and that musically this period is also one in which a forceful Kimberley identity begins to appear in music and associated activity. Stompen Ground (actually the Kimberley Aboriginal Arts and Culture Festival) began in 1992; a three CD set representative of Kim-berley Aboriginal music (*All this Spirit in the Land; Singing up the*

Local festivals and events are important components of the music scene in the Kimberley. While some, such as Stompen Ground, are explicitly Indigenous, others feature Aboriginal performers alongside non-Aboriginal performers.

Country; Walking along the Edge) that presents music associated with 'the Kimberley region [which] is a very special part of the planet' (*Singing up the Country*, album notes) was recorded in 1992/1993; it is in the 1990s that music products from the region – not only Jimmy Chi's two stage musicals *Bran Nue Dae* (1990) and *Corrugation Road* (1996), but an increased recorded output by numerous musicians – have helped define the region through musical output.

Regionalist thinking is also mirrored in other ways in music in the Kimberley. The first of these is in the activities of Goolarri Media/ BAMA, the Broome-based broadcast and production house of the Kimberley member of the National Indigenous Media Association of Australia (NIMAA). Goolarri Media/BAMA works as a regionally based Indigenous broadcast and recording studio. Statements of objectives by Goolarri/BAMA are regional in their ambit and clearly implicate musical expression as a means through which regionalism is addressed:

> Goolarri Media is the operating name of the Broome Aboriginal Media Association. Goolarri's vision is to provide a culturally dynamic and technically efficient environment to stimulate and support the cultural strengths of Aboriginal people in the Kimberley region of Western Australia. Goolarri incorporates facilities for media and multi media production, digital sound recording, events management, performing arts training, and leading edge integrated computer technology (Goolarri Media Enterprises, nd);

> We record music festivals, sports carnivals and other community events throughout the region using crews of community operators ... many hours of local indigenous music have been recorded in this way since 1996 with regular coverage of Nindji Nindji Festivals in Hedland, Derby Moonrise Rock Festivals, Munumburra Festivals in Wyndham, and Stompen Ground in Broome (Goolarri Media Enterprises, 2001 website).

This regionalist identity is reified in the output of Goolarri, as the body behind the running of Stompen Ground and in recordings. The first recording issued through Goolarri is *Didj'un: Singer/Songwriters from*

244 Deadly sounds, deadly places

the Kimberley, which includes a song commissioned for the album, 'Any-
where in the Kimberley (is home sweet home to me)' by Kevin Gunn.
Recordings from other companies also have regionalist themes – CDs of
festivals (*Kimberley Moonrise Rock Festival 2000; Munumburra Songwriters' Festival 1999*), and albums (for example, *Kimberley Country*
by the Benning Brothers Band). Numerous musicians have recorded
songs that address the Kimberley. Typical of these is 'Kimberley born
and bred' by the Young Guns. This song is about 'the big differences
between living in the Kimberley and living in the city. Kimberley people
are proud of who they are and where they come from' (*Munumburra
Songwriters' Festival 1999*, album notes).

The strongest musical sense of region, however, is that presented collectively in the three CD set *All this Spirit in the Land; Singing up the
Country;* and *Walking along the Edge*, mentioned above in relation to
'Milliwindi Rise'. Not only do these CDs include songs about the Kimberley (for example, 'My Place' by Ken Prousse; 'Kimberley Riders' by
Laurie Shaw), they make continual reference to language speaking
communities and specific places. Throughout these CDs, this acts as a
form of accretion to build up a composite expression of the region as a
whole – a map, as it were, inscribed through music.

Conclusion

While exhibiting similarities with contemporary music by Aborigines
from other parts of Australia, that from the Kimberley seems to create
its own regional space. This is achieved through the accretion of references to locations in the Kimberley in song, through recording projects
that focus listeners' attention on regional compilations of music, and
through continual references to places and country in recordings. The
fact that some songs openly praise the Kimberley only adds to this. That
the agendas of musicians and the media networks through which their
music is recorded and released coincide with public calls by prominent
Indigenous personalities for a Kimberley Aboriginal ethos assists in the
sense of a concerted intention to define the Kimberley as a regional
entity, and to use this regionalism as a force against government policy
at state and federal levels. In linking music activity to regional politics,
documentation of bodies such as the Kimberley Land Council have been
significant means for locating agendas. At times the terms in these doc-

uments mirror those of song lyrics, while at others they outline support policies for the role of Indigenous musical expression as cultural mainte-nance and for stressing cultural links to country. These agendas not only address the present, they posit ongoing activity and ways of utilising music and other forms of cultural expression as one medium for future security and self-management.

Suggested listening

Kev Carmody ▲ *Bloodlines*

Lazy Late Boys ▲ *Freedom Day*

Our Home ▲ *Our Land*

Rebel Voices from Black Australia

Red Sunset ▲ *Nangu Songs*

Sunrize Band ▲ *Lunggurrma*

Yothu Yindi ▲ *Homeland Movement*

CHAPTER 11

Reclaiming country

In *World Music – The Rough Guide*, Breen (1994) provides a potted history of contemporary Aboriginal music as it interacts with Australian
post-colonisation history and politics. The theme of his chapter is that
contemporary Aboriginal music is primarily protest music – his glossing
of Martin Luther King's famous 'I have a dream ...' statement in the title
of his chapter, 'I have a Dreamtime', clearly sets the tone for a description
of Aboriginal music as protest and linked to black rights. Land rights are
one of the areas Breen identifies as central to his reading of Aboriginal
popular music, and he positions land as 'the primary issue addressed by
Aboriginal artists' (659). Distinction needs to be be drawn, however,
between types of protest. In some ways, all contemporary Aboriginal
music can be read as protest through its continual reminder of Aboriginal presence, thus of Aboriginal histories and the situations deriving
from them. Far from dominating contemporary Aboriginal music, however, heavy handed protest statements are in the minority. Certainly,
songs calling for the return of land exist. While Coloured Stone's plea
'This land, it belongs to the Aborigine ... please give it back to me' ('This
Land' on *Black Rock from the Red Centre*, 1986), resonates with Sunrize
Band's 'Let's stand up for our land rights, cause it's part of the Dreamtime' ('Land Rights' on *Lunggurrma*, 1993), earlier performers had
broached the subject in other ways. One of these is through statement of

events. This can be seen in the Gus Williams and Country Ebony song, 'A Land he Calls his Own'. Although uncompromising in its intent to be clear that land had been lost, this song functions by recounting the removal of people from their lands and expressing disappointment at treatment of Aboriginal opinion – 'When sacred soil was plundered and the elders made a stand, Their sacred words rejected and thrown in the sand'.

A distinction can be drawn between songs which call for the return of land, and those which raise the issue by stating the events through which it had been lost. Neil Murray, from Warumpi Band, sees a differ-ence in this respect between songs by urban Aboriginal musicians and those by musicians living in or closer to non-urban communities. He explained this as follows:

> groups, like No Fixed Address, are city blacks so their concerns are different from ours. They're very political – land rights and such issues, which we care about but not to the same militant extreme. We don't go about hitting people over the head with it because it isn't our nature to be like that. We do have songs that could be said to be about land rights though they never mention the word at all, they talk about something else (interview, 1988).

Murray's comment that Warumpi Band songs broach the topic of land rights by singing 'about something else' can be seen in songs discussed in this chapter. Here we focus on three land-related events in Aboriginal history and musical responses to them. This would bear out Breen's com-ment above that 'land is the primary issue addressed by Aboriginal artists', but at the same time demonstrate the range of ways this is achieved. The three events for discussion are the Wave Hill strike, the homeland movement, and the Mabo decision of the High Court of Aus-tralia. In the concluding section of the chapter we consider ways in which despite advances in land law guaranteed by the Mabo decision and the subsequent *Native Title Act* of 1993, country continues as a major topic of Aboriginal contemporary music.

The Wave Hill strike

One of the best known songs to emanate from Aboriginal perspectives on country and recounting of specific events in one land-based

Aboriginal/non-Aboriginal confrontation is 'From Little Things Big Things Grow', co-written by Kev Carmody and Paul Kelly. This song tells of the 1966 Wave Hill strike by the Gurindji people, but as its concluding verse indicates is about more than recording one event:

> That was the story of Vincent Lingiari
> But this is the story of something much more
> How power and privilege cannot move a people
> Who know where they stand and stand in their law.

The Gurindji lands are in the northwestern part of the Australian continent in the Victoria River region. Cattle stations owned by non-Aborigines were set up in this area in the late nineteenth century, after which many Gurindji settled and became station workers on one of them, Wave Hill owned by the Vestey family (Horton, 1994). In 1966, 200 Gurindji workers at Wave Hill went on strike over pay and conditions. They were led by (Tommy) Vincent Lingiari and set up camp at one of their traditional sites, Daguragu, known also as Wattie Creek. The next year they unsuccessfully petitioned the governor-general for ownership of their lands for the purpose of establishing their own cattle station. The dispute between the Gurindji, the Vestey family and various government departments continued for twenty years until 1986 when unalienable freehold title to lands in the region were accorded to the Gurindji. This twenty-year period was punctuated with a series of events. In 1968 a government township was set up for the Gurindji at Wave Hill; most Gurindji remained at Wattie Creek. In 1971 the Murramulla Gurindji Company was established to apply for land grants. In 1972, the Prime Minister, William McMahon, allocated money for the purchase of lands – at this point Lord Vestey agreed to allow the Gurindji people 60 square kilometres of land. In 1975, land at Wattie Creek was acquired by the Gurindji, and in the following year a claim was made for adjacent land. In 1981 Gurindji claims to land were recognised by the Aboriginal Land Commission.

In a spoken introduction to a 1970 recording by Galarrwuy Yunupingu, later Chairman of the Northern Land Council, of 'Gurindji Blues', a song by non-Aborigine Ted Egan, the leader of the initial action, Gurindji elder Vincent Lingiari, describes some of the situation surrounding the Wave Hill strike. The appeal to knowledge of land ownership passed to him from earlier generations that resurfaces in many Aboriginal statements of land ownership forms part of this introduction:

> My name Vincent Lingiari, came from Daguragu, Wattie Creek Station ... [speaks in an Aboriginal language] ... . that mean that I came down here to ask all these parliament people about the land right. I got story from my old father or grandpa that land belong to me, belong to Aboriginal man before the horse and cattle come over on that land where I'm sittin' now. Well, that's what I bin keepit on my mind, I still got it on my mind. That's all the word I can tell you.

In the two and a half decades between the Wave Hill strike and the Mabo decision of 1992, country remained a constant theme of the output of Aboriginal musicians. In some songs, this is through a view of Australia being sold from under Aboriginal feet – in songs such as 'Australia for Sale' by Casso and the Axons, and Amunda's 'Ain't Right to Me', where this is linked to cultural loss: 'to sell the land that ain't for sale and watch our culture die'. No Fixed Address stress the longevity of Aboriginal possession of Australia in their '40,000 Years', while Coloured Stone, alongside overt calls for return of land, long for the pre-contact world in 'Take Me Back to the Dreamtime'. Throughout this period, Aboriginal country singers continue to sing about land and its importance to the ways they saw their lives. One album from this period, *Rebel Voices from Black Australia* (released by Imparja/CAAMA in the early 1980s), compiles songs which stress Aboriginal protest positions. Some songs on this album are explicitly about land, but as in the overall repertoire of contemporary Aboriginal song, blatant calls for the return of land are not the primary means through which this album functions, rather it functions through what Neil Murray called 'something else'. What it presents is longing for a former way of life, pride in named places and sadness at the loss of culture that attends the loss of land. This is best summed up in one of its tracks, a musical setting by Les Collins of Oodgeroo Noonuccal's (Kath Walker) poem 'No More Boomerang':

> No more boomerang, no more spear
> Now we all civilised, colour bar and beer.
> No more corroboree, gay dance and din
> Now we got the movies, pay to go in.

Three decades after the Wave Hill strike, it continues to act as the topic of songs, as can be heard on Lazy Late Boys album, *Freedom Day*, which includes numerous references to the Gurindji action of the late 1960s. This album's cover carries the slogan, 'Gurrindji Freedom Day 1966' providing a clue to the album's title; the band's members are listed as from the 'Gurindji mob'; songs on the album specifically address the Wave Hill strike and the ways Gurindji achieved ownership of their lands – 'Daguragu/Wattie Creek' recalls the 1966 walk-off, 'Freedom Day' celebrates Gurindji land rights, and 'Sun Comes Up' commemorates the Wave Hill strike:

> I think of my people
> Who walked off ...
> Back in '66
> Tryin' to find our home.

The Wave Hill strike, and the subsequent successful Gurindji land claim, is one of the signposts of the history of Aboriginal land rights. It can be read as one of a continuing series of land claims, government reports, Acts of Parliament and other official policies affecting Aborigines. Of these, five have significantly influenced the nature of Aboriginal politics and subsequent expressions of Aboriginality as statements of identity and a means of protest. These are the case of *Milirrpum and Others vs Nabalco and the Commonwealth*, 1968–1971; the 1988 Australian Bicentennial; *The Report on the Problems and Needs of Aborigines Living on the New South Wales–Queensland Border* (Toomelah Report, 1988); the Royal Commission into Aboriginal Deaths in Custody (Black Deaths in Custody, 1991); and the case of *Mabo and Others vs State of Queensland* (Mabo decision, 1992). While the last of these, the Mabo decision, acts as a watershed in Indigenous land claims, it also sparked further entrenchment of the attitudes of conservative political parties to Indigenous land claims activity. In the Indigenous popular music industry it became the focus of songs and, in 1995, of a commemorative CAAMA double CD album, *Our Home, Our Land*, covering a range of musical responses to land as an issue of Indigenous identity. However, as songs produced after Mabo demonstrate, the handing down of a decision favourable to Indigenous assertion of land ownership has not been a reason for country to cease as a central topic of contemporary Aboriginal music. Before analysing the contents of *Our Home, Our Land* we explain another land-based musical case study – one which falls between the period of the Wave Hill strike and the 1992 Mabo decision and which is reflected in songs on Yothu Yindi's first album.

The homeland movement

The homeland movement (or outstation movement) was an Aboriginal initiated and government sanctioned return to traditional lands. In the late nineteenth and early twentieth centuries, among many other ways they were dispossessed of their lands, groups of Aborigines were moved onto church missions or were taken on as workers on cattle stations. For many, this involved movement away from traditional lands. For others, the possibility of remaining on or close to their country as workers in the cattle industry, despite problems of ownership and paucity of payment, allowed continued cultural practice; some links to land could thus be maintained. This changed after 1965 when the Northern Territory Cattle Station Industry Award Case (commonly referred to as the Equal Wages Case) mandated that Aboriginal workers be paid the same wages as non-Aboriginal workers (Stevens, 1981). Decided with the best of intentions towards equality, this decision in fact subverted the *de facto* arrangements by which many Aboriginal people had managed to stay on traditional lands and thus maintain links to them through continued cultural practice. Widespread unemployment and removal to fringe areas of country towns resulted (Bunbury, 2002). Social problems, alcohol abuse, dependence mentality, and loss of language and culture which followed eventually engendered a movement back to country and the setting up of Aboriginal communities intent on controlling lifestyle and reinforcing land-based cultural identity. Symbiotically with the Equal Wages Case, other events of the time, such as the Freedom Rides of 1963, the 1966 Wave Hill strike and the 1967 Referendum, added to a national focus on the conditions of Aborigines, and perhaps to some inkling of the importance of land to Aboriginal ideologies.

The first groups to achieve the successful setting up of homeland movement settlements were from Yirrkala and Maningrida in northern Arnhem Land, Amata in South Australia, and Derby in Western Australia (Lippmann, 1991; Keen, 1994), followed by members of the Pitjantjatjara in northern South Australia (Toyne & Vachon, 1984), and subsequently numerous other groups. The homeland movement is a form of cultural revival, a means of gaining control over decision-making, denying European lifestyles, and re-establishing Aboriginal identity through links with country. As such, Yothu Yindi, from Yirrkala, chose in 1989 to make it the topic of their first album, *Homeland Movement*, and specifically to refer to it in a song about the relationships between land ownership and cultural revival and survival:

> Back in the 1970s there was movement on the land
> Yolngu people moved back to their promised land ...
> Power to the people, power to their land
> Power for culture revival, power for survival ...

A compilation of both contemporary and traditional songs, *Homeland Movement* keeps these two types of song separate. This is unlike subse-quent Yothu Yindi albums, where interspersing of traditional and con-temporary song makes it possible to find links between the two genres. The presence of both on an album, levels of information about the Gumatj and Rirratjingu backgrounds of material, multilingualism in song lyrics, songs about Yolngu people, and explanation of Yolngu cosmology in the notes accompanying *Homeland Movement* (as discussed in chapter 8), imply that for this group an album ostensibly of rock music is more than this format had meant to that point. Released through Mush-room/Festival Records, the album was guaranteed a degree of national recognition, and set the agenda for developments in the Aboriginal con-temporary music scene of the following decade. It ends with a satirical, quasi-folk ballad accompanied with clapsticks, didjeridu and guitar, 'Luku-Wängawuy Manikay (1788)', in which criticism of colonisation of Australia and statement about Yolngu ownership of land go hand in hand with notice that Yolngu culture is strong.

The meaning of outstations to Aborigines is also used as the explana-tion of an album by musicians from the communities of Garmadi and Manmoyi in the Top End. This album, *Manmoyi – Garmadi: Black Gospel*, released in 1994, contains Christian choruses and songs accom-panied by acoustic guitar. Although outstations are not the topics of songs here, the album notes explain that people in Garmadi and Man-moyi outstation communities 'live in a mixture of traditional and contem-porary lifestyles ... the music in this tape was recorded at the request of

Yothu Yindi's first album, *Homeland Movement*,
celebrated the return of Aboriginal communities
to their traditional lands.

the communities [as part of] a strategy to ... record important songs and
stories'. The explanation of the album also notes that the songs on the
album are intended to assist in understanding 'how the people blend traditional beliefs with more Western methodology to make an extended
spiritual life that assists with the pressures of modern Aboriginality'
(*Manmoyi – Garmadi: Black Gospel*, album notes). Unlike the explicit
positioning of Yothu Yindi on the homeland movement as symbolic of
Aboriginal reclamation of identity, this album focuses on the outstation
community ethos of Garmadi and Manmoyi people and how songs can be
used to demonstrate lifestyles that require balance between the traditional and the contemporary.

Mabo

The Yolngu figure strongly in both the history of land rights claims and,
principally through the work and success of Yothu Yindi, in musical

expression of Aboriginal positions on land. They were the first Aborigines to mount a legal appeal against dispossession of their lands (Bartlett,
1993). This occurred in 1968 when Yolngu of the Gove Peninsula
brought an action in the Supreme Court of the Northern Territory
against the Swiss mining company, Nabalco, to stop bauxite mining on
Yolngu traditional lands (*Milirrpum and Others vs Nabalco and the
Commonwealth*, Northern Territory Supreme Court, 1971). The case
was lost, Blackburn, the presiding judge, disallowing Aboriginal law and
its expression of land ownership (Rowley, 1986; Williams, 1986;
Brennan, 1991; Lippmann, 1991; Bartlett, 1993). Although this case
was unsuccessful, it led to revised federal government policies on Aboriginal issues and paved the way for subsequent legal contests over land
ownership.

The loss of the Milirrpum case occurred under a federal Liberal government that in 1972 lost the next election to the Labor Party. One of
the most significant actions taken by the incoming Labor government
was to establish an Aboriginal Lands Commission, in response to the loss
of the Milirrpum case. The new Commission's role was to decide which
Aboriginal groups should receive land, not whether such action was jus-
tified. This ushered into Australian politics a new period of land rights
activity.

Despite the obvious presence of Aborigines in Australia, the doctrine
of *terra nullius* stood as a legal precept in Australia until 1992 when it
was overturned in the Mabo decision. Clearly a reason for celebration
among Australia's Indigenous peoples, the Mabo decision became the
topic of songs by numerous musicians – Yothu Yindi's 'Mabo' only one of
them:

> Terra nullius, terra nullius
> Terra nullius is dead and gone
> We were right, that we were here
> They were wrong, that we weren't here.

The appearance of this song serves as a pivotal point – it sums up a history of Aboriginal land rights songs, but simultaneously signals the
beginning of a second wave of Indigenous activity to reclaim country.

The Mabo case was an action by Eddie Koiki Mabo, from the island of
Mer (also known as Murray Island) in the Torres Strait, against the state

of Queensland. It challenged non-Indigenous ownership of lands Mabo claimed were his by right of continued ancestral occupation and use. The findings of the case of *Mabo and Others vs the State of Queensland* (Bartlett, 1993) were that the Meriam people 'are entitled as against the whole world to possession, occupation, use and enjoyment of the island of Mer ...' (Bartlett, 1993, 170). The subsequent *Native Title Act* (1993) responded to this in legislation, establishing frameworks for Aboriginal and Torres Strait Islander access to, use and occupation of traditional country, with different applications depending on local conditions.

The victory of Aboriginal and Torres Strait Islander peoples in the Mabo case was celebrated by CAAMA in the 1995 release of a two CD set, *Our Home, Our Land*. Unlike other CAAMA recordings which present musicians from a region loosely defined as 'central Australian', this album combines Indigenous artists from across Australia in a focused statement on Aboriginal and Torres Strait Islander belief in land and its significance. The album's provenance in CAAMA and its identity as a statement of core belief in land exemplifies CAAMA's wider agenda of working with Indigenous music on a national level. The significance of this album is explained in the opening comments of its accompanying notes:

> Australia is a country of immeasurable power and beauty – from the waters and mountains, the deserts and forests to the cities and outstations ... [The songs on] *Our Home, Our Land* tell of the powerful attachment to the land shared by Australia's Aboriginal and Torres Strait Islander peoples, of a rich cultural history extending more than 60,000 years. They tell of the ongoing struggle for land rights and the hope for a future in which all of this nation's peoples live in a more just and equitable society ... The Mabo decision and its acknowledgment of native title rights recognised the essential, inextricable bond between life and land ... This CD is for all Australians, all who live in this land (*Our Home, Our Land*, album notes).

Our Home, Our Land contains twenty-four tracks, three of which are by non-Aborigines with strong links to Indigenous music and musicians: 'Solid Rock' by Shane Howard of Goanna; 'Tjapwurrung Country' by Neil Murray; 'Nukkanya' by Paul Kelly. The remaining twenty-one tracks fall into different types of Aboriginal songs about land. 'Land Rights', by Sunrize Band, is the closest to an outright protest song on the set. It addresses the listener directly, using phrases such as 'stand up for our rights', phrases which recur in numerous Aboriginal songs:

> Don't like someone to take my home
> Give me back my freedom
> Give me back my home
> So let's stand up for our land rights ...

In contrast to this, 'Nitmiluk', by Blekbala Mujik, celebrates the 1989 return of a specific place, Nitmiluk, to its Aboriginal owners. This song exemplifies hand-back of land as a recurring topic of Aboriginal rock songs about land. Alongside happiness at the return of land, it expresses the wish that all people will share the land (see chapter 9). Other songs are also about specific places, often stating the singer's closeness to a locale. For example, 'Big Mountain Wilpena Pound', by Artoowarapana Band, expresses pride in and attachment to a place:

> When I was just a kid I used to play around
> A Flinders Ranges mountain I call home ...
> Near the foothills of the place I love
> Called Wilpena Pound ...

The majority of songs on *Our Home, Our Land* state the Indigenous position that loss of land is equal to loss of culture. For example, in 'Angerwuy' by female group Raven, this process is dated from the advent of white people in Australia:

> You never, never, never gave a damn about us
> You can't stop us from dancing.

The linking of land and culture is also made in Warumpi Band's 'We Shall Cry', but here with the added dimension of reference to Aboriginal children:

> We have travelled to so many places
> Heard many sad stories of our people's struggles
> As we try to hang on to our land, our culture, our children.

Singing about country, which runs throughout this double album, is one level through which Aboriginal musicians spread messages about land ownership and the importance of land to Aborigines and Torres Strait Islanders. Singing a song about a land-related topic is only one way that this achieves a point. There is another agenda implicit in this album, and perhaps in all Aboriginal contemporary songs about land, and this is the idea of 'singing the land', not singing about the land, but singing the land into existence. In the title track of this double album, 'Our Home, Our Land', by Melbourne-based Tiddas member Lou Bennett, the lyrics include the statements

> We sing our home, our home, our home
> We dance our land, our land
> Where we stand together,

expressing something of the way that an Aboriginal song acts as a means by which the land is referred to and called into day-to-day Indigenous existence. The land is the past ('always was') and the present at the same time; to its owners, it is the future ('always will be'). A song about land sings the past into the present and projects it into the future: we sing our home, we dance our land.

Our Home, Our Land is above all a tribute to Eddie Mabo, and this is demonstrated by the inclusion on the album of four songs about him and the legal case named after him. Through these songs the specificity of one land claim is embodied and tribute is made to the separate legal actions undertaken by individual Indigenous Australians through which the concept of land reclamation is kept alive. Yothu Yindi's 'Mabo' adopts a position of Aboriginal vindication that what Indigenous Australia had stated for just over two centuries had been recognised officially, while two songs, 'Respect for Eddie Mabo' by Tasmanian group Rygela Band, and 'Koiki, Father Dave and James' by Sydney-based Peter Yananda McKenzie, express indignation that Aborigines and Torres Strait Islanders were forced to resort to the Australian legal system to prove their identity and right to land; in the words of 'Respect for Eddie Mabo', 'we've adopted legalities instead of our rights'. The second of these songs calls on Aborigines and Torres Strait Islanders to take the example of the Merriam people and stand up for their rights. This call to Australian Indigenous peoples is made by addressing them through the regional names by which they popularly refer to themselves – Murries (from southern Queensland and northern New South Wales), Yolngu (from northeast Arnhem Land), Koories and Nungas (New South Wales and Victoria), Yapa and Nyoongahs (from Western Australia):

> Now you Murries and Yolngu too
> Koories and Nungas there
> Yapa and Nyoongahs from the west
> Stand up and say you care.

The fourth song about Eddie Mabo and the Mabo case is 'Mabo' by the Mills Sisters, from Thursday Island:

> A humble man with heart to see
> The shining light of liberty
> And dawning of equality – Mabo.

The Mills Sisters' song contextualises Eddie Mabo's struggle in description of the natural beauty of the Torres Strait Islands, interpreting the Mabo decision in global terms as 'the dawning of equality'.

Conclusion – beyond Mabo

> Won't you stand tall by me
> Stand and fight
> Won't you stand and fight by me
> For we are the land

> (Richard Frankland, 'We are the Land' on *Meeting One*,
> The Charcoal Club, 2002).

Analysis of the contents of *Our Home, Our Land* can give the impression that the Mabo decision was an endpoint in Indigenous land rights. While the double CD set celebrates the decision of the High Court, and through collecting songs about country written over a number of years provides a convenient documentation of events and responses to them, reactions within the Indigenous community to the outcome of the Mabo case remain equivocal. As Aboriginal songs written since 1992 demonstrate, the need to express feelings about country, to affirm identity through singing about a place, or adding to the repertoire of songs about land remains a mainstay of contemporary Aboriginal musical expression.

To some Aboriginal spokespeople, the Mabo decision was a case of 'giving an inch, but taking another mile' (Mansell, 1995, 322). How it would be applied by the federal government was not trusted, lack of consultation with Indigenous peoples in the process was criticised, and calls were made for qualifications to statements within it. These issues were especially listed in the Eva Valley (NT) statement, drawn up in 1993 by a national Indigenous forum as a response to Mabo. The statement notes the need to acknowledge that Indigenous land title 'cannot be extinguished by grants of any interests', that these would require 'informed consent of all the relevant title holders', and 'total security for sacred sites and heritage areas' must occur (Moores, 1995, 364–65). To Noel Pearson, at that time Executive Director, Cape York Land Council, the decision was not only belated, but also cautious. His interpretation of the decision raised further, problematic issues of sovereignty, compensation and leasing arrangements. Further, he noted that far from solving the situation prior to 1992, the Mabo decision clearly kept land on the agenda as the focus of the process of reconciliation:

> Mabo compels the nation to confront fundamental issues concerning the indigenous people of Australia, issues which have been largely avoidable to date ... (1) that as a consequence of their ownership of Australia prior to 1788 ... they have been deprived without any form of settlement, and (2) that Aboriginal people had ownership of the entire country (and were deprived of) protecting their ownership ... the unavoidable subject matter for negotiation must at least be indigenous rights to land ... (Pearson, 1995, 354).

As the 2002 failure of a land claim by the Yorta Yorta demonstrates, the initial welcoming of the Mabo decision was not to be followed by the unilateral success of Indigenous applications for rights to land (Paul & Gray, 2002).

After it gained power in 1996, the conservative Howard government reacted to the Wik decision by amending the *Native Title Act*, making it much more difficult for Indigenous Australians to claim co-existence of native title alongside pastoral activity. At the same time, funding for Aboriginal services and programs was cut. The federal government's refusal to apologise for past treatment of Indigenous Australians, structural 'reforms' to ATSIC that made it less autonomous from ministerial inter-ference, and the appointment of conservative judges to the Australian High Court, all combine to demonstrate that the political climate sur-rounding Aboriginal Affairs in Australia has deteriorated substantially since the Mabo decision.

This is a major reason for the continuance of land as the focus of Indigenous politics, and also its continuance in song. When Lajamanu Teenage Band sing about land in their 'Leave my Grandpa's Land' (on their 1995 album, *Echo Voices*), they connect with a tradition of rock songs by central Australian music groups over a period of some decades. Similarly, country features in songs by artists such as Phil Moncrieff, who sings of the importance of land in his 1996 song 'This Land's Worth More than Gold and Silver' (on *One Mob, Many Mobs*). Another member of the latest generation of young Aboriginal singer-songwriters, Jason Lee Scott, sings that 'Now it's time for me to go back to the land' (on *From the Desert to the Sea*, 2002). Wider pan-Aboriginal sentiments related to country also appear in his songs, such as 'Nunga Down Under':

> This is our nation and our home
> This is the country we come from
> This is the culture our spirits gave
> This is the land of the boomerang.

As with the recordings of many contemporary Aboriginal musicians, the album notes accompanying Scott's *From the Desert to the Sea* contain numerous references to both his own Aboriginality ('I was born in Ceduna, South Australia, and my tribal connections link to the Kokatha, Wirangu, Mirning clans') and to other, widespread ones ('Nunga from South Australia, Arnungu from the Pit[jantjatjara] lands ... Nyungar from Western Australia, Yolngu from Arnhem Land ... Koori from Vic-toria ... and Murri from Queensland. Whatever you are, shout it out with pride').

In the repertoire of Aboriginal musicians it is still common to hear songs that address community, country, land, place and site as continua-tion of a tradition of singing about land. On *Wild Brumbys*, Daniel Brumby and Ted Kunia sing about Areyonga in 'Ngura Utunya'; Black-shadow Band include a song about Irantji waterhole on their 2001 self-titled album; the song 'It's Our Home' appears on Ltyentye Apurte Band's album from 2001, *It's Our Home – Santa Theresa*; The Lazy Late Boys sing about Wattie Creek in their 'Daguragu/Wattie Creek' and about members of the Gurindji in songs such as 'Gurindji Girl' on their *Freedom Day*. For this group, 'the boys like to write and sing songs about their mob, the Gurindji' (*Freedom Day*, album notes). Place also continues to recur in the work of urban Aboriginal musicians, for example, Bart Willoughby sings about the Block (a section of Sydney inner-city housing) in his song 'Don't Knock the Block' on his *Frequencies* album released in 2000:

> The block was the heartland of Aboriginal life
> If you'd just come to Sydney or were in a bit of strife
> The community was always there for Koori peoples' needs
> And Gough Whitlam said it was their land in 1973.

Thus Aboriginal connections to land, the histories behind those connections and Aboriginal reactions to attempts to counter them continue to resurface in contemporary songs in various ways. The final word on this aspect of contemporary Aboriginal music can best be made by the members of Red Sunset on their 1998 album *Nangu Songs*:

> All the songs are about the land and its Tribal People ... The songs talk about how objects appeared on the land and are about our dreaming and totems. Nangu is our country ...

Discography

This discography lists recordings and performers discussed in this book. It is organised alphabetically by artist name or by title for compilation recordings and those that do not indicate an artist. Entries show: performer/title if no performer – title – label – serial number – date. The lack of details in some entries indicates that these are not shown on a recording.

Aboriginal Choirs of Central Australia. CAAMA.
AIM 4 More, *AIM 4 More.* Jamalga Music, JCM100, 1997.
All this Spirit in the Land – Traditional Songs Recorded Live in the Kimberleys, Western Australia. Garnduwa Amboorny Wirnan Inc, JCK92CD2, 1992.
All You Mob! ABC Music, 12872, 2002.
Amunda, *Civilised World.* CAAMA, 223, 1991.
—— *Pedlar Ave.* STUN007, 1995.
Andhannaggi – Walker River Clan Songs. CAAMA, 243, 1995.
Anu, Christine, *Stylin' Up.* White Records, D24345, 1995.
Areyonga Desert Tigers, *Light On.* Imparja.
Aroona, *Aroona.* Imparja, 1985.
Artoowarapana Band, *Adnyamathanha Way.* Dex 3567.
—— *Artoowarapana Country.* Imparja,1986.
Atkins, Mark, *Didgeridoo Concerto.* Larrikin, LRF 338, 1994.
Atkins, Shelly, *Shell.* CAAMA, 348.
Barambah, Maroochy, *Aborigine.* Daki Budtcha Records, DBPL 003, 1995.
—— *Mongungi – Modern Tribalism.* Daki Budtcha Records, DBPL 1001123DS, 1994.

Benning Brothers, *The Benning Brothers Band*. Pindaroo, PIN503, 1998.
—— *Kimberley Country*. Pindaroo, PIN503CD, 1998.
The Best of Koori Classics. Enrec/Larrikin, LRF 399, 1996.
Black, Alastair, *Didgeridoo Dreaming*. Larrikin, LRF260, 1991/1992.
Blackshadow Band, *Blackshadow Band*. CAAMA, 344, 2001.
Blekbala Mujik, *Blekbala Mujik*. CAAMA, 244, 1995.
—— *Come-n-Dance*. CAAMA, 226, 1993.
—— *Midnait Mujik*. CAAMA, 213, 1990.
—— *Nitmiluk!* CAAMA, 209, 1990.
—— *Walking Together*. CAAMA, 261.
Bran Nue Dae. BND Records, BNDCD002, 1993.
Bridge, Ernie & Noel, *200 Years Ago*, DR 9401, 1994.
Broken English, *Broken English – The Studio Sessions*. Skinnyfish Music, SFBE001, 2001.
Brumby, Daniel & Ted Kunia, *Wild Brumbys*. CAAMA, 341.
Buried Country: The Story of Aboriginal Country Music. Larrikin, D46509, 2000.
Carmody, Kev, *Bloodlines*. Festival, D30954, 1993.
—— *Eulogy for a Black Person*. Festival, D30692, 1991.
—— *Images and Illusions*. Festival, D31380, 1995.
—— *Street Beat*. Festival, D11344, 1992.
Cassar–Daley, Troy, *Beyond the Dancing*. Columbia, 4782112, 1994.
—— *Big River*. Columbia, 495236 2, 1999.
—— *True Believer*. Columbia, 486872 9, 1997.
Casso and the Axons, *Australia for Sale*. Greg Castillon, 1987.
Charcoal Club, *Meeting One*. Taram Records, TRCD001, 2002.
Coloured Stone, *Barefeet Dancing*. 1995.
—— *Black Rock from the Red Centre*. RCA, SPCD 1209, 1986.
—— *Bunna Lawrie's Best of Coloured Stone*. CAAMA, 313, 1997.
—— *Coloured Stone*. Imparja.
—— *Crazy Mind*. RCA, VPK1 0821, 1989.
—— *Human Love*. RCA, SPCD1208, 1986.
—— *Inma Juju: Dance Music*. RCA, VPCD 0847, 1991.
—— *Island of Greed*. RCA, SPCD 1088, 1985
—— *Koonibba Rock*. RCA, SPCD 1087, 1985.
—— *Songs from the Nullabor*. 1995.
—— *Wild Desert Rose*. RCA, SPCD 1206, 1988.
Corroboree: Australian Aborigines of Noonkenbah.
Corrugation Road. Angoorabbin Records, AR8, 1996.
Country Wranglers, *Kintore Gospel*. CAAMA.
Cox, Kerrianne, *Just Wanna Move*. KC111.
—— *Opening*. KC333.
Dargan, Ash, *Aphrodijiac*. Holborne/Indigenous Australia, IA2026D.
—— *Wirrimbah*. Holborne/Indigenous Australia, IA2031D.

Dargin, Alan, *Bloodwood — The Art of the Didjeridu*. Natural Symphonies, NS 331, 1991.

Demurru Hits — Maningrida Soundtracks. Maningrida Media, OM 9014D, 1995.

Didj'un — Singer/Songwriters from the Kimberley. Goolarri Music, GMCD001, 1998.

Fitzroy Xpress, *Little Bit Country, Little Bit Rock & Roll*. Fitzroy Xpress, 2000.

From the Bush. CAAMA, CD214, 1990.

Geia, Joe, *Yil Lull*. Dex 3695, 1988.

Gudju Gudju, *Follow One Track*. Larrikin, LRX375, 1995.

Hardy, Col, *Black Gold*. Opal Records, OLLP 501.

—— *Remember Me*. Opal Records, OLLP536, 1991.

Hermannsburg (Aranda) Ladies Choir, *Hermannsburg Ladies Choir*. Imparja.

How Could I Know — the AIDS Album. CAAMA, 203, 1989.

Hudson, David, *Didgeridoo Spirit*. Oceanic Music, OM9013D, 1996.

—— *Guardians of the Reef*. Indigenous Australia, IA2002D.

—— *Gudju Gudju — Songs Inspired by the Tjapukai Language*. Holborne/Indigenous Australia, IA 2005 D.

—— *A Postcard from David Hudson*. Holborne/Indigenous Australia, IA2064.

—— *Woolunda — Ten Solos for Didgeridoo*. Celestial Harmonies, 13071–2.

Hunter, Ruby. *Thoughts Within*. White/Aurora, D31108, 1994.

Ilkari Maru, *Ilkari Maru*. Imparja.

Indijjinus, *On the Outskirts*. Larrikin, LRF 376, 1995.

Inkamala, Irwin, and the Country Lads, *Hermannsburg Mountain*. CAAMA, 211, 1990.

Janke, Toni, *Hearts Speak Out*. Toni Janke Productions, CD TJP001, 1993.

Kimberley Moonrise Rock Festival 2000.

Kintore Gospel Band, *Western Desert Gospel*. Imparja.

Knox, Roger, *Give it a Go*. Enrec, ENC 001, 1983.

—— *The Gospel Album*. Enrec, ENC 020, 1986.

—— *Warrior in Chains*. Enrec, EN 160, 1998.

Koori Classic, Vol 3 — The Girls. Enrec, ENC 043.

Koorie (Archie Roach, Ruby Hunter, Wayne Thorpe). Victorian Aboriginal Cultural Heritage Trust, 1989.

Kulumindini Band, *History*. Marlinja Music, 1995.

—— *Marlinja Music*. Marlinja Music.

—— *You're Not Useless*. Marlinja Music, 1993.

Lajamanu Teenage Band, *Echo Voices*, CAAMA, 247, 1995.

Langford, Andrew, *Didgeridoo Tracks*. Larrikin, LRF 404, 1995.

Laughton, Herbie, *Herbie Laughton*, Imparja.

The Lazy Late Boys, *Freedom Day*. CAAMA.

Letterstick Band, *An-Barra Clan*. CAAMA.

Lewis, Tony, *Passage*. Move Records, MD 3103, 1990.

Little, Jimmy, *Jimmy Little Sings the Country and Western Greats*. Festival, F22000, 1971.

—— *Messenger*. Festival, D3206, 1999.

—— *Yorta Yorta Man*. Monitor, CA 90014, 1995.

Little Piggies, *Dreaming in Broome*. Little Piggies, LP-CD1, 1997.

Logan, Ronal 'Tonky', *Singing a Memory*. Gracie Records, SNR 018.

Ltentye Apurte Band, *It's Our Home – Santa Theresa*. CAAMA, 365, 2001.

McGrady, Ceddy, *Culture Country*. Enrec, ENC 131.

McLeod, Bobby, *Culture Up Front*. Larrikin, LRF 262, 1992.

—— *Spirit Mother*. Larrikin, LRF 275, 1993.

Manmoyi – Garmadi: Black Gospel. Manmoyi and Garmadi Communities/Kakadu Label, 1994.

Marr, Danny, *Raining on the Rocks*. Moondog, MDCD8701.

Marrugeko, *Mimi*. MIM101, 1997.

Meinmuk – Music from the Top End. ABC Music, 7243 8 33193 2 9, 1997.

Mimi Band, *Nawallarbik*.

Mixed Relations, *Love*. Redeye Records, 519086-2, 1993.

Moncrieff, Phil, *One Mob, Many Mobs*. Phil Moncrieff, 1996.

Morton, Tex, *Tex Morton: Yodelling Cowboy*. Kingfisher Cassettes, KF AUS-31.

Mt Liebig Band, *Western Desert Gospel*. Imparja.

Munumburra Songwriters' Festival 1999. Moondog, MD9905, 1999.

Nabarlek, *Bininj Manborlh*. Skinnyfish Music, SFM133, 2001.

—— *Munwurrk – Bushfire*. NB001.

Nangu, *Red Sunset*. CAAMA, 325, 1998.

No Fixed Address, *From My Eyes*, Mushroom, 19696, 1992.

Nokturnl, *Haterz*. Sputnik Records, 020342, 2001.

—— *Neva Mend*. Sputnik Records/FMR, 019432.

North Tanami Band, *Travelling Warlpiri*. CAAMA, 250, 1995.

—— *Warlpiri, Warlpiri People*. CAAMA, 212, 1990.

Our Home, Our Land. CAAMA, 253, 1995.

Page, David, *Ochres – The Music*. Larrikin, LRF 406, 1996.

Passion of Flamenco and Didjeridu. Holborne/Indigenous Australia, IA2025D.

Patten, Herb, *Born an Aussie Son*. Coral Music, CD CM 002.

Pigram Brothers, *Saltwater Country*. Jigil Records, JR CD004, 1997.

Randall, Bob, *Bob Randall*. Imparja.

Rebel Voices from Black Australia. Imparja.

Red Sunset, *Nangu*. CAAMA, 325, 1998.

Roach, Archie, *Charcoal Lane*. Aurora, D30386, 1990.

—— *Jamu Dreaming*. Aurora, D30851.

—— *Looking for Butter Boy*. Aurora/Mushroom, MUSH33008.2, 1997

—— *Spiritual Being*. Mushroom Records, 335192, 2002.

Roadblock Band, *On Top of the Mountain*.

Ross, Adrian, *Bridge the Gap*. Steve Parish Music Australia, 1997.

—— *Didgeridoo Dancing*. Steve Parish Music Australia, 1997.

—— *Didgeridoo Dreaming*. Steve Parish Music Australia, 1997.

Rrurrambu, George, *Nerbu Message*. TRGR732, 2000.
Scott, Jason Lee, *From the Desert to the Sea*. Desert Sea Music, JLSM2002CD, 2001.
Scrap Metal, *Broken Down Man*. Jigil Records, AS J002.
—— *Just Looking*.
—— *Pub Sweat 'n' Tears*. Jigil Records, SMJ00, 1992.
—— *Scrap Metal*. ABC Records, 846 519–2,1990.
Shakaya, *Shakaya*. Sony Music, 5097552000, 2003.
Sing Loud – Pay Strong. CAAMA, 206, 1990.
Singing up the Country – Traditional and Contemporary Songs from the Kimberleys, Western Australia. Garnduwa Amboorny Wirnan Inc, JCK92CD1, 1992.
Soft Sands, *Soft Sands*. Imparja.
Songs from the Kimberleys. Australian Institute of Aboriginal Studies, AIAS/13, 1968.
SPIN.fx, *Uluparru*. CAAMA, 374, 2002.
Stiff Gins, *Origins*. Stiff Gins, 2001.
Sunrize Band, *Lunggurrma*. ABC Music, 518 832-2, 1993.
—— *Sunset to Rize!* SUN 001.
Tableland Drifters, *On the Road*. CAAMA, 219, 1991.
Thomas, Josh, *Thylacine Live*. CAAMA, 258, 1995.
Thylacine, *Nightmare Dreaming*. CAAMA, 262, 1996.
Tibet-Australia: Sounds of Peace. Myra Records, NWCD 830, 1991.
Tiddas, *Sing about Life*. Mercury, 518 3482, 1993.
—— *Lethal by the Kilo*. Mercury, 538 277-2, 1998.
—— *Tiddas*. Mercury, 5327992, 1996.
Titjikala Desert Oaks Band, *Titjikala Desert Oaks Band*. CAAMA, 204, 1989.
Tjapukai, *Storywaters*. Holborne/Indigenous Australia, IA3000D.
Tjapukai Dancers, *Proud to be Aborigine* Jarra Hill Records, CDJHR2012, 1989.
Torres, Michael, *Full Moon over Broome*. Goolarri Media, 1997.
Tribute to Noonkanbah People. Moondog, CD9809, 1998.
Ulpanyali Band, *Ulpanyali Band*. CAAMA, 220, 1991.
Unte Nthenherenye? (Where Do You Come From?) Contemporary Arrernte Music. Institute for Aboriginal Development.
Uwankara Palyanku Kanyintjaku – A Strategy for Life. CAAMA, 208, 1989.
Wairuk. *Right from the Start*. CAAMA, 222, 1992.
Walking along the Edge – Contemporary Music from the West Kimberleys, Western Australia. Garnduwa Amboorny Wirnan Inc, JCK93CD3, 1993.
Walley, Richard, *Waitch*. TWA Records, SMACD13, 1996.
Wama Wanti – Drink Little Bit. CAAMA, 124, 1988.
Warumpi Band, *Big Name, No Blankets*, Festival Records, D 38935, 1985.
—— *Jailanguru Pakarnu/Kintorelakutu*, Hot Records, Hot 703, 1984.
—— *Too Much Humbug*, CAAMA, 260, 1996.
—— *Warumpi Band Go Bush!* Festival Records, D 38707, 1987.
Webb, Brenda, *Little Black Girl*. Republic Records, RR2001CDS, 1993.

—— *Melting Pot.* Republic Records, RR2002CDS.

Wedgetail Eagle Band, *Wedgetail Eagle.* Imparja.

Wellington, Bill, *Memories of Alice.* CAAMA, 239, 1994.

Western Desert Band, *Western Desert Band.* CAAMA, 217, 1991.

Western Desert Gospel (Kintore Gospel Band & Mt Liebig Band). Imparja.

Wild Brumbys, *Lasseters Highway.* CAAMA, 224, 1992.

Wild Honey Dreaming (Riley Lee & Matthew Doyle). New World Productions, NMCD 710, 1993.

Wild Water, *Baltpa.*

Williams, Gus, and Country Ebony *Through the Years.* Hadley, CRS 147 CD.

Williams, Harry, and Wilga and the Country Outcasts, *Harry and Wilga Williams and the Country Outcasts.*

Williams, Warren, *Country Friends and Me.* CAAMA, 309.

Williams, Warren, and Country Ebony, *I'm Trying to Forget.* Ntjalka.

Willoughby, Bart, *Pathways.* CAAMA, 303, 1997.

—— *Frequencies.* Streetwise, SW20017, 2000.

Wirrinyga Band, *Dreamtime Shadow.* CAAMA, 215, 1990.

—— *Dreamtime Wisdom, Modern Time Vision.* CAAMA, 249, 1996.

Yamma, Frank, *Solid Eagle.* CAAMA, 1997.

Yamma, Frank, and Piranpa, *Playing with Fire – Warungku Inkanyi.* CAAMA, 326, 1999.

Yothu Yindi, *Birrkuta – Wild Honey.* Mushroom, TVD93461, 1996.

—— *Freedom.* Mushroom, TVD93380, 1993.

—— *Garma.* Mushroom, 332822, 2000.

—— *Homeland Movement.* Mushroom, D38959, 1989.

—— *One Blood.* Mushroom, MUSH33229.2, 1999.

—— *Tribal Voice.* Mushroom, TVD93358, 1992.

Young, Dougie, *The Songs of Dougie Young.* AIATSIS/National Library of Australia, AIAS 19CD.

Yunupingu, Galarwuy, *Gurrindji Blues/This Tribal Land.* RCA, 101937, 1970.

References

Aboriginal and Torres Strait Islander Commission (1997a) *Annual Report, 1996–97.* Aboriginal and Torres Strait Islander Commission, Canberra.

—— (1997b) *National Aboriginal and Torres Strait Islander Tourism Industry Strategy.* Aboriginal and Torres Strait Islander Commission, Canberra.

—— (1997c) *National Aboriginal and Torres Strait Islander Cultural Industry Strategy.* Aboriginal and Torres Strait Islander Commission, Canberra.

Ajuria, P (1997) Artist fears for 'didge trees'. *Koori Mail,* 15 Jan, p. 11.

Alice Springs Town Council (1998) *Strategic Directions Beyond 2000.* Alice Springs Town Council, Alice Springs.

Allan, Monika (1988) *The Tamworth Country Music Festival.* Monika Allan, Nestley (SA).

Allen, P (1992) An unbroken tradition – A tradition that adapts. *Tjunguringanyi* 12 (2): 14–17.

Altman, Jon (1989) Tourism dilemma for Aboriginal Australians. *Annals of Tourism Research* 16(4): 456–76.

Anderson, Gregory (1992) *Mularra: A Clan Song Series from Central Arnhem Land.* PhD thesis, University of Sydney.

Anderson, Kay (1998) Reflections on Redfern. In E. Stratford (ed.) *Australian Cultural Geographies.* Oxford University Press, Melbourne (in press).

Andrew, Stephen (1997) Archie Roach. *Rhythms* 62: 10.

Arthur, JM (1996) *Aboriginal English: A Cultural Study.* Oxford University Press, Oxford.

Attwood, Bain (1996) Mabo, Australia and the end of history. In Bain Attwood (ed.) *In the Age of Mabo: History, Aborigines and Australia.* Allen & Unwin, Sydney, pp. 100–16.

Australian Broadcasting Corporation (2003) Maintaining culture through dance. >http://www.abc.net.au/arts/performance/stories/s642378.htm<.

Australian Bureau of Statistics (1997) *The Business of Music.* Australian Bureau of Statistics, Canberra.

—— (2000) *Work in Selected Culture/Leisure Activities.* Australian Bureau of Statistics, Canberra.

Bachelard, M (1997) *The Great Land Grab: What Every Australian Should Know About Wik, Mabo and the Ten-Point Plan.* Hyland House, Melbourne.

Bailey, John (2001) *The White Divers of Broome: The True Story of a Fatal Experiment.* Macmillan, Sydney.

Bangarra Dance Theatre (2002) *The Totem Program* (promotional flyer). Bangarra Dance Theatre, Sydney.

Basile, A (1994) Ruby's thoughts. *On the Street,* 19 Apr, p. 17.

Beckett, Jeremy (1958) Aborigines Make Music. *Quadrant,* 8, Spring 32–38.

—— (1981) *Modern Music of Torres Strait.* Australian Institute of Aboriginal Studies, Canberra.

—— (1993) 'I don't care who knows': The songs of Dougie Young. *Australian Aboriginal Studies* 2: 34–38.

Bartlett, Richard (1993) *The Mabo Decision with Commentary by Richard Bartlett and Full Text of the Decision in Mabo and Others vs State of Queensland.* Butterworths, Sydney.

Bell, Diane (1998) *Ngarrindjeri Wurriwarrin: A World that Is, Was, and Will Be.* Spinifex, Melbourne.

Benterrak, Krim, Muecke, Stephen & Roe, Paddy (1984/1996) *Reading the Country: Introduction to Nomadology.* Fremantle Arts Centre Press, Fremantle.

Berndt, Ronald & Berndt, Catherine (1988, 5th edn) *The World of the First Australians: Aboriginal Traditional Life: Past and Present.* Aboriginal Studies Press, Canberra.

Biracree, T (1993) *The Country Music Almanac.* Prentice Hall, New York.

Bird, Jimmy (1989) They can't break us down. In Paul Marshall (ed.) *Raparapa Kularr Martuwarra: Stories from the Fitzroy River Drovers.* Magabala Books, Broome.

Bohemia, Jack & McGregor, Bill (1995) *Nyibayarri: Kimberley Tracker.* Aboriginal Studies Press, Canberra.

Bottoms, Timothy (1999) *Djabugay Country: An Aboriginal History of Tropical North Queensland.* Allen & Unwin, Sydney.

Bowden, Ros (1990) *Being Aboriginal: Comments, Observations and Stories from Aboriginal Australians.* Australian Broadcasting Commission, Sydney.

Bran Nue Dae Productions (1991) *The Making of Bran Nue Dae* (TV documentary). Bran Nue Dae Productions, Broome.

Breen, Marcus (ed.) (1989) *Our Place – Our Music.* Aboriginal Studies Press, Canberra.

—— (1992) Desert dreams, media, and interventions in reality: Australian Aboriginal music. In Reebee Garofalo (ed.) *Rockin' the Boat: Mass Music and Mass Movements*. South End Press, Boston, pp. 149–70.

—— (1994) I have a dreamtime: Aboriginal music and black rights in Australia. In S Broughton, M Ellingham, D Muddyman & R Trillo (eds) *World Music: The Rough Guide*. Rough Guides, London, pp. 655–62.

Brennan, Frank (1998) *The Wik Debate – Its Impact on Aborigines, Pastoralists and Miners*. University of NSW Press, Sydney.

Broughton, S, Ellingham, M, Muddyman, D & Trillo, R (eds) (1994) *World Music: The Rough Guide*. Rough Guides, London.

Brown, M (1997) Aboriginal players swap didgeridoo for 10-gallon hat. *Sydney Morning Herald*, 11 Jan, p. 5.

Bucknall, Gwen, & Bucknall, John (1994) 'We want to keep that language ...': What is happening with Aboriginal languages in the Aboriginal independent community schools in Western Australia. In Deborah Hartman & John Henderson (eds) *Aboriginal Languages in Education*. IAD Press, Alice Springs, pp. 257–75.

Bulletin of Immigration and Population Research (1994) The Yothu Yindi family. *Bulletin of Immigration and Population Research* 11: 26–27.

Bunbury, Bill (2002) *It's Not the Money, It's the Land: Aboriginal Stockmen and the Equal Wages Case*. Fremantle Arts Centre Press, Fremantle (WA).

Butler, J (1990) *Gender Trouble: Feminism and the Subversion of Identity*. Routledge, London & New York.

CAAMA (nd.a) *Aboriginal Choirs of Central Australia* (press release). Central Australian Aboriginal Media Association, Alice Springs.

—— (nd.b) *Blekbala Mujik* (press release). Central Australian Aboriginal Media Association, Alice Springs.

—— (nd.c) *Australian Music Recognises its Black Soul* (press release). Central Australian Aboriginal Media Association, Alice Springs.

—— (nd.d) *From CAAMA Music* (press release). Central Australian Aboriginal Media Association, Alice Springs.

—— (nd.e) *How Could I Know – The AIDS Album* (press release). Central Australian Aboriginal Media Association, Alice Springs.

—— (nd.f) *Strong Culture* (press release). Central Australian Aboriginal Media Association, Alice Springs.

—— (nd.g) *Walker River Clan – Andhanaggi* (press release) Central Australian Aboriginal Media Association, Alice Springs.

—— (nd.h) *Wama Wanti – Drink Little Bit* (press release). Central Australian Aboriginal Media Association, Alice Springs.

—— (1988) *Sing Loud – Play Strong* (video). CAAMA, Alice Springs.

—— (1989) *CAAMA – Prospectus*. Central Australian Aboriginal Media Association, Alice Springs.

—— (1990) *Media Release – May 1990*. Central Australian Aboriginal Media Association, Alice Springs.

Cape York Unity News (1997) Lockhardt River vox populi. 8 Dec, p. 30.

Carmody, Kev (1996) Carming end to fringe festival. *The Concrete Press*, 26, 9 Jul, p. 4.
—— (1996) interview with Chris Gibson, Sydney.
Carney, G (1974) Bluegrass grows all around: the spatial dimensions of a country music style. *Journal of Geography* 73 (4): 34–55.
Casimir, John (1994) Islands come to the city on wings of song. *Sydney Morning Herald*, 15 Oct, p. 13A.
Castellano, M, L Davis, & L Lahache (2000) *Aboriginal Education: Fulfilling the Promise*. University of British Columbia Press, Vancouver.
Castles, John (1992) *Tjungaringanyi*: Aboriginal rock. In Phil Hayward (ed.) *From Pop to Punk to Postmodernism: Popular Music and Australian Culture from the 1960s to the 1990s*. Allen & Unwin, Sydney, pp. 25–39.
Chadwick, N (1975) *A Descriptive Study of the Djingili Language*. Aboriginal Studies Press, Canberra.
Chi, Jimmy & Kuckles (1991) *Bran Nue Dae*. Currency Press/Magabala Books, Sydney/Broome.
Christie, Michael (1994) Yirrkala community education centre and the Laynha homelands schools. In Deborah Hartman & John Henderson (eds) *Aboriginal Languages in Education*. IAD Press, Alice Springs, pp. 117–26.
Chryssides, Helen (ed.) (1993) *Local Heroes*. Collins Dove, Melbourne.
Clarke, D (1995) *The Rise and Fall of Popular Music*. Penguin, Hammondsworth.
Clugston, C (1998) Music fills minds, minds make a difference. *Revolver* 22 Jan, p. 17.
Clunies Ross, Margaret (1983) Two Aboriginal oral texts from Arnhem Land, North Australia, and their cultural context. In Stephen Knight & S Mukherjee (eds) *Words and Worlds: Studies in the Social Role of Verbal Culture*. Sydney Studies in Society and Culture, No. 1, University of Sydney, pp. 3–30.
Cohen, A (1985) *The Symbolic Construction of Community*. Routledge, London.
Commonwealth of Australia (1991) *National Report of the Royal Commission into Aboriginal Deaths in Custody*. Commonwealth of Australia, Canberra.
—— (1992) *Aboriginal Deaths in Custody – Overview of the Response by Governments to the Royal Commission*. Commonwealth of Australia, Canberra.
Condie, T (1997a) Surviving. *Koori Mail*, 12 Feb, p. 15.
—— (1997b) City of soul. *Koori Mail*, 8 Oct, p. 15.
—— (1998) In celebration of our survival. *Koori Mail*, 10 Feb, p. 12.
—— (1999) Festival the best yet! *Koori Mail*, 13 Jan, p. 13.
—— (2000a) 8000 people enjoy the music and culture. *Koori Mail*, 9 Feb, pp. 17–22.
—— (2000b) NoKTuRNL lads support the Rollins Band. *Koori Mail*, 19 Apr, p. 45.
—— (2001) McLeod album is a paradox. *Koori Mail*, 19 Sept, p. 33.
—— (2002a) A meeting of minds. *Koori Mail*, 4 Sept, p. 22.
—— (2002b) Lookin' solid, feelin' deadly. *Koori Mail*, 30 Oct, pp. 24–25.
—— (2003) One-stop muso. *Koori Mail*, 26 Mar, p. 36.
Connell, John (1999) My island home: The politics and poetics of the Torres Strait. In R King and J Connell (eds) *Small Worlds, Global Lives: Islands and Migration*. Pinter, London, pp. 195–213.

Connell, John & Gibson, Chris (2003) *Sound Tracks: Popular Music, Identity and Place*. Routledge, London.

—— (forthcoming) World music: Deterritorialising place and identity. *Progress in Human Geography*.

Coombs, Anne & Varga, Susan (2001) *Broometime*. Sceptre, Sydney.

Coombs, HC, H McCann, H Ross & M Williams (eds) (1989) *Land of Promises*. Centre for Resource and Environmental Studies and Aboriginal Studies, Canberra.

Corn, Aaron (1999) The didjeridu as a site of economic contestation in Arnhem Land. *Newsletter – The Centre for Studies in Australian Music* 10, December: 1–4.

—— (2002) *Burr-Gi Wargugu ngu-Ninya Rrawa*: Expressions of ancestry and country in songs by the Letterstick Band. *Musicology Australia* 25: 76–101.

Corn, Aaron & Gumbula, Neparrnga (2002) Nurturing the sacred through Yolngu popular song. *Cultural Survival Quarterly* 26(2): 40–42.

Cosgrove, D & Jackson, P (1987) New directions in cultural geography. *Area* 19(2): 95–101.

Cross, K (2002) Bundjalung renew an ancient tradition. *Koori Mail*, 9 Jan, p. 17.

Country Music Association of Australia (1997) *Australian Country Online*. >http://www.countrymusic.asn.au<.

Coupe, Stuart (1985) The deserving Warumpis. *Sun Herald*, 19 May.

Crawford, Ian (2001) *We Won the Victory: Aborigines and Outsiders on the North-West Coast of the Kimberley*. Fremantle Arts Centre Press, Fremantle.

Creswell, T (1985) Aboriginal band for PNG. *Sydney Morning Herald*, 11 September.

Crough, Greg (1993) *Visible and Invisible: Aboriginal People in the Economy of Northern Australia*. North Australia Research Unit and the Nugget Coombs Forum for Indigenous Studies, Darwin.

Crough, Greg & Christophersen, Christine (1993) *Aboriginal People in the Economy of the Kimberley Region*. North Australia Research Unit – Australian National University, Darwin.

Davey, Stan & Dixon, Rod (1987) The Noonkanbah story – Two reviews. *Aboriginal History*, 11 (2): 171–77.

Davis, Jack, Muecke, Stephen, Narogin, Mudrooroo & Shoemaker, Adam (eds) (1990) *Paperbark: A Collection of Black Australian Writings*. University of Queensland Press, Brisbane.

Davis, S & Prescott, J (1992) *Aboriginal Frontiers and Boundaries in Australia*. Melbourne University Press, Melbourne.

Dawson, S (1985) *Smoky Dawson: A life*. George, Allen & Unwin, Sydney.

Deadly Vibe (1999) The rhythm is in the nature. 31: 21.

Deadly Vibe (2003) Singing in the shower. 72: 6–7.

De Certeau, Michel (1984) *The Practice of Everyday Life*. University of California Press, Berkeley.

Delaney, B (2001) Hip-hop artist brings global perspective to black struggle. *Sydney Morning Herald*, 23 Jul, p. 3.

Deleuze, G & Guattari, F (1987) *A Thousand Plateaus: Capitalism and Schizo-phrenia*. Translated by B Massumi. University of Minnesota Press, Minneapolis.

Department of Employment Education and Training (1995) *Alive and Deadly: Reviving and maintaining Australian Indigenous Languages*. Commonwealth of Australia, Canberra.

Dillon, Michael (1991) Interpreting Argyle: Aborigines and diamond mining in north-west Australia. In John Connell & Richard Howitt (eds) *Mining and Indigenous Peoples in Australasia*. Sydney University Press, Sydney, pp. 139–52.

Dixon, R (1980) *The Languages of Australia*. Cambridge University Press, London.

—— (1984) Dyirbal song types. In Jamie Kassler & Jill Stubington (eds) *Problems and Solutions: Occassional Essays in Musicology Presented to Alice M Moyle*. Hale & Iremonger, Sydney, pp. 206–27.

—— (1980) *The Languages of Australia*. Cambridge University Press, Cambridge.

Dixon, R & Martin Duwell (eds) (1990) *The Honey-Ant Men's Love Song and Other Aboriginal Song Poems*. Brisbane, University of Queensland Press.

Djirrimbilpilwuy, Frank (1997) Album dedication, *Meinmuk – Music from the Top End*. ABC Music/Triple J, Sydney.

Dodson, Mick (1995) *Indigenous Social Justice: Strategies and Recommendations*. Submission to the Parliament of the Commonwealth of Australia on the Social Justice Package, Aboriginal and Torres Strait Islander Social Justice Commis-sioner, Sydney.

Donaldson, Tamsin (1995) Mixes of English and ancestral language words in southeast Australian Aboriginal songs of traditional and introduced origin. In Linda Bar-wick, Allan Marett & Guy Tunstill (eds) *The Essence of Singing and the Sub-stance of Song: Recent Responses to the Aboriginal Performing Arts and Other Essays in Honour of Catherine Ellis (Oceania Monograph 46)*. University of Sydney, Sydney, pp. 143–58.

Dudrah, R (2002) Birmingham (UK): Constructing city spaces through black popular cultures and the black public sphere. *City*, 6(3): 335–50.

Duffy, Michelle (2000) Lines of drift: Festival participation and performing a sense of place. *Popular Music* 19: 51–64.

Dunbar-Hall, Peter (1994) *Style and Meaning: Signification in Contemporary Aborig-inal Popular Music, 1963–1993*. PhD thesis, University of New South Wales.

—— (1995) *Discography of Aboriginal and Torres Strait Islander Performers*. Sounds Australian, Sydney.

—— (1996) Rock songs as messages: Issues of health and lifestyle in central Australian Aboriginal communities. *Popular Music and Society* 20 (2): 43–68.

—— (1997a) Continuation, innovation and dissemination: The didjeridu and Aborig-inal rock groups. In K Neuenfeldt (ed.) *The Didjeridu: From Arnhem Land to Internet*, John Libbey/Perfect Beat Publications, London/Sydney, pp. 69–88.

—— (1997b) Music and meaning: The Aboriginal rock album. *Australian Aboriginal Studies* 1: 38–47.

—— (1997c) Site as song – song as site: Constructions of meaning in an Aboriginal rock song. *Perfect Beat* 3(3): 55–74.

—— (1997d) The uses of reggae by Aboriginal musicians. In T Hautamäki & H Järviluoma (eds) *Music on Show: Issues of performance*. Tampere (Finland): Dept of Folklore, pp. 73–78.

Dunbar-Hall, Peter & Gibson, Chris (2000) Singing about nations within nations: Geopolitics and identity in Australian Indigenous rock music. *Popular Music and Society* 24(2): 457–64.

Dunne, S (1995) Hip hope. *Sydney Morning Herald – Metro*, 24–30 Nov, p. 13.

Dusty, Slim & J McKean (1996) *Slim Dusty: Another day, another town*. Macmillan, Melbourne.

Dyer, P, Aberdeen, L & Schuler, S (2003) Tourism impacts on an Australian indigenous community: A Djabugay case study. *Tourism Management* 24: 83–95.

Dyer, R (1997) *White*. Routledge, London & New York.

Edwards, Hugh (1984) *Port of Pearls: Broome's First Hundred Years*. Author, Swanbourne (WA).

Elder, Bruce (1993) The beat behind bars. *Sydney Morning Herald*, 7 July.

—— (1995) Sophistication from the heartland. *Sydney Morning Herald*, review used as promotional material for Blekbala Mujik by CAAMA.

Eliezer, C (1996) Blekbala Mujik – Blekbala Mujik. *The Herald Sun*, 19 May, unpaginated.

Ellis, Catherine (1969) Structure and significance in Aboriginal song. *Mankind* 7(1): 3–14.

—— (1985) *Aboriginal Music: Education for Living*. Queensland University Press, Brisbane.

Ellis, Catherine & Barwick, Linda (1989) Antikirinja women's song knowledge 1963–1972: Its significance in Antikirinja culture. In P Brock (ed.) *Women: Rites and Sites*. Allen & Unwin, Sydney, pp. 21–40.

Ellis, Catherine, Brunton, Mary & Barwick, Linda (1988) From the Dreaming Rock to Reggae Rock. In A McCreddie (ed.) *From Colonel Light into the Footlights*. Pagel Books, Norwood (SA), pp. 151–72.

Evorall, T (1999) Mentorship program at Songlines. *Koori Mail*, 10 Feb, p. 22.

—— (1999) Blackfire sweeps Chinese market. *Koori Mail*, 19 May, p. 31.

Feld, Steven (1994) From schizophonia to schismogenesis: On the discourses and commodification practices of 'world music' and 'world beat'. In Charles Keil & Steven Feld (eds) *Music Grooves: Essays and Dialogues*. University of Chicago Press, Chicago, pp. 257–89.

Feld, S & Basso, K (eds) (1996) *Senses of Place*. School of American Research Press, Snata Fe, New Mexico.

Ferrier, Elizabeth (1990) Mapping power: Cartography and contemporary cultural theory. *Antithesis* 4(1): 35–49.

Finlayson, J (1995) *Aboriginal Employment, Native Title and Regionalism*. Centre for Aboriginal Economic Policy Research Discussion Paper 87, Canberra.

Form Guide (1996) Tiddas. *The Form Guide*, 25–26 Sept, p. 35.

Forrest, Peter (1985) *Springvale's Story and the Early Years at the Katherine*. Murranji Press, Darwin.

Fraser, D (2001) 'Murri country on the airwaves'. *Australian*, 25 Sept, p. 5.

Garofalo, Reebee (ed.) (1992) *Rockin' the Boat: Mass Music and Mass Movements*. South End Press, Boston.

Garton, Stephen (1989) Aboriginal history. In James Walter (ed.) *Australian Studies: A Survey*. Oxford University Press, Melbourne, pp. 189–205.

George, J (1992) Black music. *Twelve to Twenty-Five* 2(2): 34–37.

Gibson, Chris (1997a) The Tamworth Country Music Festival: Whiting out the margins in the social construction of place. Paper presented at Urban Life/Urban Culture – Aboriginal/Indigenous Experiences conference, Goolangullia Centre, University of Western Sydney, November.

—— (1997b) 'Nitmiluk': *song-sites and strategies for empowerment*. Paper presented at the Association for the Study of Australian Literature conference: Land and Identity, University of New England, September.

—— (1998) 'We sing our home, we dance our land': Indigenous self-determination and contemporary geopolitics in Australian popular music. *Environment and Planning D: Society and Space*, 16: 163–84.

—— (1999) Cartographies of the colonial and capitalist state: The geopolitics of Indigenous self-determination in Australia. *Antipode* 31(1): 45–79.

—— (2003) Cultures at work: Why 'culture' matters in research on the 'cultural' industries. *Social and Cultural Geography* 4(2): 201–15.

Gibson, Chris & Connell, John (2000) Artistic dreamings: Tinseltown, sin city and suburban wasteland. In John Connell (ed.) *Sydney: The Evolution of a World City*. Oxford University Press, Sydney, pp. 292–318.

—— (2002) Indigenous cultural industries in remote Australia: A case study of popular music. Paper presented at the Institute of Australian Geographers conference: Shaping Grounds, Canberra, July.

—— (2004) *Music and Tourism*. Channel View, Clevedon.

Gibson, Chris & Davidson, Deborah (2004) 'Tamworth, Australia's "country music capital": Place, marketing, rurality, and resident reactions'. *Journal of Rural Studies* (in press).

Gibson, Chris & Dunbar-Hall, Peter (2000) Nitmiluk: Place and empowerment in Australian Aboriginal popular music. *Ethnomusicology* 44(1): 39–64.

Gibson, C, Murphy, P & Frestone, R (2002) Employment and socio-political relations in Australia's cultural economy. *Australian Geographer* 33(2): 173–89.

Gill, Andy (1993) Yothu Yindi: Freedom. *The Independent*, 30 May, p. 17.

Gilroy, Paul (1993) *The Black Atlantic: Modernity and Double Consciousness*. Verso, London.

Gledhill, H (1996) Black sounds from the Centre. *On the Street*, 18 Dec, p. 12.

Goodwin, A & Gore, J (1995) World beat and the cultural imperialism debate. In R Sakolsky and F Ho (eds) *Sounding Off! Music as Subversion/Resistance/Revolution*. Autonomedia, New York, pp. 121–32.

Goolarri Media Enterprises (2001) website >http://www.gma.com.au<.

—— (nd) *Goolarri Media Enterprises* (promotional catalogue).

Grossberg, Lawrence (1984) Another boring day in paradise: Rock and roll and the empowerment of everyday life. *Popular Music* 4: 225–58.

Gummow, Margaret (1987) The square dance song as an Aboriginal performing art. Paper presented at Popular Music Seminar, University of New England.

—— (1992) *Aboriginal Songs from the Bundjalung and Gidabal Areas of South-Eastern Australia*. PhD thesis, University of Sydney.

—— (1994) The power of the past in the present: Singers and songs from northern New South Wales. *The World of Music* 36(1): 42–50.

—— (1995) Songs and sites/moving mountains: A study of one song from northern NSW. In Linda Barwick, Allan Marett & Guy Tunstill (eds) *The Essence of Singing and the Substance of Song: Recent Responses to the Aboriginal Performing Arts and Other Essays in Honour of Catherine Ellis (Oceania Monograph 46)*. University of Sydney, Sydney, pp. 121–32.

—— (2002) Yawahr: Corroboree for everybody. *Musicology Australia* 25: 48–75.

Hall, M (2000) In Alice, hope springs Nokturnl. *The Weekend Australian*, 10–11 Jun, p. 3.

Hanna, M (1999) *Reconciliation in Olympism: Indigenous Culture in the Sydney Olympiad*. Walla Walla Press, Sydney.

Hansen, Kenneth & Hansen, Lesley (1977) *Pinutpi/Luritja Dictionary*. Institute for Aboriginal Development, Alice Springs.

Haraway, D (1991) *Simians, Cyborgs and Women: The Reinvention of Nature*. Free Association Books, London.

Harley, JB (1988) Maps, knowledge and power. In D Cosgrove & S Daniels (eds) *The Iconography of Landscape*. Cambridge University Press, Cambridge, pp. 277–312.

Harris, Stephen (1990) *Two-Way Aboriginal Schooling*. Aboriginal Studies Press, Canberra.

Hartman, Deborah & Henderson, John (eds) (1994) *Aboriginal Languages in Education*. IAD Press, Alice Springs.

Hawke, Steve & Gallagher, Michael (1989) *Noonkanbah: Whose Land, Whose Law*. Fremantle Arts Centre Press, Fremantle.

Hayward, Phil (ed.) (1992) *From Pop to Punk to Postmodernism: Popular Music and Australian Culture from the 1960s to the 1990s*. Allen & Unwin, Sydney.

—— (1993) Safe, exotic and somewhere else: Yothu Yindi, 'Treaty' and the mediation of Aboriginality. *Perfect Beat* 2 (2): 33–42.

Hayward, Philip & Neuenfeldt, Karl (1998) Yothu Yindi: Context and significance. In Philip Hayward (ed.) *Sound Alliances: Indigenous Peoples, Cultural Politics and Popular Music in the Pacific*. Cassell, London, pp. 175–80.

Heath, Jeffrey (1978) *Linguistic Diffusion in Arnhem Land*. Australian Institute of Aboriginal Studies, Canberra.

Hemphill, P (1970) *The Nashville Sound: An Intimate Portrait of the Country and*

Western Music Scene. Simon & Schuster, New York.

Henry, R (2000) Dancing into being: The Tjapukai Aboriginal Cultural Park and the Laura Dance Festival. *The Australian Journal of Anthropology* 11(3): 322–32.

Hesmondhalgh, D (2002) *The Cultural Industries.* Sage, London.

Hiatt, L (1965) *Kinship and Conflict: A Study of an Aboriginal Community in Northern Arnhem Land.* Australian National University Press, Canberra.

Hill, Barry (2002) *Broken Song: TGH Strehlow and Aboriginal Possession.* Knopf/Random House, Sydney.

Hill, Ernestine (1943) *The Great Australian Loneliness.* Robertson & Mullens, Melbourne.

Hinkson, M (2002) New media projects at Yuendumu: Inter-cultural engagement and self-determnination in an era of accelerated globalization. *Continuum: Journal of Media and Cultural Studies* 16(2): 201–20.

Holden, A & Duffin, R (1998) *Negotiating Aboriginal Interests in Tourism Projects: The Djabugay People, The Tjapukai Dance Theatre and the Skyrail Project.* Research paper No. 4, Centre for Australian Public Sector Management, Griffith University, Brisbane.

Hollinsworth, D (1996) *Nama tarkendi:* Indigenous performing arts opening cultural doors. *Australian–Canadian Studies* 14(1): 55–68.

Horton, D (ed.) (1994) *The Encyclopedia of Aboriginal Australia,* Aboriginal Studies Press, Canberra.

House of Representatives Standing Committee on Aboriginal and Torres Strait Islander Affairs (1992) *Language and Culture – A Matter of Survival: Report of the Inquiry into Aboriginal and Torres Strait Islander Language Maintenance.* Commonwealth of Australia, Canberra.

Howes, C (1999) Qld singer goes 'Black to Reality'. *Koori Mail,* 24 Feb, p. 25.

—— (2001) 'Emu Tracks' making dreams come true. *Koori Mail,* 17 Oct, p. 19.

Huggan, Graham (1989) Decolonizing the map: Post-colonialism, post-structuralism and the cartographic connection. In B Ashcroft et al (eds) *The Post-Colonial Studies Reader.* Routledge, London & New York, pp. 407–11.

Hume, Lynne (2002) *Ancestral Power: The Dreaming, Consciousness and Aboriginal Australians.* Melbourne University Press, Melbourne.

Hunter, A (1996) Bob Geldof in rock and roll payback. *On the Street,* 5 Aug, p. 12.

Iveson, K (1997) Partying, politics and getting paid: Hip-hop and national identity in Australia. *Overland* 147: 39–47.

Jackson, P (1989) *Maps of Meaning: An Introduction to Cultural Geography.* Unwin Hyman, London.

Jacobs, JM (1993) Shake 'im this country: The mapping of the Aboriginal sacred in Australia – the case of Coronation Hill. In P Jackson & J Penrose (eds) *Constructions of Race, Place and Nation.* UCI Press, London, pp. 100–18.

—— (1995) 'That dangerous fantasy of authenticity': A review of the JC Slaughter Falls community arts project, Brisbane. *Ecumene* 2(2): 211–14.

Janke, T (1999) *Our Culture, Our Future: Report on Australian Indigenous Cultural and Intellectual Property Rights.* Michael Frankl & Co, Sydney.

Jawoyn Association (1993a) *Jawoyn People, Land and Life,* Jawoyn Association Training Section, Katherine (NT).

—— (1993b) Mabo: Putting the big stick to one side?, Speech presented at the 1993 Aboriginal Culture and Heritage Conference: People Place Law, Sydney, 8–11/9/1993.

—— (1994a) *Rebuilding the Jawoyn Nation: Approaching Economic Independence.* Green Ant Publishing, Darwin.

—— (1994b) Interim training and employment strategy. Unpublished policy document, Jawoyn Association, Katherine (NT).

Jensen, J (1998) *The Nashville Sound: Authenticity, Commercialisation and Country Music.* Country Music Foundation Press and Vanderbilt University Press, Nashville.

Johnson, Colin (1979) *Long Live Sandawara.* Hyland House, Melbourne.

Johnson, Kim (1994) The Djabugay Language at Kuranda State School. In Deborah Hartman & John Henderson (eds) *Aboriginal Languages in Education.* IAD Press, Alice Springs, pp. 40–44.

Jopson, Debra (1999) Poor fellow, my culture. *Sydney Morning Herald,* 22 Sept, p. 14.

—— (2002) Toning down Scarytown. *Sydney Morning Herald,* 27 Aug, p. 9.

—— (2003) History in the remaking. *Sydney Morning Herald,* 11 Feb, p. 9.

Jordan, S (1995) 'Blekbala Mujik' *Rolling Stone,* May 90.

Kartomi, Margaret (1988) Forty thousand years: Koori music and Australian music education. *Australian Journal of Music Education* 1: 11–28.

Kassler, Jamie & Jill Stubington (eds) (1984) *Problems and Solutions: Occassional Essays in Musicology Presented to Alice M Moyle.* Hale & Iremonger, Sydney.

Katherine Town Council (1983) *The Katherine.* Victor G Feros Town Planning Consultants, Brisbane.

Kearney, William (1987) *Jawoyn (Katherine Area) Land Claim.* Report by the Aboriginal Land Commission to the Minister for Aboriginal Affairs and to the Administrator of the Northern Territory.

Keen, Ian (1994) *Knowledge and Secrecy in an Aboriginal Religion: Yolngu of North-East Arnhem Land.* Oxford University Press, Melbourne.

Keenan, Michael (2000) *Wild Horses Don't Swim.* Bantam Books, Sydney.

Keillor, E (1996) The voices of First Nations women within Canada: Traditionally and presently. *Australian–Canadian Studies* 41(1): 33–39.

Keogh, Ray (1989) *Nurlu* songs from the Kimberley: An introduction. *Australian Aboriginal Studies* 1: 2–11.

—— (1990) *Nurlu Songs from the West Kimberley.* PhD thesis, University of Sydney.

—— (1995) Process models for the analysis of *nurlu* songs from the western Kimberleys. In Linda Barwick, Allan Marett & Guy Tunstill (eds) *The Essence of Singing and the Substance of Song: Recent Responses to the Aboriginal Performing Arts and Other Essays in Honour of Catherine Ellis (Oceania Monograph 46).* University of Sydney, Sydney, pp. 39–52.

Kibby, M (1999) The didj and the web: Networks of articulation and appropriation. *Convergence* 5(1): 59–75.

Kidd, Rosalind (1997) *The Way We Civilise: Aboriginal Affairs – The Untold Story.* Queensland University Press, Brisbane.

Kimberley Land Council (1993) *Kimberley Land Council Yearly Report, 1992–1993.* Kimberley Land Council, Derby.

—— (1998) *The Kimberley: Our Place – Our Future.* Kimberley Land Council, Derby.

Kimberley Land Council & Waringarri Resource Centre (1991) *Report of the Conference on Resource Development and Kimberley Land Control (Crocodile Hole Report).* Kimberley Land Council, Derby.

Knopoff, Steven (1997) Accompanying the Dreaming. In K Neuenfeldt (ed.) *The Didjeridu: From Arnhem Land to Internet,* John Libbey/Perfect Beat Publications, London/Sydney, pp. 39–68.

Knox, Roger (1988) We call it Koori music. In A Rutherford (ed) *Aboriginal Culture Today.* Dangaroo Press, Sydney. 236–43.

Kolig, Erich (1987) *The Noonkanbah Story.* University of Otago Press, Otago.

—— (1990) Government policies and religious strategies: Fighting with myth at Noonkanbah. In Robert Tonkinson & Michael Howard (eds) *Going it Alone? Prospects for Aboriginal Autonomy.* Aboriginal Studies Press, Canberra, pp. 219–34.

Kong, L (1995) Popular music in geographical analyses. *Progress in Human Geography* 19(2): 183–98.

Koori Mail (1997) Franklands tells his stories on new CD. *Koori Mail,* 8 Oct, p. 21.

—— (1998) Focus on the Woodford Folk Festival. *Koori Mail,* 14 Jan, pp. 15–17.

—— (1998) Qld rappers aim to tackle youth issues. *Koori Mail,* 14 Jan, p. 19.

—— (1999) All set for Survival 99. *Koori Mail,* 13 Jan, p. 8.

—— (1999) International line-up for '100 year' corroboree. *Koori Mail,* 20 Oct, p. 12.

—— (1999) Bangarra troupe is back home. *Koori Mail,* 17 Nov, p. 29.

—— (1999) NSW, Victoria to host festivals. *Koori Mail,* 17 Nov, p. 29.

—— (1999) Raukkan takes a step back in time. *Koori Mail,* 1 Dec, pp. 14–15.

—— (2001) A man of many talents. *Koori Mail,* 30 May, p. 17.

—— (2001) Didgeridoo's popularity has an ecologial downside. *Koori Mail,* 13 Jun, p. 38.

—— (2001) Cheetham takes a bow at ceremony. *Koori Mail,* 27 Jun, p. 35.

—— (2001) Little G's looking good. *Koori Mail,* 11 Jul, p. 27.

—— (2001) A busy time for Rachel. *Koori Mail,* 22 Aug, p. 19.

—— (2001) The wait is over for J-Boy. *Koori Mail,* 5 Sep, p. 23.

—— (2001) Deb's word. *Koori Mail,* 19 Sep, p. 32.

—— (2001) Darug history in song. *Koori Mail,* 3 Oct, p. 22.

—— (2002) New releases: This is woman. *Koori Mail,* 26 Jun, p. 43.

—— (2002) Not so 'burnt out black.' *Koori Mail,* 4 Sep, p. 31.

—— (2002) Blow 'im: A blast from the past. *Koori Mail,* 2 Oct, p. 33.

—— (2002) Vic is a survivor. *Koori Mail,* 17 Apr, p. 60.

—— (2002) Brothablack's on track. *Koori Mail,* 27 Nov, p. 33.

—— (2002) Wire hip-hops back from UK. *Koori Mail,* 12 Jun, p. 47.

—— (2003) Agnes makes it happen. *Koori Mail,* 12 Feb, p. 30.

Kukoyi, Ade (1999) The significance of an Indigenous-owned recording and publishing company in Australia. In Gerry Bloustein (ed.) *Musical Visions: Selected Conference Proceedings from the 6th National Australia/New Zealand IASPM and Inaugural Arnhem Land Performance Conference, Adelaide, 1998.* Wakefield Press, Kent Town (SA), pp. 77–81.

Langton, Marcia (1993a) 'Well I Heard it on the Radio and I saw it on the Television ...': *An Essay for the Australian Film Commission on the Politics and Aesthetics of Filmmaking by and about Aboriginal People and Things.* Australian Film Commission, Sydney.

—— (1993b) Rum, seduction and death: 'Aboriginality' and alcohol. *Oceania* 3: 195–206.

Latta, D (1991) *Australian Country Music.* Random House, Sydney.

Lawe Davies, Chris (1993a) Aboriginal rock music: Space and place. In T Bennet, S Frith, L Shepherd & G Turner (eds) *Rock and Popular Music: Politics, Policies, Institutions.* Routledge, London, pp. 249–62.

—— (1993b) Black rock and Broome. *Perfect Beat* 1 (2): 48–59.

Leyshon, A, Marless, D & Revill, G (1995) The place of music. *Transactions, Institute of British Geographers,* 20: 423–33.

Lippman, Lorna (1991) *Generations of Resistance: Aborigines Demand Justice.* Longman Cheshire, Melbourne.

Lipsitz, George (1994) *Dangerous Crossroads: Popular Music, Postmodernism and the Poetics of Place.* Verso, London.

Little, J (1999) Otherness, representation and the cultural construction of rurality. *Progress in Human Geography* 23: 437–42.

Macmillan, A (1988) *Strict Rules.* Hodder & Stoughton, Sydney.

Magowan, Fiona (1994) The land is our *märr* (essence), it stays forever: the *yothu–yindi* relationship in Australian Aboriginal traditional and popular musics. In Martin Stokes (ed.) *Ethnicity, Identity and Music: The Musical Construction of Place.* Berg, Oxford, pp. 135–56.

—— (1996) Traditions of the mind or the music video: Imaging the imagination in Yothu Yindi's *Tribal Voice. Arena* 7: 99–110.

McCabe, K (1995) In his own image. *The Daily Telegraph Mirror,* 2 Nov, p. 51.

McDowell, L (1992) Multiple voices: Speaking from inside and outside 'the project'. *Antipode* 24(1): 56–72.

McFarlane, Ian (2000) Fifty influential Australian rock albums. *Rhythms* 90: 6–13.

McGrath, K (1996a) Debbie gives voice to a powerful message. *Koori Mail,* 31 Jul, p. 18.

—— (1996b) Ruby Hunter looks for a bright future. *Koori Mail,* 4 Dec, p. 29.

McLaren, P (1995) Gangsta pedagogy and ghetto ethnicity: The hip-hop nation as counterpublic sphere. *Socialist Review* 25(2): 9–16.

McLeod, Don (1984) *How the West was Lost.* Don McLeod, Port Hedland (WA).

Malone, B (1985) *Country Music USA: A Fifty Year History*. University of Texas Press, Austin.

Mansell, Michael (1995) The Mabo Case. In Irene Moores (ed.) *Voices of Aboriginal Australia – Past, Present, Future*. Butterfly Books, Springwood (NSW), pp. 322–31.

Manuel, Peter (1988) *Popular Musics of the Non-Western World: An Introductory Survey*. Oxford University Press, Oxford.

Marett, Allan (1994) Wangga: Socially powerful songs? *The World of Music* 36(1): 67–81.

Marshall, Paul (ed.) (1989) *Raparapa Kularr Martuwarra: Stories from the Fitzroy River Drovers*. Magabala Books, Broome.

Maxwell, Ian (1997a) Hip hop aesthetics and the will to culture. *The Australian Journal of Anthropology* 8: 50–70.

—— (1997b) On the flow – dancefloor grooves, rapping 'freestyle' and 'the Real Thing'. *Perfect Beat* 3(3): 15–27.

Meadows, Michael (2002) 'Tell me what you want and I'll give you what you need': Perspectives in Indigenous media audience research. In Mark Balnaves, Tom O'Regan & Jason Sternberg (eds) *Mobilising the Audience*. University of Queensland Press, Brisbane, pp. 253–65.

Michaels, Eric (1986) *The Aboriginal Invention of Television in Central Australia 1982–1986*. Australian Institute of Aboriginal Studies, Canberra.

—— (1989) *For a Cultural Future: Francis Jupurrurla Makes TV at Yuendumu*. Art & Text Publications, Sydney/Melbourne.

Mitchell, Don (2000) *Cultural Geography: A Critical Introduction*. Blackwell Publishers, Cornwell.

Mitchell, S (1996) Mates, Mabo and Warumpi. *Green Left Weekly* 24 Jul, p. 28.

Mitchell, Tony (1992) World music, Indigenous music and music television in Australia. *Perfect Beat* 1(1): 1–16.

—— (1993) World music and the popular music industry: An Australian view. *Ethnomusicology*, 37(3): 309–38.

—— (1996) *Popular Music and Locality Identity: Rock, Pop and Rap in Europe and Oceania*. Leicester University Press, London.

—— (1999) Another root: Australian hip-hop as 'glocal' subculture – Reterritorialising hip-hop. In Gerry Bloustein (ed.) *Music Visions: Selected Conference Proceedings from the 6th National Australian/New Zealand IASPM and Inaugural Arnhem Land Performance Conference*. Wakefield Press, Kent Town (SA), pp. 85–94.

Moores, Irene (ed.) (1995) *Voices of Aboriginal Australia – Past, Present, Future*. Butterfly Books, Springwood (NSW).

Morphy, Howard (1984) *Journey to the Crocodile's Nest: An Accompanying Monograph to the Film, Madarpa Funeral at Gurkawuy*. Australian Institute of Aboriginal Studies, Canberra.

—— (1991) *Ancestral Connections: Art and an Aboriginal System of Knowledge*. University of Chicago Press, Chicago.

Moyle, Alice (nd) *Songs from North Queensland.* Australian Institute of Aboriginal Studies, Canberra.

—— (1959) Sir Baldwin Spencer's recordings of Australian Aboriginal singing. *Memoirs of the National Museum of Victoria* 24: 7–36.

—— (1960) Two native song-styles recorded in Tasmania. *Papers and Proceedings of the Royal Society of Tasmania* 94: 73–78.

—— (1972) *Songs from Yarrabah.* Australian Institute of Aboriginal Studies, Canberra.

—— (1974) *Songs of the Northern Territory.* Australian Institute of Aboriginal Studies, Canberra.

—— (1977) *Songs from the Kimberleys.* Australian Institute of Aboriginal Studies, Canberra.

—— (1978) *Aboriginal Sound Instruments.* Australian Institute of Aboriginal Studies, Canberra.

—— (1984) Aboriginal music and dance: Reflections and projections. In Jamie Kassle & Jill Stubington (eds) *Problems and Solutions: Occassional Essays in Musicology Presented to Alice M Moyle.* Hale & Iremonger, Sydney, pp. 14–30.

—— (1985) The Torres Strait phonograph recordings: A preliminary listing of contents. *Australian Aboriginal Studies* 2: 53–57.

Moyle, Richard (1979) *Songs of the Pintupi: Musical Life in a Central Australian Society.* Australian Institute of Aboriginal Studies, Canberra.

—— (1986) *Alyawarra Music: Songs and Society in a Central Australian Community.* Australian Institute of Aboriginal Studies, Canberra.

—— (1997) *Balgo: The Musical Life of a Desert Community.* Callaway International Resource Centre for Music Education, Perth.

Mudrooroo (1997) *Indigenous Literature of Australia – Milli Milli Wangka.* Hyland House, Melbourne.

Muecke, Stephen (1992) *Textual Spaces: Aboriginality and Cultural Studies.* New South Wales University Press, Sydney.

Muecke, Stephen, Rumsey, Alan & Wirrunmarra, Banjo (1985) Pigeon the outlaw: History as texts. *Aboriginal History* 9: 81–100.

Mulvaney, J, Morphy, H & Petch, A (eds) (1997) *My Dear Spencer: The Letters of FJ Gillen to Baldwin Spencer.* Hyland House, Melbourne.

Munro, K (2002) Hansen reaches legend status. *Koori Mail,* 26 Jun, p. 42.

Munro, P (2002) Mob rules. *Sydney Morning Herald,* 30 Nov–1 Dec, p. 5.

Murray, Neil (1988) interview with Peter Dunbar-Hall, Sydney.

—— (1996) interview with Chris Gibson, Sydney.

—— (1993) *Sing for Me, Countryman.* Hodder & Stoughton, Sydney.

Mudrooroo (1997) *The Indigenous Literature of Australia: Milli Milli Wangka.* Hyland House, Melbourne.

Myers, F (1989) Burning the truck and holding the country: Pintupi forms of property and identity. In E Wilmsen (ed) *We Are Here: Politics of Aboriginal Land Tenure.* University of California Press, Berkeley, pp. 15–42.

Narogin, M (1990) *Writing from the Fringe: A study of modern Aboriginal literature.* Hyland House, Melbourne.

National Board of Employment, Education and Training (1996) *The Land Still Speaks: Review of Aboriginal and Torres Strait Islander Language Maintenance and Development Needs and Activities*. Commonwealth of Australia, Canberra.

National Indigenous Media Association of Australia (nd) *NIMAA: The Voice of Our People*. National Indigenous Media Association of Australia, Brisbane.

Nettl, B (1983) *The Study of Ethnomusicology: Twenty-nine Issues and Concepts*. University of Urbana Press, Chicago.

Nettle, Daniel & Romaine, Suzanne (2000) *Vanishing Voices: The Extinction of the World's Languages*. Oxford University Press, Oxford.

Neuenfeldt, Karl (1993a) The didjeridu and the overdub: Technologising and transposing aural images of Aboriginality. *Perfect Beat* 1 (2): 60–77.

—— (1993b) Yothu Yindi and ganma: The cultural transposition of Aboriginal agenda through metaphor and music. *Journal of Australian Studies* 38(1): 1–11.

—— (1994) The essentialistic, the exotic, the equivocal and the absurd; The cultural production and use of the didjeridu in world music. *Perfect Beat* 2(1): 88–104.

—— (1995) The Kyana corroboree: Cultural production of indigenous ethnogenesis. *Sociological Inquiry* 65(1): 21–46.

—— (1996) Songs of survival: Ethno-pop music as ethnographic indigenous media. *Australian–Candian Studies* 14(1): 15–31.

—— (ed.) (1997) *The Didjeridu: From Arnhem Land to Internet*. John Libbey/Perfect Beat Publications, London/Sydney.

—— (1998) Yothu Yindi: Agendas and aspirations. In Philip Hayward (ed.) *Sound Alliances: Indigenous Peoples, Cultural Politics and Popular Music in the Pacific*. Cassell, London, pp. 199–208.

—— (2001a) Cultural politics and a music recording project: Producing 'Strike Em!' – *Contemporary Voices from the Torres Strait*. *Journal of Intercultural Studies* 22(2): 133–45.

—— (2001b) The 'Saving Grace of Social Culture': Early popular music and performance culture on Thursday Island, Torres Strait, Queensland. *Queensland Review* 8(2): 1–20.

—— (2002) Examples of Torres Strait songs of longing and belonging. *Journal of Australian Studies* 75: 111–16.

Newsome, Jennifer (1998) Indigenous music in the academy: Whose music, whose identity? In Gerry Bloustein (ed.) *Musical Visions: Selected Conference Proceedings from the 6th National Australia/New Zealand IASPM and Inaugural Arnhem Land Performance Conference, Adelaide, 1998*. Wakefield Press, Kent Town (SA), pp. 95–103.

Nicol, Lisa (1993) Culture, custom and collaboration – The production of Yothu Yindi's 'Treaty' videos. *Perfect Beat* 1(2): 23–32.

Nokturnl (2003) website >http://www.nokturnl.com<.

Northern Territory Government (1989) *Northern Territory Parliamentary Record*, 16 May, p. 6056.

—— (1999) *Foster Partnerships in Aboriginal Development: Foundations for our*

Future. Northern Territory Government, Darwin.

Northern Territory Supreme Court (1971) *Milirrpum and Others vs Nabalco and the Commonwealth*.

Ohrlin, G (1989) *The Hellbound Train*. University of Illinois Press, Urbana.

Olliffe, M (1995) Substance over image. *On the Street*, 30 Oct, p. 29.

On the Street (1995) Something for everyone. *On the Street*, 24 Jan, p. 33.

Patterson, J (2002) Djakapurra back home. *Koori Mail*, 6 Mar, p. 5.

Patterson, M (1996) Native music in Canada: The age of the seventh fire. *Australian–Canadian Studies* 14(1): 41–53.

Patton, Paul (1995) Post-structuralism and the Mabo debate: Difference, society and justice. In M Wislon & A Yeatman (eds) *Justice and Identity –Antipodean Practices*. Allen & Unwin, Wellington, pp. 153–71.

Paul, Mandy & Gray, Geoffrey (eds) (2002) *Through a Smoky Mirror: History and Native Title*. Aboriginal Studies Press, Canberra.

Payne, H (1989) Rites for sites or sites for rites?: The dynamics of women's cultural life in the Musgraves. In P Brock (ed.) *Women: Rites and Sites*. Allen & Unwin, Sydney, pp. 41–59.

Pearce, Trevor (1979) Music and the settled Aboriginal. In Jennifer Isaacs (ed.) *Australian Aboriginal Music*. Aboriginal Artists Agency, Sydney, pp. 41–48.

Pearse, R (1997) Baltpa. *Sounds Australian* 15(50): 28–29.

Pearson, Noel (1995) 204 Years of Invisible Title. In Irene Moores (ed.) *Voices of Aboriginal Australia – Past, Present, Future*. Butterfly Books, Springwood (NSW), pp. 338–61.

Pedersen, Howard & Woorunmurra, Banjo (1995) *Jandamarra and the Bunuba Resistance*. Magabala Books, Broome.

Peterson, R (1997) *Creating Country Music: Fabricating Authenticity*. University of Chicago Press, Chicago.

Pile, S & Thrift N (eds) (1995) *Mapping the Subject: Geographies of Cultural Transformation*. Routledge, London.

Pollak, A (1984) Relevance without sentiment. *Sydney Morning Herald*, 22 June.

Pritchard, Bill & Gibson, Chris (1996) *The Black Economy: Regional Development Strategies in the Northern Territory*. North Australia Research Unit Report Series No 1. Australian National University and the Northern Land Council, Darwin.

Regev, Motti (1997) Rock aesthetics and musics of the world. *Theory, Culture and Society* 14(3): 125–42.

Rhydwen, Mari (1996) *Writing on the Backs of Blacks: Voice, Literacy and Community in Kriol Fieldwork*. University of Queensland Press, Brisbane.

Riley, V (1998) Girls at our best? *Real Time* 27: 43.

Rintoul, S (2002) Songmen. *The Weekend Australian*, 13–14 Jul, pp. 16–17.

Robertson, T (1983) Nor-west group has a message. *Weekend News*, 23–24 April, p. 26.

Robinson, DC, Buck, EB & Cuthbert, M (1991) *Music at the Margins: Popular Music and Global Cultural Diversity*. Sage Publications, London.

Robinson, Fergus & York, Barry (1977) *The Black Resistance: An Introduction to the Abo-*

rigines' Struggle Against British Colonialism. Widescope Publishing, Melbourne.

Rogers, Jimmie (1989) *The Country Music Message; Revisited.* University of Arkansas Press, Fayatteville.

Roosens, E (1989) *Creating Ethnicity: The Process of Ethnogenesis.* Sage, Newbury Park.

Rose, AM (1996) A place for indigenous music in formal music education. *International Journal for Music Education* 26: 39–54.

Rose, Deborah Bird (1992) *Dingo Makes Us Human: Life and Land in an Aboriginal Australian Culture.* Cambridge University Press, Cambridge.

Rose, T (1994) *Black Noise: Rap Music and Black Culture in Contemporary America.* Wesleyan University Press, Hanover.

Rowley, CD (1970) *The Destruction of Aboriginal Society.* Australian National University Press, Canberra.

—— (1986) *Recovery: The Politics of Aboriginal Reform.* Penguin, Ringwood, Victoria.

Rowse, Tim (1995) *After Mabo: Interpreting Indigenous Traditions.* Melbourne University Press, Melbourne.

—— (2002) *Indigenous Futures: Choice and Development in Aboriginal and Islander Australia.* University of NSW Press, Sydney.

Rrurrambu, George (1996) interview with Chris Gibson, Sydney.

Rutherford, A (1988) *Aboriginal Culture Today.* Dangaroo Press, Sydney.

Ryan, C & Huyton, J (2000) Who is interested in Aboriginal tourism in the Northern Territory? A cluster analysis. *Journal of Sustainable Tourism* 8(1): 53–87.

Ryan, Robin (1994) Tracing the urban songlines: Contemporary Koori music in Melbourne. *Perfect Beat* 2(1): 20–37.

—— (1999) Gumleaf playing competitions – Aboriginal and non-Aboriginal performance styles and socio-cultural contexts. *Perfect Beat* 4(3): 66–85.

Schmidt, Annette (1993) *The Loss of Australia's Aboriginal Language Heritage.* Aboriginal Studies Press, Canberra.

Scott, Eric (1999) interview with Peter Dunbar-Hall, Tamworth.

Shaw, Bruce (ed.) (1992) *When the Dust Come in Between: Aboriginal Viewpoints in the East Kimberley Prior to 1982.* Aboriginal Studies Press, Canberra.

Smith, Graeme (1994) Australian country music and the hillbilly yodel. *Popular Music.* 13(3): 297–311.

Smith, Graeme & Dunbar-Hall, Peter (1993) *Yothu Yindi: 'Treaty'.* Sounds Australian, Sydney.

Smith, J (1984) *The Book of Australian Country Music.* Berghouse Floyd Tuckey Publishing, Sydney.

Smith, L (1999) *Decolonizing Methodologies: Research and Indigenous Peoples.* University of Otago Press, Dunedin.

Smith, Michael (1996a) Blekbala songlines. *The Drum Media,* Jan, unpaginated.

—— (1996b) Tiddas: Bridge of voices. *The Drum Media,* 6 Aug, p. 20.

—— (1999a) Coloured Stone: Rock'n'roll survivors. *The Drum Media,* 19 Jan, p. 28.

—— (1999b) Singin' up triumphant survival. *The Drum Media*, 19 Jan, p. 28.

—— (2000) The nurturing experience of Yothu Yindi. *Drum Media*, 17 Oct, p. 32.

Smith, Ollie & Plater, Diana (2000) *Raging Partners: Two Worlds, One Friendship*. Magabala Books, Broome.

Stapleton, J (1985) Warumpi Band wins a Pacific guernsey. *Financial Review*, 30 Aug.

Steggels, S (1992) Nothing ventured, nothing gained: Midnight Oil and the politics of rock. In P Hayward (ed.) *From Pop to Punk to Postmodernism: Popular Music and Australian Culture from the 1960s to the 1990s*. Allen & Unwin, Sydney, pp. 139–48.

Stephens, M (1998) Babylon's natural mystic: the North American music industry, the music of Bob Marley, and the interpretation of transnationalism. *Cultural Studies* 2: 139–67.

Stevens, Frank (1981) *Black Australia*. Australian Publishing Co-operative, Sydney.

Stevenson, Deborah (2000) *Art and Organisation: Making Australian Cultural Policy*. University of Queensland Press, Brisbane.

Stokes, J, de Gruchy, I & Hobba, L (nd) *Aboriginal Country Music Festival 1979*. No details.

Strehlow, Theodor (1971) *Songs of Central Australia*. Angus & Robertson, Sydney.

Streit-Warburton, Jili (1995) Craft, raft and lifesaver: Aboriginal women musicians in the contemporary music industry. In R Sakolsky & FW Ho (eds) *Sounding Off! Music as Subversion/Resistance/Revolution*. Autonomedia, New York, pp. 307–19.

Stubington, Jill (1978) *Yolngu Manikay: Modern Performances of Australian Aboriginal Clan Songs*. PhD thesis, Monash University.

—— (1979) North Australian Aboriginal music. In J Isaacs (ed.) *Australian Aboriginal Music*. Aboriginal Artists Agency, Sydney, pp. 7–19.

—— (1982) Song performance and Aboriginal polity: A northeast Arnhem Land example. *Musicology Australia* August: 84–103.

—— (1994) Yolngu *manikay* at Yirrkala: The construction of a research field. *The World of Music* 36(1): 82–98.

Stubington, Jill & Dunbar-Hall, Peter (1994) Yothu Yindi's 'Treaty': *Ganma* in music. *Popular Music* 13 (3): 243–59.

Sullivan, Chris (1988) Non-tribal music and song: From first contact to citizen rights. *Australian Aboriginal Studies* 1: 64–67.

Sutton, Peter (1995) *Country: Aboriginal Boundaries and Land Ownership in Australia (Aboriginal History Monograph No. 3)*. Aboriginal History Incorporated, Canberra.

Sutton, P, Coltheart, L & McGrath, A (1983) *The Murranji Land Claim*. Northern Territory Land Council, Darwin.

Sweeney, Philip (1991) *The Virgin Directory of World Music*. Virgin, London.

Thomas, N (1994) *Colonialism's Culture: Anthropology, Travel and Government*. Polity Press, Cambridge.

Thompson, Liz (1990) *Aboriginal Voices: Contemporary Aboriginal Artists, Writers and Performers*. Simon & Schuster, Sydney.

Thompson, L (1997) A song of protest. *Pacific Islands Monthly* 67(1): 48–49.

Thusi, N (2002) Cairns duo have a date with destiny. *Koori Mail*, 6 Feb, p. 32.

Tichi, C (1994) *High Lonesome: The American Culture of Country Music*. University of North Carolina Press, Chapel Hill.

Toomelah Report: Report on the Problems and Needs of Aborigines Living on the New South Wales–Queensland Border (1988). Human Rights Australia.

Toussaint, Sandy (1995) Western Australia. In Ann McGrath (ed.) *Contested Ground: Australian Aborigines under the British Crown*. Allen & Unwin, Sydney, pp. 240–68.

Toyne, P & D Vachon (1984) *Growing Up the Country: The Pitjantjatjara Struggle for their Land*. McPhee Gribble, Melbourne.

Trudgen, Richard (2000) *Why Warriors Lie Down and Die: Towards an Understanding of Why Aboriginal People of Arnhem Land Face the Greatest Crisis in Health and Education Since European Contact – Djambatj Mala*. Aboriginal Resources and Development Services, Darwin.

Turnbull, David (1993) *Maps are Territories, Science is an Atlas: A Portfolio of Exhibits*. Deakin University, Geelong.

Valentine, G (1995) Creating transgressive space: The music of kd lang. *Transactions of the Institute of British Geography* 20: 474–85.

van Toorn, Penny (1990) Discourse/patron discourse: How minority texts command the attention of majority audiences. *Span* 30: 102–15.

Waitt, Gordon (1997) Selling paradise and adventure: Representations of landscape in the tourist advertising of Australia. *Australian Geographical Studies* 35: 47–60.

—— (1999) Naturalizing the 'primitive': A critique of marketing Australia's indigenous people as 'hunter-gatherers'. *Tourism Geographies* 1(2): 142–63.

Walker, Clinton (1993) Archie Roach. *Rolling Stone*, Mar, pp. 78–81.

—— (2000) *Buried Country: The Story of Aboriginal Country Music*. Pluto Press, Sydney.

Walsh, Michael & Yallop, Colin (eds) (1993) *Language and Culture in Aboriginal Australia*. Aboriginal Studies Press, Canberra.

Wark, M (2000) Messenger beyond the middle class. *The Australian*, 21 Jun, p. 43.

Warner, W (1937) *A Black Civilization: A Social Study of an Australian Tribe*. Harper & Brothers, New York.

Watson, Eric (1975) *Country Music in Australia*. Rodeo Publications, Sydney.

—— (1983) *Country Music in Australia. Volume 2*. Cornstalk, Sydney.

—— (1987) Country Music: The voice of rural Australia. In Marcus Breen (ed.) *Missing in Action: Australian Popular Music in Perspective*. Verbal Graphics, Melbourne, pp. 47–77.

Watson, Helen, Yolngu community at Yirrkala & Chambers, David (1989) *Singing the Land, Signing the Land: A Portfolio of Exhibits*. Deakin University, Geelong.

Wells, Edgar (1982) *Reward and Punishment in Arnhem Land, 1962–1963*. Australian Institute of Aboriginal Studies, Canberra.

Whiteley, Sheila (ed.) (1998) *Sexing the Groove: Popular Music and Gender*. Routledge, London.

Wilcannia Community Working Party (2001) *Wilcannia Community Working Party Issues Paper*. Wilcannia Community Working Party, Wilcannia.

Wild, Stephen (1984) Warlbiri music and culture: Meaning in a central Australian song series. In Jamie Kassler & Jill Stubington (eds) *Problems and Solutions: Occassional Essays in Musicology Presented to Alice M Moyle*. Hale & Iremonger, Sydney, pp. 186–204.

—— (1994) Reflections on field research in Aboriginal Australia: Central Australia and Arnhem Land. *The World of Music* 36(1): 51–58.

Williams, Nancy (1986) *The Yolngu and their Land: A System of Land Tenure and the Fight for its Recognition*. Australian Institute of Aboriginal Studies, Canberra.

Williams, S (1997) Flat note sounds for black Songlines. *The Weekend Australian*, 25–26 Jan, p. 14.

Wilson, A (2002) A dream come true for Tonky. *Koori Mail*, 4 Sep, p. 32.

Wilson, S (2003) Hip hop and hope. *Sunday Telegraph Magazine*, 3 Feb, pp. 14–17.

Winchester, H, Kong, L & Dunn, K (2003) *Landscapes: Ways of Imaging the World*. Pearsons, Sydney.

Wright, F (1999) *The Art and Craft Centre Story, Vol 1*. Desart & ATSIC, Alice Springs.

Wright, F & Morphy, H (2000) *The Art and Craft Centre Story, Vol 2: Summary and Recommendations*. Desart & ATSIC, Alice Springs.

Yothu Yindi (2003) website >http://www.yothuyindi.com/ourhome/html<.

Yu, Peter (1997) Multilateral agreements: A new accountability in Aboriginal affairs. In Galarwuy Yunupingu (ed.) *Our Land is Our Life*. University of Queensland Press, Brisbane, pp. 168–80.

Yunupingu, Galarwuy (1997) Introduction. In Galarwuy Yunupingu (ed.) *Our Land is Our Life: Land Rights – Past, Present and Future*. University of Queensland Press, Brisbane, pp. xv–xviii.

Yunupingu, Mandawuy (1996) Birrkuta (album note). *Birrkuta – Wild Honey*. Mushroom Records, TVD93461.

Yunupingu, M, West, D, Anderson, I, Bell, J, Lui, G, Corbett, H & Pearson, N (1994) *Voices from the Land: 1993 Boyer Lectures*. ABC Books, Sydney.

Zeppel, H (2001) Aboriginal cultures and indigenous tourism. In N Douglas & R Derrett (eds) *Special Interest Tourism*. Wiley, Sydney, pp. 232–59.

Index